SECRET VICTORY
THE INTELLIGENCE WAR THAT BEAT THE IRA

To colleagues murdered while serving and protecting others, and to those who suffer in silence.

William Matchett

Matchett, Belfast, UK, 2016 (International Edition).

Front cover is a joint Police/Army patrol, Jonesborough market, south Armagh, 1986. The police officer is a detective constable in Special Branch and the soldier is SAS.
The Special Branch insignia is above the title. This consists of an eagle holding a tourniquet in front of an outline of Northern Ireland. Operation Eagle and Tourniquet were the first two covert operations by an updated Special Branch, also known as 'E' department.

Foreword

The armed conflict in Northern Ireland otherwise known as the 'troubles' generated a massive media and academic interest in all aspects of Irish terrorism and the State's response. The interest has not diminished as we now struggle to deal with the legacy of that terrible violent past.

Central to the current debate has been an increased scrutiny of the State's role, in particular the intelligence services and with a distinct focus on Special Branch - the department within the Royal Ulster Constabulary G.C. charged with responsibility for intelligence matters. Whilst considerable coverage has been given to the alleged exploits of Special Branch there still exists only a superficial understanding of its structure, role and operational contribution to the war against terrorism. The public's knowledge is limited about how this helped to create a security environment that enabled political negotiations to take place to end the conflict.

SECRET VICTORY by Dr William Matchett is the first book on the Northern Ireland scene to provide that comprehensive insight. And in doing so the author lifts the veil on the complex world of intelligence in response to armed conflict within the state's borders and beyond.

The book's uniqueness lies in the fact that it is written by an insider, a person who has worked for many years at the coalface and observed at first hand the professionalism of his colleagues in responding to the many and varied challenges ranging from life threatening situations through to the unceasing demand for more and better intelligence.

SECRET VICTORY is a 'go to' reference point for all as it corrects many of the more fanciful and lurid descriptions of the work of Special Branch. These have gained unwarranted credence over the years simply because they were not corrected at the time. The book sets out in accessible format a comprehensive look at a complicated and contentious topic - intelligence gathering and its multiple applications. It takes the reader on a guided tour of the factors that influenced the development of Special Branch in a constantly changing terrorism landscape.

It is a book that will challenge many previously held concepts about Special Branch as, the author has been candid and forthright about its shortcomings as well as its successes. But the scope and insight that he provides is a testimony to the professionalism of ordinary men and women of the Royal Ulster Constabulary G.C. who when called upon in extraordinary circumstances had the capacity and the endurance to successfully deliver.

Raymond White
5 September 2016

Retired Assistant Chief Constable OBE. BEM. LLB. (Hons)

Contents

ABBREVIATIONS

ACC	Assistant Chief Constable
AQ	Al Qaeda
AQI	Al Qaeda in Iraq
ASU	Active Service Unit
CCTV	Close Circuit Television
CIA	Central Intelligence Agency
CID	Criminal Investigation Department
COP	Close Observation Platoon
CTTSO	Combating Terrorism Technical Support Office
DC	District of Colombia
DCI	Director and Co-ordinator of Intelligence
Det	Detachment (14 Intelligence Company)
DMSU	Divisional Mobile Support Unit
DV	Develop Vetted
E4A	'E' department (Special Branch) Alpha (surveillance)
E4 HMSU	'E' department (Special Branch) Headquarters Mobile Support Unit
ETA	Euskadi Ta Askatasuna
EU	European Union
FARC	Fuerzas Armadas Revolucionarias de Colombia
FBI	Federal Bureau of Investigation
FRU	Force Research Unit
GAA	Gaelic Athletic Association
GB	Great Britain
GHQ	General Headquarters
GOC	General Officer Commanding
GPMG	General Purpose Machine Gun
HET	Historical Enquiries Team
HMI	Her Majesty's Inspector
HMIC	Her Majesty's Inspectorate of Constabulary
HMSU	Headquarters Mobile Support Unit
HQ	Headquarters
HSB	Head of Special Branch
HUMINT	Human Intelligence
IED	Improvised Explosive Device
INLA	Irish National Liberation Army
IPLO	Irish Peoples Liberation Army
IRA	Irish Republican Army
ISAF	International Security Assistance Force
ISIS	Islamic State in Iraq and Syria
IWS	Irregular Warfare Support
MI5	Military Intelligence 5 (also known as the Security Service)
MOD	Ministry of Defence
MRF	Military Reaction Force
NCND	Neither Confirm Nor Deny
NHS	National Health Service
NGO	Non-Governmental Organisation

NI	Northern Ireland
NICRA	Northern Ireland Civil Rights Association
NIM	National Intelligence Model
NIO	Northern Ireland Office
OC	Officer Commanding
OIRA	Official Irish Republican Army
OOB	Out Of Bounds
OTR	On-The-Run
PIRA	Provisional Irish Republican Army
PLO	Palestinian Liberation Organisation
POW	Prisoner of War
PSF	Provisional Sinn Féin
PSNI	Police Service of Northern Ireland
PT	Physical Training
QGM	Queen's Gallantry Medal
QRF	Quick Reaction Force
RAF	Royal Air Force
RHC	Red Hand Commandos
RHSB	Regional Head of Special Branch
RIC	Royal Irish Constabulary
ROI	Republic of Ireland
RPG	Rocket Propelled Grenade
RUC	Royal Ulster Constabulary
SAS	Special Air Service
SB	Special Branch
SDLP	Social Democratic and Labour Party
SMG	Sub Machine Gun
SPG	Special Patrol Group
SSU	Special Support Unit
SWAT	Special Weapons and Tactics
TCG	Tasking and Co-ordination Group
UDA	Ulster Defence Association
UDR	Ulster Defence Regiment
UK	United Kingdom
UN	United Nations
US	United States
USC	Ulster Special Constabulary
USMC	United States Marine Corps
UVF	Ulster Volunteer Force
WW1	World War 1
WW2	World War 2

Introduction

In 1982, I was a police officer stationed in the IRA heartland of south Armagh. At 18 it was a rude awakening to the reality of armed conflict. Up to then, joining the police was a boyish adventure that left my mother distraught. In south Armagh every day had drama. You relied totally on your mates and never went out without a good reason. I was shot at, caught in roadside bombs and mortared. I lost some good friends. I would lie if I said I was not afraid. I knew the IRA men who were doing this, we all did, but we could not prove it.

The IRA and their Sinn Féin apologists were two sides of a well-oiled machine. No one called it an insurgency, but it was. One did murders, the other excused them. The problem for me was trying to understand why so many locals supported them. At the same time, far more did not. The ones on my side could not be seen talking to me, or the IRA would kill them. Away from prying eyes they passed on condolences after a police officer or soldier was killed and told you to avoid certain roads. I saw the worst and the best in people.

When the IRA hit us they fled into the Republic. The border was a stone's throw away and we could not cross it. On the other side the police or military were rarely out. Dublin did not see the IRA as I did. I was clueless about the politics of it all. It was simple stuff in my eyes; Provos were terrorists and their killings were murders.

In 2007, I worked on police-building programmes in Anbar province, Iraq, the heartland of al-Qaeda in Iraq, and then in 2009, Helmand province, Afghanistan, the Taliban's heartland. A fundamental ideology legitimising murder, with the police top of the list, was not unique to the IRA. Helmand and Anbar were south Armagh on a bigger scale. Tribal allegiances were exploited with great effect. Insurgency thrives in a political wasteland. For people like me, sadly, it was very familiar.

In all three countries the military fought an insurgency with the aim of stabilising the environment to a point where local police could take over. In Northern Ireland this took seven years. Fourteen years after US-led interventions in Afghanistan and Iraq this has still to happen. With so many relevant parallels, how has this been so difficult to achieve? I am not saying the police model at the centre of Northern Ireland's security response is perfect, but it is a lot better than anything else that has been used or proposed.

Winning the intelligence war beat the IRA, leaving Sinn Féin intact to join a devolved government they had tried to destroy. Half the IRA was in prison and most of the rest were fugitives living in the Irish Republic. By the early 1990s, the IRA had run out of road. They needed a face-saving way out, which they got. Effective security in tandem with politics brought about the peace. The IRA wanted their people out of prison and amnesties for their on-the-runs. This is also the type of ending in store for the Taliban and Islamic State, eventually. Politically, it is the wise thing to do but hard to stomach for those who have been on the receiving end.

In Iraq and Afghanistan, police from mostly the US and Europe advised military commanders. None I met had policed a conflict, and many were uninterested in what this looked like. As far as they were concerned, they had been hired for their police knowledge and whether that was based on policing Boston, Birmingham or Berlin was beside the point. They knew best practice, the latest guidelines and modern techniques. This is why they were hired. They were the experts.

In one place I worked, Haditha, Iraq, most of the Iraqi police officers had been wiped out in one incident for want of basic guidance, none of which appears in modern guidelines. To anyone from my background, what was needed was obvious. Iraqis and Afghans, like all police officers, love stories. They want to know what you did with a situation they now face. If you have never walked in their shoes, how do you do this? For the US and UK military this is easy; they have extensive experience in fighting small wars. But this is not the case for police officers.

A police organisation in a conflict must get ahead of the threat if it is to defeat it. Reacting is losing. Modern police services are obese bureaucracies unfit for this purpose. Political correctness has paralysed police-building efforts. Police officers cannot afford to police with the fear of being sued, which is what most of this bureaucracy is for. Had the police force of which I was a member been given the guidance Iraqis and Afghans received, the Troubles would still be raging.

In 1982, I joined a police force in a time of conflict and in 2014 left a police service in a time of peace. They are remarkably different organisations. Most of my career was in Special Branch, an intelligence agency despised by a sectarian IRA, the Islamic State of its day. To them, I was part of the problem and a reason why they took up arms. Currently, some of the IRA men I helped to put behind bars are in politics. The Belfast Agreement gave them a platform to promote their views. The result has been a tsunami of criticism about the police force they hated. They and political opportunists wishing to market the politics of the Northern Ireland 'peace process' on the world stage have suppressed the security dimension as an essential ingredient. The policing 'lessons' never reached places like Iraq and Afghanistan in any significant shape. At what cost to the lives of officers in both countries we will never know.

In an irregular conflict a tough police force can bridge the gap between war and peace to consolidate hard won military gains. This happened in Northern Ireland. The rule of law approach endured. In Iraq and Afghanistan, the police issue was an after-thought. All attention was on the military. Commercial companies filled the void and made enormous profits. Governments contracted 'police experts' to deliver police-building programmes. It all became very confused and inept.

In writing this book, the ultimate aim is to inform. The intelligence war waged against the IRA and managed by Special Branch is the most widely misunderstood aspect of the Northern Ireland conflict. These pages put the record straight. The best counter-terrorism weapon from the Troubles has been left on the shelf.

Loughgall did not swell the ranks of the IRA,
quite the opposite.

Chapter 1

Loughgall: The Inside Story

From the mid-1970s the Provisionals followed a long war strategy that depended on using the Republic of Ireland as a safe haven. Cross-border IRA brigades were the main protagonists and isolated border police stations their main targets. The main soft targets were local off duty security forces, border Protestants and civilian contractors helping to rebuild security bases. By the 1980s gun and bomb attacks on police stations were common, such as the destruction of Ballygawley police station that left two constables dead, George Gilliland (34) and William Clements (52), and a mortar attack on Newry police station that killed nine police officers: Alexander Donaldson (41), John Dowd (31), Sean McHenry (19), Geoffrey Campbell (24), Paul McFerran (33), Rosemary McGookin (27), David Topping (22), Denis Price (22) and Ivy Kelly (29). The brigades responsible operated in border areas each side of south Armagh. And it was the instability South Armagh IRA had created that these neighbouring brigades were looking to copy.

Cross-border brigades contained the IRA's top killers.

It was the extreme that suppressed less radicalised views within the organisation. By the mid 1980s a successful cross-border IRA murder spree threatened to destabilise the entire state by plunging Northern Ireland into a full blown sectarian civil war, which was the aim of cross-border brigades. Any hope of achieving this, however, was extinguished on the 8th May 1987 when the most ambitious brigade - East Tyrone/Monaghan IRA - suffered a humiliating setback at Loughgall. Not only did the Loughgall incident signal the decline of the IRA cross-border offensive, it also signalled the decline of the IRA terrorist campaign.

East Tyrone/Monaghan IRA contained irreconcilables like James Lynagh and Patrick McKearney. Both were on-the-runs, fugitives from the law in Northern Ireland who lived in border counties in the Republic of Ireland. Much to the frustration of the British, the Republic did not treat on-the-runs as terrorists. Lynagh and McKearney were the driving force behind most IRA murders in Tyrone and many others in the neighbouring counties for at least a decade prior to the Loughgall incident. For younger brigade members, Lynagh and McKearney were living legends, republican icons, someone they aspired to be. To Special Branch, they were streetwise homicidal maniacs and the main impediment to ending the conflict.

Most law-abiding citizens believed people like Lynagh were unstoppable and beyond the reach of the law. Lynagh also believed this, which meant he had a false sense of his own operational value. McKearney was similarly deluded. This is because Lynagh and McKearney confused murdering soft targets in surprise attacks with combat. They were criminals not combatants. Psychopaths not soldiers. They were intoxicated by republican myths and had lost touch with reality. They did not appreciate that the first time they came up against soldiers trained in combat without having the element of surprise as an advantage, would be their last.

South Armagh IRA was the terrorist organisation's most effective brigade. Within its area of operations it had eliminated vehicle police patrols through the extensive use of roadside bombs. In south Armagh, for the police and Army this restricted patrolling to foot and air, which the IRA was also targeting with deadly results. The police could not operate without the close support of the Army. This is what success looked like for the IRA – forcing the police to focus more on security duties than normal policing duties thereby limiting normal interaction with the public. The ploy is to physically and socially exclude police from the area. The last thing the Provisionals wanted was a police officer having a friendly chat with a local and coming across as someone decent looking to serve and protect them.

A retired SB officer who served in south Armagh describes what it was like: "I have never experienced such a feeling of helplessness. We were totally on the back foot." He goes on to show that the police had to be measured in how they responded to any incident as the threat was always directed at the security forces. Something as seemingly benign as attending a road traffic accident was a potential terrorist ambush. Outside of incidents involving Army or police casualties, a cautious approach meant the police usually responded slowly or not at all. In one incident he recalls:

As soon as we got the bodies away that was it. There was no scene, no forensics, no door-to-door. It was too dangerous. Anytime we ever did door-to-door, few doors opened. You got nothing. Nobody ever saw anything. That's the way it was. You were getting no help. I'm not saying they all wanted us dead, but many were happy to see you walk into something, having a brave idea that it was there. A lot just totally hated us. Here's the bottom line, the murder file was easily held in one hand. You know what I mean? It tells you everything.

Despite good personal and professional relationships between police intelligence agencies each side of the border, as one former SB officer wryly observed, "It was all one-way. Very little came back and certainly nothing you didn't already know." Of this the Richards Report, Co-ordination of the Security Effort (1981), notes:

Garda shortcomings are sometimes attributed to a combination of a lack of willingness to proceed against PIRA and sometimes a lack of professional capability ... The most significant deficiencies in this technically unsophisticated and basically unarmed force include a lack of resources to acquire and process intelligence, an inadequate surveillance capability and general shortages of manpower and material.

Besides commending Special Branch the report also links inadequate security policies on the southern side of the border to "very few convictions in the Republic of terrorists from border areas." The report also illustrates how politics intruded: "It must not be forgotten that Irish politics play a large part in senior Garda appointments and that the force as a whole is sensitive to changes in political leadership and policy." Richards assessed cross-border police liaison as limited and too reliant on a political dimension on the Irish side that extends to "attitudes of the judiciary, the impediment of the Irish constitution, extradition, the working of extra-territorial legislation and the incompatibility of North/South laws and procedures." Cross-border security co-operation, whilst harmonious, was cosmetic.

Maintaining a permanent police presence was a perilous task in hostile border areas but was crucial to defeating the IRA. Yet Dublin insisted the border was not an issue. The daily enmity experienced by constable Tracy Doak in Newry prior to her murder typifies on-the-ground difficulties the police faced. Constable Doak was a 21-year old with deep Christian beliefs, committed to treating everyone fairly and with compassion. She was one of four officers, inspector William Wilson (28), constable Steven Rodgers (19) and constable David Baird (22) murdered by a bomb placed on a parked lorry on the 20th May 1985 in the process of delivering 'normal' policing. She was due to get married in several months.

Exasperated by nationalist leaders withholding support for his officers and Dublin's anaemic stance on border security Chief Constable Sir John Hermon took the unusual step of issuing several statements based on scientific fact (tachograph read-out of the lorry the bomb was on) that the bomb was manufactured in and detonated from the Republic of Ireland. Dublin and the SDLP, unaware of the source of the Chief Constable's information, quickly contradicted these. The replies were factually baseless, indicating a consciousness and sensitivity to any notion that nationalist leaders were in some way to blame.

In a divided society experiencing a sectarian conflict where the police was portrayed by extremists on one side as anti-nationalist, it did not matter how even-handed or professional officers like Tracy Doak were or how 'normal' the policing; nationalist leaders were never going to give her their support. This was due to historic animosity of the British presence in Ireland and the police being at the cutting edge against IRA terrorism and on the receiving end of Sinn Féin propaganda. In a conflict, communities withholding consent for policing is compensated for by intelligence. But gathering quality intelligence relies on how these communities perceive frontline officers – the public face of policing. Which is why constable Doak and officers like her made a profound difference.

Explaining how intelligence was crucial to countering cross-border IRA brigades and at the same time progressing normal policing is the Loughgall incident. Loughgall was a Protestant village in county Armagh on the county boundary with Tyrone. It comprised a small number of houses and a couple of shops along a main street that was routinely quiet. Its residents supported the police. The centre of the village was in a hollow, which is where a relatively unprotected police station the size of a large detached family house was located. The station provided a policing service to the village and adjoining nationalist areas. East Tyrone/Monaghan IRA considered the station and the four or five police usually within it an ideal target. As it turned out, things did not go to plan. Eight terrorists were shot dead by the SAS: James Lynagh (32), Patrick McKearney (32), Patrick Kelly (32), Gerard O'Callaghan (29), Eugene Kelly (25), Michael Gormley (25), Declan Arthurs (21) and Seamus Donnelly (19). An innocent Catholic civilian, Anthony Hughes (36), was also shot dead by the SAS.

In a violent ten minutes the entire brigade command had been wiped out. All the assailants killed were known to SB and linked to previous murders. Unknown to Special Branch beforehand was exactly who would participate, as there were other active members (some of who were killed in later covert operations). What was likely, however, was that Lynagh and McKearney would be involved. For the IRA it was the largest loss of life in a single incident during the conflict and came at a time IRA confidence was high.

When the attack occurred the only people in Loughgall police station were two constables of SB's specialist firearms team - E4 HMSU (Headquarters Mobile Support Unit) - and six SAS. Also present was a uniform constable stationed there, according to one of the E4 HMSU officers involved. All those who would normally have been in the station, with the exception of one, had been replaced by covert specialists. What follows is largely a synopsis of one of the E4 HMSU officer's experience. He states that he and his colleague had volunteered to be in the station, as had the local officer who was essential to the plan. The rest of the E4 HMSU performed an outer cordon for the SAS as a Quick Reaction Force (QRF), as opposed to being close in and part of the immediate response. Twenty-six SAS were involved in total, with those outside hiding in fields and woodland close to the station.

Both E4 HMSU officers had to protect the local uniform officer when anyone called at the station, as there was concern that an insurgent pretending to be an innocent caller would trigger the attack by shooting the first officer he met. Despite Loughgall being limited opening, which meant it closed at 7pm to the public, 7.00pm to 8.00pm was guaranteed to have several officers inside doing paperwork. IRA reconnaissance would have yielded this fact. Throughout the day, to any passer-by there was a visual appearance that there was no change of routine. The attack took place at 7.30 pm.

Patrick McKearney and a few more were wearing concealed body armour. Some attackers had ammunition magazines tapped together for quick reloads and others had extra ammunition magazines and loose rounds carried in their pockets. All of them wore balaclavas, surgical gloves and many had socks over their shoes, all of which was to guard against being identified or leaving forensic evidence behind. The attack had all the hallmarks of preparing for a close-quarter shoot. One of their weapons, a Ruger revolver, was taken off constable Clements' dead body at Ballygawley and had been used in three murders since. Ballistic traces on the rest of the firearms would almost certainly evidence similar provenance.

Several hours prior to the attack the terrorists took a Ford digger at gunpoint from a family and concealed a 400lb bomb in its bucket. Around the same time a blue Hiace van, which was to transport the gun team, was acquired in similar fashion. The van parked outside the station and the gun team debussed, directing sustained fire at the station during which the digger got into position. Six attackers armed with automatic military rifles all fired. A loaded pistol was recovered in the rubble near the digger (driven by Declan Arthurs) and a spare pump action shotgun was in the van. The van driver, Eugene Kelly, fired constable Clements' Ruger revolver. Seconds after the terrorists opened fire the Ford digger with its raised bucket crashed through the fence. Within seconds an explosion destroyed most of the building and injured all those inside, the most serious being an E4 HMSU officer who suffered severe head injuries. The soldiers outside believed no-one inside had survived; such was the enormity of the blast. And everyone inside was amazed they were still alive. Having observed the immediate build up in the village those in the police station knew that they were about to be attacked. Yet, even then, what happened took them totally by surprise.

The SAS commander was in the station. Initially on the first floor, after the blast he ended up on the ground floor, but somehow collected himself and was the first to return fire. It took a few seconds for the attackers to realise they were taking incoming fire. The IRA expected little if any resistance. They believed a constable and several part-time reserve constables (schoolteachers and farmers in their early-50s) would be present and easily overwhelmed by the sheer force and suddenness of the assault. What they did not expect were soldiers of the world's foremost elite regiment. Had it not been for the SAS commander the assailants would have entered the wrecked building and killed two police officers incapacitated on the ground floor. And this was the plan – covering fire for a car bomb, storm the station, kill everyone inside and steal weapons and documents. But it was also about demoralising the police and sending out a loud signal to Westminster that Northern Ireland was ungovernable, a failed state. As it was, it had the opposite effect.

Unfortunately Anthony Hughes and his brother Oliver, who were dressed similar to the terrorists (navy overalls), appeared in a white Citroen car just as the attackers had started shooting. The coincidence and timing could not have been any worse. The SAS killed Anthony and seriously injured Oliver, the latter receiving emergency medical treatment from either the SAS or E4 HMSU. Within minutes an ambulance was called and fronted by a police escort to the hospital. Oliver survived. The SAS 'cut-offs' broke cover and exposed themselves to great danger in order to protect three women in a car that the attackers had fired at, moving it away from harm. Another car driven by a woman containing a young child was dealt with similarly and a third involved protecting a man who had run from his car. In total, eight innocent civilians in four separate vehicles were caught up in the shooting. Even with the benefit of hindsight the opinion of the E4 HMSU officer is that the speed and scale of the assault meant that the area could not have been cordoned off any better. All three police were hospitalised. None returned fire. No attackers escaped. The incident lasted between five and ten minutes.

Special Branch assessed that E4 HMSU could not counter this type of unit without dramatically increasing the risk to officers and the public. The heaviest calibre weapon E4 had was a .223 calibre Heckler and Koch 33 rifle, which was less powerful than the 7.62 NATO calibre weapons used by the terrorists at Loughgall or the 50 Calibre weapons and RPGs available to cross-border IRA brigades. In contrast the SAS had superior firepower to East Tyrone/Monaghan IRA, chiefly in two general purpose machine guns (GPMGs) of 7.62 NATO calibre. The GPMG is a belt-fed weapon that fires 750 rounds per minute and is accurate up to distances of just over a mile. Both were sited in a wooded area overlooking the station approximately 300-400 yards away. Precise short bursts of three to four rounds fired from each were the decisive factor. Over 1,000 rounds were fired by the SAS, the majority from the GPMGs, which left both barrels smoking hot. The SAS also had the latest Heckler and Koch (7.62 NATO calibre) rifles, which were very powerful.

Relevant to examining the Loughgall incident is how eight terrorists of the same brigade led by Lynagh attacked the home in Tynan of 86-year old Sir Norman Stronge and his son James (a part-time police reservist) with machine guns and grenades in 1981. Both victims were shot in the head at close range and their family home burnt down. Hearing the explosions local police responded but were ambushed. A short gun battle ensued in which the police came a poor second. The security response on the southern side was suspiciously slow and allowed the terrorists to escape back across the border, vindicating Lynagh's decision to shoot it out and adding to his belief that he and his men were invincible. It was a view many police shared, especially when considering the murders perpetrated by East Tyrone/Monaghan IRA in the following years without any sign of them being stopped. There was nothing in law enforcement anywhere in the world capable of tackling seasoned killers in heavily armed gangs like the IRA's cross-border brigades.

In the Loughgall incident the Regional Head of Special Branch (RHSB) had been horribly injured in a terrorist attack when in CID. The IRA had targeted him because he was a tough pro-active cop and a thorn in their side. They also targeted him because he was a Catholic. His investigative background made him a formidable Special Branch commander. An inspirational leader, he was totally committed to his work and demanded the same of others. While the intelligence for Loughgall was compelling it was not definitive. The assessment of it was quite brilliant.

According to a close colleague, who was also a senior SB

officer, having got the raw intelligence - which was shortly before the incident and unconnected to other attacks - the RHSB consulted with his senior tactical advisor. Under one roof SB had world-class police and military specialists at hand 24/7. The tactical plan was pushed up the chain of command.

For such a plan, the Chief Constable authorises it based on a briefing by the Head of Special Branch (HSB), an assistant chief constable (ACC) at HQ, and requests resources from the Army. Senior uniform and CID officers, the Permanent Under Secretary of State in the NIO and Director and Co-ordinator of Intelligence (MI5) are informed. The latter two brief the Northern Ireland Secretary of State who briefs the Prime Minister. It is a dynamic and fast ground-up process. There is no political interference. The police are very much in charge.

A consortium of expert opinion, having considered the tactical menu, assessed the SAS was the best tactical option and the only viable response available in the circumstances. The plan of action was deemed proportionate. Another important factor considered was the Irish dimension - the Garda's lacklustre track record against on-the-runs, limited capacity to conduct surveillance and unimpressive response in the Tynan incident (murder of Sir Norman Stronge and his son James). Equally, in examining other tactical options in practical terms, in a situation where SB knew about a munitions hide (which did not apply to Loughgall) they needed to balance this against terrorist units positioning these in locations they could monitor. Terrorists were surveillance-aware and suspicious of strange vehicles or faces, as the murder of five surveillance operators by the IRA demonstrates.

As an example of a risk associated with surveillance, a year after Loughgall the same IRA brigade conspired to murder unionist politician Ken Maginnis and his police close protection team. Maginnis was an outspoken critic of the IRA. SB was aware of the location of the munitions hide, but surveillance on the hide suffered a soft compromise. A soft compromise is where personnel engaged in covert activity have been detected in a manner that poses no real or immediate threat to them, but exposes what they are at. Usually, this means the covert operation is blown and an overt security response takes over.

The soft compromise near Maginnis' home alerted the terrorists who then abandoned the operation. Consequently, local police recovered automatic rifles and an RPG-7. Follow-up arrests did not result in criminal prosecutions and were never likely to. Losing weapons was not a major setback due to Gadaffi's generosity in this regard. Surveillance of this type, much like agents (or what the republican movement called 'touts'), has its limitations. Being tempted to discover more can jeopardise the opportunity to exploit what you already have and risks shifting the attack to an unknown venue and time thereby increasing the risk to life, particularly if there is little prospect of future intelligence updates.

The penalty of the Maginnis compromise was that, those involved went on to commit more murders due to insufficient evidence to link them to the crime. Overt tactical options like pre-emptive arrests aimed to prevent, or covert tactical options like surveillance aimed at gathering more intelligence, were unsuited at Loughgall.

The E4 HMSU officer injured in the attack on Loughgall police station says that, the SB commander or SAS commander would not have put personnel into the station in the manner that they did had they known what was to happen. The fact SB did not have control of the explosives or knew the nature of the attack is corroborated by the size of the bomb and what actually happened. Had they known these details, they would have put in place easy measures to protect their men inside the station. That none of this happened shows how little knowledge and control the police had.

A member of the SAS who operated alongside US special forces in Iraq and Afghanistan was first briefed on "kill or capture" in these later conflicts. He did not experience any briefing in Northern Ireland or hear of one from others where "arrest" was not the primary aim of the mission. The intent was always to arrest, which the SAS did most of the time despite being up against the UK's most prolific serial killers. Soldiers opened fire because they believed their lives or others were in danger and not as a preprogrammed action. It was not about facilitating a clean kill, but how could killing be avoided with men like Lynagh?

The largest security dividend from Loughgall was not eight top terrorists being killed, although this was significant, but that the Provisionals were totally clueless about how Special Branch knew. This 'not knowing' aggravated Provo paranoia about agents, severely curtailing future East Tyrone/Monaghan IRA terrorist activity. Whatever the next planned attack was they could never be sure if Special Branch knew. Their thinking was no longer offensive but defensive. Perhaps an agent was involved, but there is as much chance that the information came from a technical source – eavesdropping device in a home, building or vehicle or a telephone intercept. Surveillance on a suspect could have picked up on him or her taking interest in Loughgall prior to the attack? A member of the public could have reported suspicious activity in enough detail for SB to suspect Loughgall police station was a target? Or perhaps it was none of these?

The diversity of gathered intelligence, of which agents accounted for 60%, made it difficult for terrorists holding a post-mortem to pinpoint the leak, as it could have been caused in different plausible ways. The approach was crucial to protecting well-placed sources (human and technical) and sensitive methodologies, boosted immeasurably by the IRA's irrational fear of agents. Today former Provisionals are as committed to discovering secret sources behind the intelligence attack as they were at the time. Nowhere is this desire more acute than the Loughgall incident.

To taint what happened Sinn Féin propagandists accused Special Branch of a dirty war directed by London where the SAS are murderous death squads. Yet this does not compute with the ground-up approach used and ignores the unprecedented threat to life posed by vicious cross-border brigades. Critics of the security policy also wonder why loyalist terrorists were not killed in the same way, connecting this to an injustice felt by nationalists. Unlike republicans, however, loyalists were not indoctrinated into an ideology that promoted the security forces as the enemy - legitimate targets to be killed. Republicans murdered at least 20 covert operators. Loyalists killed none. It is a simple risk analysis. Republican insurgents posed a far greater threat to life than loyalist terrorists when confronted in a covert operation. This risk was highest with cross-border IRA brigades.

In a covert operation arrests were always the explicit aim and occurred 96% of the time and 99.5% of the time overall when including disruptive/pre-emptive arrests/searches or other overt tactics usually at the local level by uniform police. Incidents like Loughgall are the very rare occasions when arrests or other preventative measures were not possible. To argue otherwise is to claim that in Northern Ireland's conflict there were no circumstances where armed insurgents engaged in terrorism could have been justifiably killed in a covert operation because other tactical options were always available.

Strategically, intelligence-led arrest operations were crippling the IRA, which tied in with Special Branch having identified 'prisoners' as the IRA's greatest vulnerability. The IRA was running out of 'volunteers' and most of those they had were not as committed as popularly portrayed, and not as committed or proficient as the security forces they were up against. Incidents like Loughgall were the closest the IRA came to proper open combat. Yet even when they fired the first shots and had the advantage of surprise, when the soldiers fired back they had no contingency because they never needed one before. The formation used to attack the station reveals that they had no concept or experience of combat. Loughgall did not swell the ranks of the IRA, quite the opposite. A former SB detective sums it up:

> They stood the entire brigade down after Loughgall. It totally wrecked them. The witch-hunt for a mole destroyed them mentally. They'd lost all confidence. Nobody was in a rush to join or at least nobody with any sense. After Loughgall they were never the same.

The Loughgall incident amplified to frontline IRA activists what they already knew, Special Branch were allowing a crime to escalate to a point where a suspect and munitions came together that regularly culminated in arrest and a long prison sentence but on rare occasions death. At grassroots level active terrorists and their families knew this and were intimidated by it. The Loughgall incident also demonstrated to the IRA leadership that involving a large number of terrorists in an attack was a strategic liability. Had the cross-border offensive not been stopped, of which the demise of East Tyrone/Monaghan IRA is the most public example, maintaining a permanent police presence in isolated rural areas and progressing normal policing would have been extremely difficult. Wider destabilisation would have resulted. More lives would have been lost.

South Armagh's cancerous instability had been prevented from spreading. South Armagh IRA would become more vulnerable and south Armagh less unstable, a dramatic turnaround from the 1970s. Success at Loughgall publicly showed where the balance of power lay in the intelligence war. It gave Special Branch vital momentum against the IRA that neither they nor their political partner could stop. For a beleaguered police force and a long-suffering public, what happened at Loughgall convinced many for the first time that the IRA was beatable. Loughgall was the beginning of the end. The intelligence attack would devastate the IRA through an arrest-centric approach interspersed infrequently with ferocious flexes of Loughgall-type hard power.

Ultimately, successful covert operations were due to professional frontline police officers. But to fully understand this, it is necessary to start at the beginning.

Insurgent networks habitually violate the laws of war.

Chapter 2

The Troubles

The old adage still stands. No two wars are the same. But we can categorise war. In thinking of war most people have in mind WW2 or WW1. These were conventional wars where soldiers dressed in the uniform of one army fought soldiers in the uniform of another army. The enemy was easily identified. It was obvious who was a soldier and who was a civilian. Both sides are required to comply with the laws of war, namely the various Geneva Conventions and associate protocols. These decree that prisoners should be treated in a humanitarian way and there should not be summary executions. Any side in flagrant disregard will be prosecuted for war crimes, such as the Nuremburg trials against the Nazis or more recent trials of Serbian forces following the breakup of Yugoslavia. This conventional war, however, is mostly a thing of the past.

The most common form of war since WW2 has been irregular war. This is the category the Troubles fall into, as do ongoing conflicts in Iraq and Afghanistan. Irregular war is a phenomenon comprised of two competing opposites – insurgency and counterinsurgency. Insurgency invariably involves a protracted campaign of terrorism and political militancy by people opposed to the state. The objective is to wear down the resolve of the existing government for the purpose of overthrowing it. In the latter part of the 20th century successful insurgencies have been conducted in Vietnam and Algeria. In none of these countries did insurgents militarily defeat the state's security forces. Rather, they made the war so unpopular in Washington (Vietnam) and Paris (Algeria) that it was politically impossible to do anything other than concede to the insurgents' demands. The main reason these insurgencies succeeded was that they were popularly supported.

The most recent insurgencies, however, fall into a category called urban insurgency. Examples are the IRA, some Islamic extremist groups in Iraq and some groups in Latin America. Urban insurgency is not popularly supported. The majority of the population oppose it. It is an unpopular uprising. A few violent extremists hold the rest of the population to ransom. Northern Ireland's conflict was not a war of the people - quite the opposite. The majority Protestant community at this time (65%), that was predominantly unionist, opposed it and while almost all those in the minority Catholic community, that was predominantly nationalist, ideologically supported the IRA cause the majority strongly disagreed with IRA terrorism.

Knowing that insurgency is a combination of terrorism and politics explains the relationship between the IRA and Sinn Féin. If one wants to be technically precise the Provisional IRA and Provisional Sinn Féin describe the terrorist and political elements, thereby PIRA/PSF accurately describes the full insurgent construct. Most people know the PIRA as the IRA, Provos or Provisionals, and Provisional Sinn Féin as just Sinn Féin. Both collaborated daily in pursuit of common goals. A significant number in Sinn Féin were also in the IRA. At leadership level the two roles often overlapped. They were all insurgents.

The IRA was a dangerous terrorist organisation proficient at guerrilla war hit and run tactics. Its political partner was even better. Sinn Féin contained superb propagandists and strategic thinkers. Politics and terrorism were two mutually supportive features of a single enterprise. This is why, arguably, the IRA/Sinn Féin combination is the world's foremost example of a modern insurgent network. Sinn Féin is a main reason why the IRA was so formidable.

Modern insurgent networks habitually violate the laws of war. In carrying out attacks they dress in civilian clothes, making them indistinguishable from the civilian population they hide amongst, which is the intent. This endangers civilians. As a rule they avoid confrontations with the security forces. Their small numbers and inferior resources dictate this. To do otherwise means early defeat. Conscious of this Sinn Féin created the illusion that IRA terrorists were combatants, misappropriating the language of war to promote them as soldiers, delivering on the IRA's crave to be seen as equals to the security forces.

Also in contravention of the laws of war and typical of groups like the IRA/Sinn Féin are torture, mutilation and the summary execution of prisoners as official policy. Gross human rights violations are the norm. In Northern Ireland, Sinn Féin's task was to hide or excuse these abuses and other sinister features in the course of legitimising IRA actions and delegitimising those of the state.

Another feature of a modern insurgency is that it deliberately incites sectarian violence to raise ethnic or religious tension between communities. The IRA prospered from purposely provoking a sectarian escalation of violence. It saw ethnic division as a weakness to exploit. IRA murders of Protestants that triggered loyalist terrorists into murdering Catholics were retaliations the IRA hoped for. Tit-for-tat murders preyed on nationalist fears that unionists were sectarian instruments of British security policy that Irish nationalists historically loathed. The intent was to pit Irish against British, nationalist against unionist, republican against loyalist and Catholic against Protestant in deepening the divide of an already divided society. In Iraq, Sunni insurgents in al-Qaeda bombed Shia mosques and murdered Shia civilians. It is what insurgents do – segregate and isolate. Splitting communities by fear. Suspicion and intolerance reign. Trust between communities evaporates. Local politics collapse. Instability is pervasive. This is how insurgents create and control their support-base.

Other characteristics of a modern insurgency include intimidating the population, murdering local police officers and soldiers and limiting their ability to respond to attacks. An urban insurgent network also strives to force the government into repressive responses, such as detention without trial (internment), Army primacy or harsh emergency laws. This is because repressive security measures allow insurgents to portray themselves as victims, thereby attracting much needed support.

Modern insurgent networks rely on a fundamental ideology capable of mixing historic animosities with current grievances (real or perceived). This blurs moral boundaries enough to convince believers that murder is justifiable. In 1969, the fundamental ideology of physical-force-republicanism dating from the late 1700s was used by a handful of impatient angry men to justify them discarding the democratic process to resolve nationalist grievances by violence. Whilst genuine grievances existed and needed to be addressed they were not severe enough to warrant a conflict. Ideology is the glue that holds together an insurgency.

Yet the IRA and Sinn Féin is only the tip of the insurgent iceberg. Beneath are active, passive and outside supports. Active support is providing safe houses, vehicles and information on the police and Army (how and where they patrol, respond to calls, and personal details like where they live, cars they drive or places they frequent). Similar information is provided on members of the judiciary or anyone insurgents deem to be the enemy.

Passive support takes the form of general admiration for insurgent activities. Sunni crowds in Iraq cheered at US deaths in the same way republicans did with the security forces in Northern Ireland. An example is the abduction, beating and executions of corporals David Howes (23) and Derek Wood (24) in west Belfast in 1988. No-one in a large republican crowd intervened. Most were happy to see the soldiers murdered and those who thought of trying to help were too scared to do so. Passive support also entails failing to assist the police, such as reporting suspicious activity or disclosing known information about terrorism.

Underpinning the IRA terrorist campaign was murdering local police. This is typical of insurgency because the police represent the rule of law, which is the main obstacle for insurgents and a democracy's first line of defence. Sinn Féin excused such murders by discrediting the police, portraying them as sectarian puppets of the British war machine and therefore 'legitimate targets.' Sinn Féin's depiction of the police conditioned nationalists into believing the police were anti-Catholic. Chief Constable Sir Hugh Annesley (1989-96) writes about this in his 1990 annual report:

> *The task of bringing terrorists to justice requires determined people of goodwill to come forward and assist the police... anything less than real support for the police carries with it the prospect, indeed certainty, that violence will continue to afflict us all.*

Like his predecessors, in coded language Annesley aimed his comments at the moderate SDLP who also largely reflected the position of the Catholic Church on policing and justice issues. Annesley saw the SDLP's refusal to fully endorse the police as having significantly contributed to the under-representation of Catholics in the police. He blamed this for helping to prolong the conflict. Annesley further writes that, "a unity between the police and the people" was critical to effective security and that this alongside politics and economics was crucial to bringing about peace. Nationalist politicians Paddy Devlin and Gerry Fitt were more forthright, arguing that the SDLP under John Hume's leadership was too close to Sinn Féin. They also argued that police professionalism and impartiality from 1972 demonstrated that the police deserved SDLP support and lamented that this was not forthcoming. The SDLP stance was passive support.

Nationalist leaders were simultaneously supporting the IRA and condemning them. The contradiction is typical of the effect created by an insurgency. In Iraq, US General David Petraeus (commander of coalition forces in Iraq and Afghanistan, and widely credited with stemming the advance of the Sunni insurgency in Iraq) claims the disengagement from political dialogue of moderate Sunni parties sustained the Sunni insurgency and had a profoundly negative impact on stability operations, the safety of local police and police recruitment. Without the passive support of moderates the IRA and Sinn Féin would not have posed the threat they did.

The SDLP stance influenced the Republic of Ireland (ROI). Despite Irish Prime Ministers like Jack Lynch and Garret Fitzgerald resenting the Provisionals and what they stood for, they were held hostage by a political fringe in Irish politics that supported the Provisionals. The Dublin government was consumed by controversy in being accused of arming the Provisionals in the early 1970s, typified by the arms trial against several government ministers. Showing how the ROI dimension impacted on security in Northern Ireland a former Special Branch senior officer said:

> *The PIRA had the benefit of placing its broad organisational support mechanism in ROI, including primary munitions hides and importation routes, training, engineering, testing, OTRs [on-the-runs], recuperation, strategic meetings etc. The PIRA at its height attracted self-sustaining core practitioner support and significant passive support from the wider nationalist community, which transcended all social and economic groups within that community.*

For the IRA, the border and territory of the neighbouring state was a strategic asset. Irish criminal courts interpreted IRA terrorism as a political act and not a crime. Extradition refusals were routine. Similarly, criminal courts in Syria regarded al-Qaeda terror suspects as political refugees and therefore refused to extradite them to Iraq. The Republic of Ireland's failings facilitated the IRA to conduct a prolonged terrorist campaign in Northern Ireland, epitomising how an insurgency influences the approach of a neighbouring state of the same religion or ethnicity.

Outside supports also involve a distant international aspect.

The sizeable Irish-American diaspora contained a small criminal element that supplied the IRA with weapons. Many Irish-Americans gave money to Sinn Féin in the misguided belief their contribution was not funding terrorism. In 1979 support from the US also translated into politics, forcing President Jimmy Carter into prohibiting the supply of weapons to the police in Northern Ireland.

As well as Irish-America, the IRA received outside support from Colonel Gadaffi's Libya. The dictator's largesse left the IRA better armed and financed than the armies of many third world nations. Gadaffi's motivation was his hatred of the US and its closest ally – the UK. Gadaffi and the IRA shared a common enemy, particularly after the UK facilitated US airstrikes in Tripoli in 1986. Dealing with violent totalitarian regimes was not new for the IRA. In WW2 they worked with the Nazis against the British, their chief of staff Seán Russell dying on a German U Boat.

When considering outside, active and passive supports, it is clear insurgency is much more nuanced than a small group of terrorists and political propagandists. Insurgency is a complex social and political web of relationships, alliances and influences in varying degrees of transparency that interact wittingly or unwittingly to impede the counterinsurgent. In the Global War on Terror, President George W. Bush viewed this as a zero sum - if you are not part of the solution you are part of the problem. Viewed in this way, the SDLP, Dublin and Irish-America were part of the problem. Not as much as insurgents and Colonel Gadaffi, but part of the problem nonetheless. Yet, all of these actors are also part of the solution.

Insurgency is a self-contained strategy within which terrorism is a main tactic to prosecute a long war. The creation of the Provos in December 1969 in Dublin was the start of Northern Ireland's long and irregular war. The IRA's first Chief of Staff, Seán MacStiofáin, copied the classic insurgency template of Mao Zedong (the founder of Communist China). He implemented Mao's three-phase strategy of defence, defence and retaliation then all-out offense. For this the IRA promoted that it was defending

Catholics and attacking oppressive British forces of illegal occupation. Unlike Mao's popularly supported peasant uprising, however, the IRA was not popularly supported. This was a major flaw in MacStiofáin's thinking. Nonetheless, a dedicated devotee of physical-force-republicanism, MacStiofáin's extensive use of terrorism in the opening stages served a valuable purpose, even though it was not well organised. Extreme and sustained terrorism highlighted the IRA cause. It was textbook insurgency designed to exploit the state's slowness to respond. Consequently the initial political and security response aggravates the situation. The net effect is to attract support to the insurgency's cause. This is what happened in Northern Ireland.

MacStiofáin was undoubtedly buoyed by the success of the Tet offensive in 1968 by the Vietcong. Events in Vietnam dramatically played out on television screens across the world, especially in the US. This was the intent. Shaping the message that went out to the public, particularly to remote audiences, was central to Sinn Féin's communications strategy. Sensational images of US troops being attacked were instrumental in forcing the US to leave Vietnam. This was MacStiofáin's phase three. Former Special Branch officers recall that at the time republicans popularly viewed Northern Ireland as Britain's Vietnam, noting the analogy was quickly dropped due to obvious sensitivities in Irish-America.

From the outset it was always going to be a lengthy affair, which the IRA did not fully appreciate. Although MacStiofáin was naïve about the IRA's capacity to quickly drive the British out of Northern Ireland - the headline aim of the IRA - he and others genuinely believed they could. In 1973 it became clear this was fantasy. Which is why MacStiofáin's original strategy was revised in the mid-1970s by a new breed of young leaders from the north who understood change was required to compensate for the IRA's unpopularity. They also better understood what was needed for a long war in Northern Ireland's unique environment.

Unlike the original leaders, a small exclusive elite of bright strategic thinkers privately knew they could never militarily defeat the British, but had to maintain the outward pretence that they could. Although deceitful it was pragmatic. The revised strategy was a protracted terrorist campaign underpinning a wider political agenda to create the optimum conditions that would benefit Sinn Féin's entry into bona fide politics. It was in the interest of Sinn Féin to deliberately extend the armed conflict. The IRA terrorist campaign, or what the IRA and Sinn Féin called the 'armed struggle,' was the means not the end.

Entering democratic politics and becoming a major political force each side of the border was the objective. But few republicans at the time would have bought into this and fewer would have understood it. As a major political force Sinn Féin would be better placed to deliver on its original promise to unite Ireland.

Similar to insurgency, counterinsurgency is broadly comprised of two main blocks - politics and security - that correspond to the political and terrorist elements of insurgency. Notwithstanding loyalist terrorist organisations and insurgent splinter groups, the remit of the police and Army in the context of the main threat was to counter the IRA. The government would deal with Sinn Féin's political militancy.

Counterinsurgency describes the totality of actions designed to defeat irregular forces like the IRA – 'defeat' being the key word. Counterinsurgency is commonly seen as 80% politics and 20% security. It seems too low a percentage for security when considering General David Petraeus believes everything depends on security. Security is the priority. The ebb and flow of conflict means security for large spells dominates. Without effective security, politics remains dysfunctional. Without effective security, there is no hope.

Security and politics are interdependent in defeating an insurgency. And as General Petraeus highlights, intelligence is crucial to security. In Northern Ireland the Whole of Government strategy that evolved in 1976 saw security pushing the IRA and politics pulling it toward peace. Because the IRA was the main protagonist and aggressor, the Whole of Government strategy was based on defeating the IRA in order to end the conflict. Politics always had primacy. The difficulty is in balancing politics, security, social, economic and governance issues with the prevailing terrorist threat at any single point in time. In this regard effective security, as General Petraeus emphasises, is essential.

Sir Frank Kitson was a British Army brigadier who served in Northern Ireland for 18-months from 1971 to 1972. He had authored books on irregular warfare based mostly on his experiences in Kenya and Malaya. His writings attracted the attention of Sinn Féin propagandists who claimed the tactics in his books were used in Belfast, based on Kitson's presence in Belfast. At the Saville Inquiry into 'Bloody Sunday' in 2001, however, Kitson testified that none of the tactics he wrote about, such as counter-gangs, was implemented in Northern Ireland. Nothing that transpired resembled Kitson's tactics. The briefest study of the counter-gang concept illustrates that it relies on co-ethnicity. This would have meant teams of proselytised Provos partnering the Army in attacking the Provos, which never happened.

What transpired from a security perspective was a rule of law approach, where the British government treated the IRA as terrorist criminals. This was broadly in keeping with classic British counterinsurgency, such as the successful approach in the Malayan Emergency (1945-60) against communist guerrillas. Central to the approach are policy, doctrine and operational procedures that comply with humanitarian principles and basic human rights norms. The aim was not to physically destroy the IRA or treat terrorists as the enemy but to prosecute them in a court of law and put them in prison. This is distinctly different to the destructive approach adopted by the French in Algeria and US in Vietnam. Both of these were military-based efforts, routinely involving air strikes and artillery bombardments against an enemy that was often invisible, hidden in open sight amongst the civilian population. Success was measured in body counts. The French approach was especially brutal. Notwithstanding that French and US forces were dealing with a popularly supported insurgency, the destructiveness of the approach was also a major reason why the insurgency succeeded. In the all-important 'hearts and minds' campaign the destructive approach is counter-productive.

Even though Northern Ireland was experiencing a de facto irregular war, the best way to reduce violence and defeat the IRA was through a robust policing action. The main benefit of this approach was that it allowed the state to stigmatise the IRA as criminals and undermined Sinn Féin promoting them as a legitimate army. The approach depicted the IRA as terrorists and not soldiers or combatants, as former US President John F Kennedy once noted:

Irregular war is another type of war, new in its intensity, ancient in its origin – war by guerrillas, subversives, insurgents, assassins, war by ambush instead of combat; by infiltration instead of aggression, seeking victory by eroding and exhausting the enemy instead of engaging him.

Criminalising the insurgency allowed the state to use common language to describe the IRA and its activities in terms the public understood. It directly contested IRA/Sinn Féin ideology and was unequivocal in projecting the IRA as wrong.

The security approach complemented the political approach. A downside was that it suppressed the reality of the conflict being an irregular war. Although not on the same scale of duplicity as the IRA/Sinn Féin leadership in the mid-1970s, or for the same reasons, it was nonetheless a necessary pretence.

For many, thinking of Northern Ireland as an irregular war between 1969 and 1998 is new. They are more familiar with it being called the Troubles. But one should not get hung up on the semantics of terminology. Viewing the Troubles as an irregular war makes it easier to see how sophisticated the IRA/Sinn Féin network was and what it took to sustain the 'armed struggle.' Only by understanding the full complexity of the threat can we ever hope to understand the response. As insurgency and counterinsurgency become familiar one begins to realise there is so much more to the Troubles than terrorists and security forces.

The Troubles did not experience the same level of violent intensity as Iraq or Afghanistan. Neither did it have the same geopolitical impact. Probably there has never been an irregular war less about armed conflict and more about politics. Nevertheless it was still a tumultuous upheaval to civil society. It devastated the lives of many people; forced governments, communities and groups into abnormal actions and prevented the normal functioning of a liberal democracy. The IRA and Sinn Féin are right in saying it was a war. This, however, is about as accurate as it gets for them. What they had to mask was how they conducted themselves, which is in keeping with how groups of this type behave. They are vulnerable to the facts.

Conversely, having adopted a rule of law approach that excludes the language of war the British government could not admit that it was a war. Once we realise the government's dilemma, the label becomes relatively unimportant. What matters is to get a complete and accurate picture of the IRA and Sinn Féin threat – strategy, tactics and operational procedures. The same applies to the security response, especially the intelligence aspect. Examining the Troubles as an irregular war does this. It also allows for relevant comparisons and analogies with similarly categorised conflicts, especially those since 9/11.

The significance of recent Irish history as it relates to the Troubles is also easier seen when viewed from an irregular war perspective. From the early 1900s the history of armed conflict in Ireland shows that a successful insurgency formula was the IRA and Sinn Féin and from the mid-1800s a successful counterinsurgency formula was a rule of law approach by local police – the Royal Irish Constabulary (RIC). Both are intelligence-based. Special Branch was central to the RIC's operational effectiveness and Michael Collins' IRA relied on spies. But the two had never really been matched up. In the Anglo-Irish Conflict (1919-22) the British adopted a destructive military-based approach as opposed to the rule of law, only realising too late that this was self-defeating, as it was in Vietnam and Algeria. RIC successes were in putting down Fenian uprisings that predated the IRA. It was therefore inevitable that the Troubles would see these proven formulas - appropriately updated - defining each side. In this regard a captured IRA document (early 1970s) is instructive. It reads:

> *Irish history has produced two extraordinary phenomena in the world of intelligence; the RIC model, which was copied all over the world, and the I.R.A. model, which was the envy of every revolutionary organisation since the 1920s. They were remarkably different in intent, yet had much in common in operation.*

The IRA was the disease. Special Branch was the cure. The intelligence war would be key to ending the conflict.

Heightening sectarian tension profited the newly formed Provisionals.

Chapter 3

Licence to Kill

At the start of the Troubles, riots between Catholic and Protestant mobs and confrontations between police and 'civil rights' protesters were common scenes on television screens across the world. Most viewers and commentators, however, did not realise they were watching the outworking of a power struggle in republicanism between rival IRA and Sinn Féin factions. Instructive and insightful in this regard is how Special Branch assessed the situation. The Special Branch annual report (1970) by the Head of Special Branch states:

> By the beginning of the year we had long-since re-oriented our target thinking and activities to cover the whole spectrum ranging from our traditional I.R.A. enemy through the various anarchist and pseudo-political groups of the Left to the far Right of extreme Protestantism. With our experience, however, we did not share some fashionable down-grading of the I.R.A. as a serious threat, and our gloomy predictions on their re-emergence as Public Enemy No. 1 were proved correct with each succeeding month.

Extreme Protestantism remained an amorphous mass of unrest and dissatisfaction against the new order of things, but lacked any cohesive organisation even remotely resembling the I.R.A.

…

It is generally believed that at the time of the split, about two-thirds of the existent membership of the I.R.A. joined the Provisional Group and its ascendency over the Official (Goulding) Group in this respect was maintained throughout the year. Its policy … proved to be more attractive to (a) the older hard line types and (b) the more militant youthful members.

Radical Provisionals had taken over from moderate Officials and now posed the main threat to national security. The report further related that Sinn Féin was involved in promoting civil disorder, which was widespread and a major drain on security resources. Sinn Féin's role in riots is highly significant. Typical of an insurgency, the last thing insurgents' want is inter-community harmony.

The Provisional IRA's political arm worked feverishly behind the scenes to influence the direction of civil rights groups. They saw fighting between Protestants and Catholics as a good thing, an opportunity to increase their appeal and standing in the Catholic community. Heightening sectarian tension profited the newly formed Provisionals and their political partner. Subtly hi-jacking the civil rights movement so that it championed a nationalist agenda was guaranteed to alienate unionists, which suited militant republicans. Inciting riots to cause violent confrontations with the police (a predominantly Protestant force) followed the same thinking. Having steered the civil rights movement down a nationalist path, any police confrontation with 'civil rights' protesters conveniently allowed Sinn Féin to portray as an attack on nationalists by an anti-Catholic police force.

The Provisionals and their Sinn Féin counterpart correctly calculated that the issue of nationalist identity would ruin the cross-community aspect of the civil rights movement, thereby preventing working class Catholics and Protestants coming together to jointly progress common grievances. They also correctly calculated that, in turn, the civil rights movement, which now represented nationalist grievances, was the perfect shop window to portray the police as a sectarian force Catholics could not trust by causing the police to confront increasingly violent 'civil rights' protesters. None of this happened by accident. An insurgent network with a hidden sectarian agenda had contrived these outcomes in order to isolate the Catholic community from any normal interaction with the Protestant community and police.

The Special Branch report also shows other characteristics of the Provisionals typical of an insurgency. An example is the Provos bombing business premises as a policy to counteract government attempts to attract investment and create jobs. Others are the supply of finance from sympathisers in the US and suspicions about personalities in or close to the Dublin government donating a large amount of cash to arm the Provisionals from the European continent.

In keeping with its insurgent character, although rioting persisted as an insurgent tactic throughout the Troubles, it was soon overshadowed by pre-meditated murders. Stones and petrol bombs gave way to bombs and bullets. The ante was upped with deadly costs. Since the start of the insurgency in 1969, in the first 20 months loyalist terrorists murdered two people (both Protestants) and republican terrorists murdered 48. Retaliatory murders of Catholics by loyalists needed to happen otherwise the Provisionals would be exposed for the sectarian, aggressive organisation they were, the opposite of the non-sectarian, defensive organisation they professed. Republicans had perpetrated 95% of all murders. This is the immediate impact the Provos had, showing their intent to escalate sectarian violence by provoking a loyalist backlash. Despite these deficiencies the 'defender' tag stuck and sectarian aspect overlooked by the republican community who preferred their approach to peaceful civil rights protests or the less violent Officials.

The first offensive action by the Provisionals that resulted in security force fatalities were the murders of constables Sam

Donaldson (23) and Robert Millar (26) in a bomb attack in August 1970 in south Armagh. This was six months prior to the IRA murdering the first soldier, Robert Curtis (20), in Belfast. The lance corporal was shot dead by an IRA sniper on his last foot patrol before he was due to go home on leave. Murdering local police distanced the police from the nationalist community and increased ethnic division because unionists viewed the Provisionals as sectarian murderers and fully supported police efforts to stop them. Murdering Protestants and police ensured republican areas had no normal contact with either, which was essential to an IRA/ Sinn Féin long war strategy based on controlling republican areas.

IRA murders of police show the Provisionals rated local police as their main threat. It proved a popular approach in an increasingly sectarian conflict and was a main reason why, by 1973, the Officials were made irrelevant by the more violent Provos.

From 1970 the Provisionals were the 'real' IRA. In turn, Provisional Sinn Féin took over from Official Sinn Féin in influencing 'respectable' groups like the Northern Ireland Civil Rights Association. The difficulty was that, constitutional nationalists like the SDLP refused to accept the nationalist character of the civil rights movement, insisting it was cross-community. Their stance compounded a similar failing in unionist leaders who refused to acknowledge that genuine civil rights grievances existed in the first place and that, although these affected Catholic and Protestant working-class communities alike, they were greater in the former. Both failings benefited the Provisionals. And it was not as if the Provisionals in 1970 were politically astute. The Special Branch 1970 report estimates that the Official IRA had a more intelligent leadership than the Provisionals and was far more politically advanced than its rival. Or as a retired Special Branch officer puts it:

When you talk to old time IRA they refer to the Provos as the 69ers, and generally that they [Provisionals] didn't have a political thought in their head at that time.

Another states: "You could have put the Provos political manifesto on a postage stamp." An enormous plus for the new version of the IRA and Sinn Féin is that they wanted to connect with grassroots nationalists and knew how to achieve this. This, however, was out of need to control a support-base to pursue a long war strategy rather than any clever calculation about securing a strong political foothold.

Ultimately, the Officials were sidelined because they refused to sink to the Provos' level of depravity. For instance, in 1970 the Official IRA abducted a police officer in Caledon but later released him unharmed. It was not in their makeup to execute prisoners. The Official IRA was also alive to the sectarianism of the Provos. In their Easter Statement in 1972 the Official IRA condemned the Provo campaign, claiming it had split society on sectarian lines and increased the threat of civil war. A Special Branch assessment (6 Jan 1972) records that the Provo bombing campaign is to be increased against Protestant businesses. An example being a car bomb that killed six Protestant civilians in Coleraine (1973). The assessment presages an escalation of this policy in subsequent years, such as the Tullyvallen massacre (1975, five Protestants murdered) and Kingsmill massacre (1976, 10 Protestants murdered). These attacks happened close to the border, leaving the former victims commissioner, Sir Kenneth Bloomfield, to conclude in 2013 that the Provisionals operated a policy of ethnic cleansing in border areas.

In broad terms, as an insurgent network one gets a grasp of what the Provisionals and Sinn Féin were at, all of which conformed to how an insurgency behaves. As such, the one aspect above all else that they put most effort into protecting themselves against was Special Branch. Emphasising this point, the Special Branch annual report (1971) notes that the Official IRA was radicalised by the Provos in only one area, legitimising the murder of Special Branch officers while opposing the murder of "normal" police officers. From 1971 to 1990 SB lost ten serving officers (seven Protestants and three Catholics) in nine separate incidents that also resulted in the deaths of three civilians. The IRA was responsible for all of these. Five of the incidents where when detectives were off duty, such as Maurice Rolston (37), a Protestant from County Longford. Married, with three children, he was killed by a bomb under his car at his Newcastle home in 1973. The bomb could have easily killed his family, as his wife also used the car. Another example is Patrick McNulty (30). A Catholic married with two children, he was off-duty in Londonderry when shot dead by two terrorists in 1977. Two of his three brothers were also in the police. At his funeral, Bishop Edward Daly said:

> *If policemen find it necessary to carry arms to protect their own lives and the lives of their family, it is not an indictment of the police, but one of society, the government and the churches. Everyone in the community must accept that he or she had played a part in the murder.*

Bishop Daly highlighted the deadly price being paid by the police for the passive and active support of the IRA by the nationalist community and the same community's refusal to fully support the police.

Prior to the Provos, mainstream republicanism did not hold such a radical view of SB. Had there been a series of covert operations that killed IRA men or innocent Catholics, or a spree of loyalist murders of Catholics, hatred of this depth could be more easily rationalised. But this was not the case. Rather, the hatred displayed was a manifestation of an historic fear of SB by militant republicans in times of conflict. For the Provos, Special Branch had to be neutered, the first step being to convince republicans and eventually nationalists that Special Branch was the worst of the worst, different to other police officers and a group to be despised and feared.

The Official IRA's new found intolerance of a selected section of the police is perhaps the clearest example of how the Provisionals and Sinn Féin successfully discriminated against Special Branch, casting it as the arch villain in a general hardening of attitudes in the republican mainstream. From the outset the IRA and Sinn Féin treated Special Branch with a level of disdain that exceeded any other aspect of the state. Unsurprisingly, therefore, in the intelligence war the purview of Sinn Féin was to discredit Special Branch. In its most primitive form tainting Special Branch was done through propaganda literature like Republican News or leaflets handed out in republican housing estates. Smearing was also done through what the Northern Ireland Secretary of State Roy Mason (1976-9) called the second front in the propaganda war.·

Special Branch training material from 1976 explains the second front as Sinn Féin's wider dissemination policy, where it often chose a respectable third party, either a front organisation under its direct control like a relatives group that promoted the republican version of victimhood, an organisation sympathetic to its aims, like a civil liberties group or NGO like Amnesty International, socialist party such as the Communist Party of Ireland, or individuals such as journalists. It reads:

Even the smallest gap between the Provisionals and the organisation or individuals making the allegations, will add disproportionately to the credibility. This is particularly true of the press and television especially where their audience is far away and largely ignorant or uncaring of the minutiae of Northern Ireland paramilitary politics. The realisation of this credibility relationship explains why the Provisionals utilize the wide range of sympathetic bodies to further their campaign. The Provisional movement in general contains accomplished propagandists who are well capable of initiating, orchestrating and disseminating a campaign of allegations based upon non-existent or flimsy evidence. They are fully appreciative of how easily a lie can be propagated and then sustained and how difficult it is to counter with the truth; the more so where the lie is simple and sensational and the truth complex and boring, where the whole situation is complicated by legal limitations which largely favour the accuser not the accused and where the situation is populated with those who have concealed sympathies and bias masquerading as the impartial and objective.

Sinn Féin's PR strategy transmitted their message to a wider audience through proxies. While Sinn Féin worked at discrediting Special Branch the IRA worked on cutting off the information supply to it by ruthlessly dealing with collaborators, a term that includes anything from informing to displaying sympathy for the police or Army. Collaborators were largely republicans who secretly gave information to the security forces, Special Branch being the Provos main worry.

In contrast to SB detectives, collaborators were people in republican areas and therefore easy to get at. An example of how the IRA dealt with collaborators is a captured IRA document found on a leading IRA figure in August 1973. It lists five ways Special Branch gathers intelligence from 'volunteers'; loose talk; informers; listening devices; movement and behaviour of volunteers; and lack of discipline. Moreover, the document outlines debriefing procedures once released from police custody: "Any volunteer found to be telling lies about his interrogation will be severely dealt with." A main reason to lie was to hide having agreed to become an informer; the ultimate sanction for which - to interpret 'severely dealt with' - was execution.

Various local instructions regarding informers and loose talk were enforced formally from the 6th September 1973 through "G.H.Q. Directive, General Order No. 1," as amended by the Provisional Army Council (PAC). This is a very polished legalistic-type document, protectively marked "classified" and "restricted to G.H.Q. and/or officers appointed by the Chief-of-Staff." General Order No. 1 details the penalties imposed for talking and not reporting this fact is to be "dismissed with ignominy" or charged with "treachery." The IRA had executed 10 'collaborators' up to the time General Order No. 1 was issued.

General Order No. 1 regulated the IRA approach to 'collaborators' and exemplifies the IRA's congenital fear and hatred of Special Branch. The Special Branch annual report (1973) reinforces this point:

The year 1973 began with a IRA Headquarters statement to the effect that there would be no let up in their campaign of violence and that the British provocateur and RUC Special Branch would be "ruthlessly struck down where and whenever found."

General Order No.1 and similar directives that preceded it resulted in at least 83 extra-judicial executions (78 Catholics and five Protestants) of 'collaborators', double the deaths caused by the police. The youngest was a 15-year old boy (Bernard Teggart) with learning disabilities. His body was placed on public show in the street. The oldest was pensioner Michael Madden, taken into his garden and shot repeatedly in the head. He was 68. The first was John Kavanagh (Jan 1971). Husband and wife Gerard and Catherine Mahon were executed together.

What follows is a list of these executions. Not included are serving members of the security forces abducted and executed by the IRA, such as constable William Turbitt (42). He was one of two police officers ambushed near Camlough by South Armagh IRA in June 1978. His colleague, constable Hugh McConnell (32) was also killed. Constable Turbitt was born in County Monaghan and was married with four children. UDR soldier James Elliot (36) is another. In 1972 the IRA left his body on the border connected to a 500lb bomb and six claymore landmines. He was married with three children.

The IRA has the unenviable record of being the only terrorist organisation to have a 100% record in executing every member of the security forces they held prisoner, even exceeding the record of the so-called Islamic State.

The security operation to check the area for bombs in order to recover a body in a rural border setting took several days and was widely reported in the media. Almost half of the incidents listed involved this type of scenario. For the IRA it tied up security resources and maximised media coverage. For the victim's family it was a traumatic ordeal. The border aspect was most prevalent from the early 1980s onward, reflecting the IRA's reliance on its cross-border brigades.

Also excluded from the list are most of the 16 'disappeared,' although seven are included. The seven were abducted, executed and secretly buried by the IRA. After the conflict ended the IRA admitted responsibility, having consistently denied this previously. The IRA/Sinn Féin denial policy for outrageous crimes like the 'disappeared' guarded against making the IRA more unpopular than it was already and protected the political prospects of Sinn Féin.

Of the 83 killings: 57 were civilians and 26 terrorists. With the exception of six murders by insurgent splinter groups the IRA committed all of these murders. Every republican terrorist murdered was a Catholic. The majority (70%) of deaths were civilians, including four young men with learning disabilities and three women. Executions peaked in 1973.

At least 1,200 people were affected by a close family member murdered by republicans having been tainted a 'tout,' a derogatory term for informer. Perhaps more than any other community, labelling someone this is the worst insult. It is an indelible stain on a family that lasts generations. All of which was designed to deter anyone co-operating with the police in any shape or form. Even to the extent of attending seriously wounded police officers or soldiers, this being interpreted as collaborating, as Jean McConville's murder shows.

Eighty-three extra-judicial executions is a damning indictment of stated IRA/Sinn Féin policy. Even more damning, however, is the frequency with which a body was defiled and a victim's reputation sullied in generally dehumanising the man, woman or boy who was murdered. The list and how executions were performed is perhaps the clearest exposé of the real Provisionals and Sinn Féin.

27 Jan 1971, Belfast. **John Joseph Kavanagh (28)**, Catholic, civilian, married with two children. Shot in the head at point blank range as a suspected Special Branch informer.

19 April 1972, Belfast. **Martin Owens (22),** Catholic, civilian, married with one child. Murdered by the IRA, shot five times from close range. His body was thrown from a car in Belfast.

1972, Belfast. **Kevin McKee (17),** Catholic, IRA, single. One of the 'disappeared'; abducted and executed by the IRA who claimed he was an Army agent and a member of the Military Reaction Force. IRA men from Belfast were brought in to execute him. His body was recovered in June 2015 (County Meath) in the same unmarked grave as Seamus Wright (4 on the list).

2 Oct 1972, Belfast. **Seamus Wright (25),** Catholic, IRA, married. One of the 'disappeared'; executed by the IRA who claimed he was a British Army agent and a member of the Military Reaction Force. His body was recovered in County Meath in June 2015 in the same grave as the body of Kevin Mckee.

2 Oct 1972, Belfast. **Edward Patrick Bonner (37),** Catholic, civilian, married with three children. Shot twice in the head from close range as a suspected Special Branch informer, picked out from 25 people forced to line up by three masked gunmen.

7 Dec 1972, Belfast. **Jean McConville (37),** Catholic, civilian, widow with 10 children. Abducted from her home while minding her children. Shot in the head by the IRA for supposedly comforting an injured soldier and being a suspected British Army informer. Her body was secretly buried and was not found until 2003 in the Republic. Because of her mixed marriage the family was intimidated out of a loyalist area, moving to the republican west Belfast. The IRA only admitted to the murder once the conflict ended. In 2006 the police ombudsman took the unusual step of announcing Jean McConville had not been an informer.

5 June 1973, Tyrone. **Terence Herdman (17),** Catholic, civilian, single with one child. He was taken to south Armagh were he was badly tortured. Shot twice in the head as a suspected informer. The word 'tout' was written on a label and placed on the blindfolded body left on the border.

9 Aug 1973, Londonderry. **Patrick Anthony Duffy (37),** Catholic, civilian, married with seven children. Shot seven times as a suspected Special Branch informer, his body found in a coffin in an abandoned car at the border. The body's condition suggested he had been immersed in water or moist earth.

21 Sept 1973, Londonderry. **James Joseph Brown (26),** Catholic, civilian, married. Shot twice in the head. His body thrown from a car as a suspected Army informer attempting to infiltrate the IRA.

1973, West Belfast. **Peter Wilson (21),** Catholic, civilian, single. One of the 'disappeared.' Described as a vulnerable person with learning difficulties. For four days before his disappearance he had lived with an Army unit. The Army was accused of using him as an informer. His remains were found in County Antrim in 2010.

13 Nov 1973, Belfast. **Bernard Teggart (15),** Catholic, civilian. A boy with a learning disability and the mental age of eight. He was beaten and shot by the IRA after witnessing the hijacking of a beer lorry, a placard with the word 'tout' pinned to the dead body. His hands and feet were tied. Not until the conflict ended 30 years later did the IRA admit to the murder, offering an apology to the family. The boy's father (Daniel Teggart) had been shot dead by the Army during crowd disorder in Belfast in 1971.

15 Dec 1973, Armagh. **Ivan Acheson Johnston (34),** Protestant, civilian, married with three children. A former policeman abducted by the IRA, interrogated and shot twice in the head for allegedly being involved in undercover activity for the occupation forces. His body was dumped at the border blindfolded and bound. Johnston was formerly in Special Branch.

1973, Belfast. **Louis Hammond (19),** Catholic, IRA, single.

Executed by the IRA who claimed he was a British Army agent and a member of the Military Reaction Force. Hammond was a native of Belfast who joined the Royal Irish Rangers in 1970. In January 1972 he deserted, joining the IRA. He was accused of being a double agent. His murder is also linked to him disclosing details to the Times newspaper about IRA leaders embezzling funds. In April 1973 he was beaten for three days by the IRA for informing before being shot several times and left for dead.

24 Feb 1974, Londonderry. **Patrick Lynch (23)**, Catholic, IRA. Shot by the IRA as a suspected Army informer after being burned and tortured with nails. His body was found bound and gagged.

20 April 1974, Belfast. **James Corbett (20),** Catholic, civilian, married. Taken from his home along with his pregnant wife and shot twice in the back of the head.

2 June 1974, Down. **Paul Tinnelly (34),** Catholic, civilian, married with seven children. A former senior figure in the Official IRA shot in front of his mother, wife and children by up to eight men, one opening fire with a submachine-gun, hitting him in the head, chest and shoulder and injuring his 65 year old mother.

11 Nov 1974, Londonderry. **Hugh Slater (29)**, Protestant, civilian. One of two Protestant civilians abducted and shot by the IRA as a suspected military intelligence agent of the UDR. His body and that of Leonard Cross were found at the side of the road bound and hooded with multiple head wounds.

11 Nov 1974, Londonderry. **Leonard Cross (18)**, Protestant, civilian. A member of the Army Cadets working as a painter. One of two Protestant civilians abducted by the IRA. The IRA accused him of being a spy, which his mother strenuously denied. His body and that of Hugh Slater was found bound at the side of the road, hooded with multiple head wounds.

1 July 1975, Belfast. **Eamon Molloy (22),** Catholic, IRA. Quartermaster in one of the IRA's three Belfast brigades, shot in the head at point blank range as a suspected informer. He is one of the 'disappeared.' His body was discovered in May 1999 in a coffin under a tree in a graveyard in the Republic having been moved from where it was originally concealed. Molloy is credited with causing the arrest of 25-30 IRA members and disclosing information to the security forces so damaging the IRA had to call a ceasefire to recover.

15 Aug 1975, Armagh. **William Meaklin (29),** Protestant, civilian, married. A former member of the police reserve, kidnapped and tortured by the IRA as a suspected Army intelligence agent. The body was dumped in south Armagh.

1 Nov 1975, Tyrone. **Columba McVeigh (17),** Catholic, civilian. Abducted and killed by the IRA as a suspected informer. His body has still to be found. Only after the conflict ended did the IRA admit carrying out the murder.

17 Jan 1976, Belfast. **Seamus Brendan O'Brien (25),** Catholic, civilian. Shot by the IRA as a suspected British agent. His body was found in a ditch.

22 Jan 1976, Tyrone. **Kieran McCann (19),** Catholic, civilian. Taken at gunpoint by the IRA who accused him of being a police informer. He was shot four times in the head.

1 July 1976, Belfast. **Brian Palmer (39),** Catholic, civilian, married. Shot in the head and chest by two masked IRA gunmen with an Armalite rifle from point-blank range. This was in a busy bar in front of his wife. Suspected as an Army agent and a member of the Military Reaction Force.

6 July 1976, Belfast. **Vincent Heatherington (21),** Catholic, civilian. Abducted from his girlfriend's home, bound, blindfolded and shot in the head by the IRA as a suspected military agent. His body was left behind a wire fence.

11 Nov 1976, Belfast. **Patrick Joseph Smyth (24),** Catholic, civilian. A former quartermaster with the IRA who allegedly gave information to police under interrogation. Shot by two IRA gunmen in a club.

9 April 1977, Belfast. **Myles Vincent McGrogan (22),** Catholic, civilian. Shot in the head by the IRA as a suspected British intelligence informer.

5 May 1977, Belfast. **James Green (22),** Catholic, civilian. Shot by the IRA while driving his cab. Accused of being a British agent.

22 Aug 1977, Armagh. **William Martin (62),** Catholic, civilian, married. Shot in the head by the IRA as a suspected police informer.

24 June 1978, Armagh. **Patrick McEntee (53),** Catholic, civilian, married with five children. Stopped with his wife by two armed men and driven across the border. Murdered by the IRA as a suspected British Army informer. Previously shot in both legs and partially crippled in 1973.

1978, Belfast. **Brendan McGraw (24),** Catholic, civilian, married. One of the 'disappeared.' Executed by the IRA who claim he confessed to being an Army agent of the Military Reaction Force. Newly married, his wife was expecting their first baby. His body was found in County Meath in 2014.

12 Feb 1979, Tyrone. **Patrick Sills (27),** Catholic, IRA. Abducted at gunpoint, driven inside the Tyrone border, beaten with a pickaxe handle and shot in both legs. He died from loss of blood. Reports placed him as an IRA leader who indoctrinated new recruits.

11 July 1979, Fermanagh. **Michael Kearney (20),** Catholic, IRA.

Abducted and tortured before being shot in the head by the IRA as a suspected informer. His body was left in south Armagh. A later IRA investigation in 2003 acknowledged that he was arrested under "General Orders" and cleared him of being an informer.

25 April 1980, Belfast. **Michael Madden (68),** Catholic, civilian. Shot six times in the head and arm in his back garden by two IRA men as a suspected police informer.

13 May 1980, Armagh. **Anthony Shields (57),** Catholic, civilian. Stopped at the border by four masked IRA gunmen, dragged from his car and shot as a suspected security forces informer. His body was not recovered by the Army for four days because of booby-trap landmines.

4 Sept 1980, Armagh. **Ross Hearst (52),** Protestant, civilian, married with five children. Abducted at the border by four armed men and shot four times by the IRA as a suspected informer. His body was found on the roadside near his burnt-out car. The IRA murdered his daughter Margaret Ann Hearst (24) in 1977.

14 Nov 1980, Belfast. **Peter Valente (33),** Catholic, civilian, married with four children. Murdered by the IRA as a suspected informer, his body dumped in the Protestant Highfield estate to make it appear a loyalist murder.

1 Jan 1981, ROI. **Eugene Simons (26),** Catholic, IRA, married with three children. Abducted and shot by the IRA who claimed he had confessed to being an informer for the Military Reaction Force. He is one of the 'disappeared.' His body was found three years later in a bog near Dundalk.

20 Jan 1981, Armagh. **Maurice Gilvarry (24),** Catholic, civilian. Shot by the IRA and dumped on a border road as a suspected informer.

22 Feb 1981, Belfast. **Patrick Gerard Trainor (28),** Catholic, civilian, married with three children. Abducted and shot by the IRA as a suspected informer. His body was found on waste ground.

26 June 1981, Belfast. **Vincent Robinson (29),** Catholic, civilian, married with two children. Shot in the head by the IRA as a suspected Special Branch informer. His body was found in a rubbish chute.

27 Sept 1981, Belfast. **Anthony Braniff (27),** Catholic, civilian, married. Shot by the IRA as a suspected police informer.

19 Jan 1982, Belfast. **John Torbett (29),** Catholic, civilian, married with four children. Shot by the IRA as a suspected police informer having been seriously wounded two weeks earlier and ordered to leave the country.

6 March 1982, Armagh. **Seamus Morgan (24),** Catholic, civilian, married with four children. Shot by the IRA as a suspected informer. His body was dumped on a border road.

3 April 1982, Belfast. **Patrick Scott (27),** Catholic, civilian. Shot in the head at point blank range by the IRA as a suspected informer. His body was found in an alley with his hands and feet tied and his eyes covered with tape.

6 May 1983, Armagh. **Eric Dale (43),** Catholic, civilian, married with five children. Abducted, tortured then shot dead by the INLA as a suspected informer. His body was dumped on a border road.

13 Feb 1984, Armagh. **James Young (41),** Catholic, civilian, married. Shot by the IRA as a suspected informer. His body was found on a border road.

26 July 1984, Armagh. **Brian McNally (25),** Catholic, IRA. Shot by the IRA as a suspected police informer, after his fingers were crushed, nails cracked and arms broken. His body was dumped in south Armagh.

23 Feb 1985, Londonderry. **Kevin Patrick Coyle (24),** Catholic, civilian, married with three children. Abducted from his home by three masked gunmen and shot twice in the head by the IRA as a suspected informer.

23 March 1985, ROI. **John Corcoran (45),** Catholic, civilian, married with eight children. Shot at point blank range in the head by the IRA as a suspected informer for the Garda.

8 Sept 1985, Belfast. **Catherine Mahon (27),** Catholic, civilian, married. An IRA gang burst into the home and beat her and her husband for a prolonged period. Shot in the back by the IRA as a suspected informer after her husband was shot in the head and she tried to run away.

8 Sept 1985, Belfast. **Gerard Mahon (28),** Catholic, civilian, married. Shot in the head by the IRA as a suspected informer.

9 Sept 1985, ROI. **James Burnett (28),** Catholic, INLA, married with three children. Abducted, bound and shot by the INLA as a suspected Garda informer. His body was dumped north of the border.

7 Oct 1985, Tyrone. **Damien McCrory (20),** Catholic, civilian. An orphan with a learning disability abducted from his home, interrogated and shot twice in the head by the IRA as a suspected police informer.

20 May 1986, Armagh. **Colm McKevitt (30),** Catholic, civilian. Abducted from his sister's home by the IRA, bundled into a van, driven 300 yards and shot as a suspected informer.

25 May 1986, Tyrone. **Frank Hegarty (45),** Catholic, civilian. Shot multiple times by the IRA as a suspected informer. His body was found on a border road with his eyes taped shut.

15 Aug 1986, Belfast. **Patrick Murray (30),** Catholic, IRA. Shot three times in the head by the IRA as a suspected police informer. His body was dumped in an alleyway, his hands tied behind his back and his eyes taped over.

10 Sept 1986, Armagh. **David McVeigh (41),** Catholic, IRA, married with three children. Shot in the head with a high velocity weapon by the IRA as a suspected informer. His body was dumped on the border.

14 March 1987, Armagh. **Fergus Conlon (32),** Catholic, IPLO, married with three children. Shot six times in the head and neck by the INLA as a suspected informer for British Intelligence. His body was dumped in south Armagh.

12 April 1987, Armagh. **Charles McIlmurray (32),** Catholic, civilian, married with two children. Shot in the back of the head at point blank range by the IRA as a suspected informer. His body was found tied up in the back of a van with a plastic bag over the head.

24 June 1987, Belfast. **Thomas Emmanuel Wilson (35),** Catholic, civilian, married with four children. Abducted from his home and shot by the IRA as a suspected informer. His body was dumped in an alleyway.

1 Sept 1987, Armagh. **Eamonn Maguire (33),** Catholic, civilian, two children. Former member of the IRA shot in the head at point blank range by the IRA as a suspected Garda informer.

19 Jan 1988, Belfast. **Anthony McKiernan (44),** Catholic, civilian, married with four children. Shot multiple times in the head by the IRA as a suspected informer, before being shot he was plied with enough alcohol to kill him.

3 Oct 1988, West Belfast. **Henry McNamee (33),** Catholic, IPLO, single. Shot by the IPLO in front of his family, accused of being a police informer. His brother Brendan McNamee (INLA) was murdered in 1975 in a republican feud.

26 Feb 1989, Belfast. **Joseph Fenton (35),** Catholic, civilian, married with four children. Shot in the head by the IRA as a suspected informer. His body was dumped in an alley.

18 July 1989, Armagh. **John McAnulty (48),** Catholic, civilian. Abducted from a Dundalk pub, beaten, burnt with cigarette ends then shot in the head by the IRA as a suspected informer. His body was dumped on the border. In 2012 he was named in the Smithwick Tribunal into IRA and Garda 'collusion' as an RUC Special Branch informer for 17 years.

26 July 1990, Armagh. **Patrick Flood (29),** Catholic, IRA, married with one child. Shot in the head by the IRA as a suspected informer. His body was found seven weeks after his disappearance on a border road in Fermanagh, bound and gagged. He had been extensively tortured.

6 June 1991, Londonderry. **Ruari Finnis (21),** Catholic, IRA. Shot three times by the IRA as a suspected informer. His body was found barefoot and blindfolded with his eyes taped shut.

21 June 1991, ROI. **Margaret Perry (26),** Catholic, civilian. Murdered as a result of injuries to her skull by the IRA because she discovered her former boyfriend, Gregory Burns, was a security forces informer (allegedly). Her body was found a year after her disappearance in a shallow grave in the ROI.

30 June 1991, Belfast. **Anthony Gerald Burns (37),** Catholic, INLA. Shot three times in the head by the INLA as a suspected informer. His body was found in the back garden of a house, his hands tied behind his back and his eyes and mouth taped.

19 July 1991, Armagh. **Thomas Oliver (37),** Catholic, civilian, married with seven children. Abducted by armed IRA men near the border and shot dead as a suspected Garda informer.

1 July 1992, Armagh. **Johnny Dignam (32),** Catholic, IRA, married with two children. Shot twice in the head by the IRA for his involvement in the murder of Margaret Perry and suspicions of being an informer. His body was found naked in south Armagh along with IRA men Gregory Burns and Aidan Starrs.

1 July 1992, Armagh. **Gregory Burns (34),** Catholic, IRA, three children. Shot twice in the head by the IRA as a suspected informer and for the murder of Margaret Perry, his former girlfriend whom he had killed when she discovered he was an informer (allegedly). His naked body was left in south Armagh.

1 July 1992, Armagh. **Aidan Starrs (29),** Catholic, IRA. Shot twice in the head by the IRA for his involvement in the murder of Margaret Perry. His naked body showed signs of torture by a hot poker. Accused of being an informer. His body was left in south Armagh.

12 Aug 1992, Belfast. **Robin Hill (22),** Catholic, IRA. Bound, gagged and shot twice in the back of the head by the IRA as a suspected informer.

22 Nov 1992, Londonderry. **Gerard Holmes (35),** Catholic, civilian. Shot twice in the head by the IRA as a suspected informer after being held captive for four days. His body was found bound in an alleyway.

12 Feb 1993, Tyrone. **Christopher Harte (24),** Catholic, IRA, married with one child. Shot multiple times in the head by the IRA as a suspected informer. His body was found hooded and tied up.

25 Mar 1993, Londonderry. **James Gerard Kelly (25),** Catholic, IRA. Shot in the head and body by the IRA as a suspected informer.

23 June 1993, Tyrone. **John Joseph Mulhern (23),** Catholic, IRA. Taken to Donegal and tortured. Shot by the IRA as a suspected informer. His body was found on a border road dressed in a boiler suit and bound by cable.

29 April 1994, Armagh. **Michael Martin Brown (23),** Catholic, civilian. Shot by the IRA as a suspected informer. His body was found close to the border dressed in a boiler suit and his hands tied behind his back.

17 July 1994, Fermanagh. **Caroline Moreland (34),** Catholic, civilian, mother of three children. Shot multiple times through the head by the IRA as a suspected informer. Her body was dumped on the Fermanagh border. The IRA tape-recorded Caroline Moreland confessing to being an informer.

27 Jan 1999, Armagh. **Eamon Collins (45),** Catholic, civilian, married with four children. One-time IRA member battered to death by unknown republicans (undoubtedly the IRA) during a walk close to his home. He suffered severe head injuries and multiple stab wounds to his upper body.

4 April 2006, County Donegal. **Denis Donaldson (56),** Catholic, civilian, married with three children. A former IRA member and senior Sinn Féin official shot dead in County Donegal where he had retreated after confessing in 2005 that he had been a police agent for more than 20 years.

In interrogating prisoners a common IRA tactic was to make them believe that admitting being an informer on tape would qualify them for release and to this end they were encouraged to tarnish Special Branch or another intelligence agency. The prisoner believed that the more they said what the interrogators wanted him or her to say the better their chances of surviving. What they did not know or refused to believe was that admitting being an informer guaranteed their death. There was to be no reprieve. To extract a taped confession torture, the threat of torture or execution was routinely used. Threats of this kind carried significant weight given the IRA's record in this respect. For the IRA the taped recording justified the execution. But its main purpose was as a propaganda tool for Sinn Féin.

Regarding loyalist terrorists, they murdered at least 19 people on suspicion of collaborating. 53% of the total were civilians and 47% loyalist terrorists. All those murdered were Protestants. The peak was 1976 (five murders) and the least violent period 1982-87 (no murders). Loyalists did not booby-trap dead bodies or perform macabre symbolism that demeaned the victim and their family. Neither did they abduct, torture and execute soldiers or police officers. The IRA outstripped loyalist terrorists in executing 'collaborators' by four to one.

Although the police ombudsman in 2003 and an IRA investigation also in 2003 declared Jean McConville and Michael Kearney, respectively, were not informers, there are significantly more than two in the list of 83. Conversely, one person was named as a Special Branch informer (John McAnulty) in the Smithwick Tribunal in 2012, which is highly unusual. Special Branch policy regarding the identity of an informer is NCND (Neither Confirm Nor Deny). Equally, divulging such information is a criminal offence under the Official Secrets Act. Five people murdered by insurgents for 'collaborating' were accused of informing to the Garda.

With the Provisional Army Council's General Order No. 1 foremost, and bearing in mind this officially sanctioned abductions, torture and executions. It is an opportune time to show how SB understood the workings of the IRA at command level in order to explain why such a policy was made and so vigorously enforced.

The IRA had an Army Executive (watchdog committee), Army Council (seven men directing the 'armed struggle'), Northern Command, Southern Command and GHQ with titles such as Chief of Staff and Quartermaster General. These bodies regularly met in the Republic in extreme secrecy. A suspected informer could not be executed unless authorised by the Army Council. In the late 1980s six senior Sinn Féin figures dominated the upper echelons of the network with three in the Army Council, which was the most important body, regarded as the first Dáil Éireann (Irish government) in waiting. Several senior figures co-ordinated these bodies and at the lower level linked in with brigade commanders. The use of brigade and battalion were nominal descriptions of areas where an Officer Commanding controlled several territorially adjacent ASUs (Active Service Units). ASUs consisted of five to six 'volunteers.'

For the IRA Northern Ireland comprised five brigade areas subdivided into 12 areas of operation. Grouping ASUs into areas is mostly an academic exercise as there are often overlaps in territorial boundaries. Over half of the brigades were cross-border in nature. As a result of the revised long war strategy in the mid-1970s the IRA was streamlined, reduced to approximately 500 active members, half being on-the-runs residing in the Republic. In 1970 the Provos had 1,400 active members.

The IRA was not democratic but despotic. Through patronage and nepotism several people manipulated the organisational structure to keep themselves continuously in power. From the mid-1970s onwards what this looked like was a permanent leadership set back from operations. A few exerted an iron grip on the many and were ruthlessly intolerant of dissenting voices. And it is this small clique that prioritised policy sanctioning the torture and murder of suspected collaborators. Those beneath them had no choice but to comply.

In the intelligence war, 83 executions and the sadistic manner of most of those were the direct result of decisions and policy implemented by the IRA/Sinn Féin leadership. A small clique of hardliners saw torture and execution as a legitimate means of deterring contact between republicans and the police, part of their wider strategy designed to demonise Special Branch and dehumanise anyone who helped them.

In a counter-society murder was accepted as a necessary policing tool.

Chapter 4

Provo Strongholds

The republican movement was the republican insurgency – the IRA and Sinn Féin. The support-base was republican enclaves; scattered communities across Northern Ireland collectively called the republican community. Within these the Provos and Sinn Féin purposely blurred legal, moral and ethical boundaries by convincing people that IRA murders were justified. Republicans were first conditioned to accepting this thinking by incidents outside of their community. A fundamental ideology had already legitimised the murder of police and soldiers or anyone associated with British rule. This included the murders of innocent Protestants being falsely passed off as accidental collateral damage. Republicans were introduced to the same philosophy within their community through General Order No. 1 sanctioning the murder of 'collaborators.'

To live in a republican enclave was to live in an environment where murder and talk of murder were commonplace and reporting any of this to the police was seen as a crime. It was impossible for anyone living in a republican area to openly co-operate with the police, such as providing a witness statement about seeing someone shoot a soldier or police officer. Say nothing, what the IRA advised their members to do when interviewed by the police, turned into a social norm in the nationalist community. IRA ideology and policies distorted the moral compass of the minority community, with the distortion strongest in republican enclaves. Here the IRA/ Sinn Féin imposed shadowy counter-societies, a modernisation of republican courts and policing from the early 1900s. It was how militant republicanism administered policing and justice.

Counter-societies are failed communities or zones of lawlessness. The concept built upon insurgents having got the tacit agreement of the republican community regarding legitimising the murders of security forces and 'collaborators' to include 'criminals' or anyone undermining the Provos. The Provisionals had the blessing of their support-base to murder anyone they wanted in the name of republicanism.

Counter-societies were a social contract between the IRA/ Sinn Féin and the republican community, a mechanism insurgents employed to indoctrinate their support-base. Of the degree of indoctrination a former SB officer states:

> *If Sinn Féin told the people of west Belfast that a spaceship was landing on the Falls Road in two hours to bring them to the planet Zog, they'd nearly all be out to get on it.*

A perverted ideology had brainwashed the majority of the republican community to an extent that they could no longer distinguish between right and wrong, fact and fiction. In a counter-society murder was accepted as a necessary policing tool. And because murder is the most serious of all crimes, legitimising it provided legitimacy for all other criminal acts committed by the IRA and Sinn Féin. The murders of Arthur McKenna (35) and Alexander McVicker (35) in Belfast in November 1970 for alleged criminality is the first example of the Provisionals flexing their muscles in a policing role. Perhaps 10 to 15 people accused of petty crimes received the same death penalty during the Troubles. The usual outcomes, however, were physical assault, expulsion from the community or kneecapping (shot in the knee).

The actual mechanics of arranging and conducting so-called punishment attacks exemplifies how closely and regularly Sinn Féin and the IRA co-operated in criminal enterprises at ground level. Punishments were arranged by appointment, usually by Sinn Féin, and carried out by an IRA civil admin team. Judgement and sentencing would have been passed by a Kangaroo court composed of several Sinn Féin and IRA representatives. Normally a complaint made to Sinn Féin by a local resident triggered the process. It was not necessary for the accused to be present at the hearing, although on occasions they were.

Most cases related to anti-social behaviour by male youths. Republican justice was dispensed swiftly and free of charge. This was its appeal. Many of the victims and their families would have known those who shot them and those involved in arranging the shooting. As always, however, to disclose this to police would have resulted in more serious consequences, which the police were acutely aware of. Saying nothing to the police despite knowing plenty constitutes criminal offences like withholding information and failing to assist the police. To investigate every incident properly would have ground policing to a halt and increased the risk to life of the person being investigated because he or she was living under the IRA/ Sinn Féin regime. Fully investigating such incidents would also have further marginalised the Catholic minority. Therefore the police turned a blind eye. This meant that the police could not and did not exploit every investigative opportunity to prosecute offenders. A former Special Branch officer states:

> *Yes, I know it's awful and nothing like what we call justice. But when it came to local hoods [criminals] the Provos rarely got it wrong. Brutal as it was most people were glad to see it, although many would not admit that today. The big problem was that it also allowed the Provos to settle personal scores and old grudges against people who had nothing to do with crime. That's the problem when you appoint yourself as judge, jury*

and executioner. You get carried away. You abuse the system for your own ends. A lot of good people were trapped in these communities. But what could they do other than play along. Don't get me wrong though. There were also plenty who were fully behind what the Provos were doing. It's a mixed bag. Moderate voices get drowned out. Extremists run the place. Speak out against them and you're card is marked. Eventually they'll hurt you or your family. Think of it like this. For the Nazis to gain power decent people sat back and did nothing, never thinking what would eventually happen. All of a sudden when the Nazis got in decent Germans wanted to do something. By then it was too late. Hitler had his henchman and systems in place. How the Provos controlled their community worked along the same lines.

An example of the numbers involved in 'punishment attacks' is contained in the Hannigan Report (1978). It states the IRA conducted 183 "punishment shootings" from January 1976 to June 1978. Loyalist terrorist organisations carried out 76 in the same period. The IRA and Sinn Féin worked together to commit approximately 2,200 'punishment shootings' during the Troubles. If one adds beatings that resulted in grievous bodily harm routinely inflicted by iron bars and hurley sticks, a more frequent form of assault, it is not unreasonable to estimate that there were around 5,000 victims of 'punishment attacks' resulting in serious injury - one attack every other day throughout the conflict. Usually no-one was convicted for these offences. The odd exception was a convicted person asking for other crimes he/she committed to be taken into consideration before being sentenced for a more serious crime, as a means of clearing the slate.

Somewhere in the middle of a wide range of IRA/Sinn Féin criminality was fraud, the most common criminal element of counter-societies. Vote fraud at election time was rife and organised by Sinn Féin. In Belfast in the 1980s this assisted Sinn Féin electoral success. Similarly, fraudulent complaints against the police by republicans were routine in any interaction with the police liable to result in criminal proceedings. Sinn Féin encouraged republicans to complain against the police, instructing what false accusations to include, such as being called derogatory sectarian names and threatened. Not to complain was treated with suspicion. Fraudulent complaints were central to Sinn Féin propaganda and would persist throughout the Troubles. A communiqué from Lieutenant General Sir John Waters to Major General Guthrie in 1989 reads:

> It is well established that the terrorists and their supporters use a base of fabricated complaints against the security forces as a means of trying to discredit them and increase their alienation from the Nationalist community.

Sinn Féin used respectable third parties as proxies to discredit the police. The Hannigan Report shows the Northern Ireland Civil Rights Association was a "prime mover in the propaganda campaign against the RUC" with a "high commitment to discrediting the RUC." Internationalising allegations entailed the Northern Ireland Civil Rights Association engaging with Soviet journalists in Belfast and in Soviet Bloc countries together with it and similar groups meeting with NORAID (Northern Aid) and Catholic Bishops in the US.

Fraud was also part of a compensation culture in republican communities regarding civil claims, social benefits, unemployment benefits, disability benefits and other social allowances. Prior to the IRA civil admin team putting a bullet in each leg Sinn Féin would have advised the victim and a member of his family how to claim for criminal injury. Sinn Féin orchestrated wide scale abuse of the British welfare system that, like IRA bombings of commercial targets, contributed to the economic war against the state. Notwithstanding that Sinn Féin also provided guidance on social and welfare benefits to legitimate claimants, for many republicans they created a dependency on state handouts through fraudulent practices.

A further example of fraud is the Provisionals holding back

in declaring someone an IRA member who was injured ₍
the police, Army or a rival terrorist organisation. The I'
admit Louis Leonard was a member until after his widow ₁₎₎
compensation (£20,000) for his murder in 1972, as to do so risked
a lesser settlement. In a BBC interview on the 17th December
2012 into a recently published HET (Historical Enquiry Team)
report into the murder the widow admitted to knowing he was in
the IRA, which was common.

The IRA used value-laden language in promoting the shooting
and beating of people they branded criminals as 'punishment
attacks' and value neutral language to describe this and the fraud
aspect as a community service. The Provisionals, however, did not
anticipate dealing with the full panoply of criminal offences. Where
they came unstuck was dealing with complaints of rape, sexual
assault, incest, unlawful carnal knowledge and indecency offences
against children. These offences usually happen in private places
away from prying eyes, are hard to prove and easy to refute. They
also require sensitive handling. Anonymity is key. For a victim of
a sex crime it takes immense courage to come forward and lodge
a complaint to the police let alone Provisionals pretending to be
the police.

Because republicans were not allowed to co-operate with the
police, sex-related crimes were seldom reported. A victim was put
off reporting it to the IRA or Sinn Féin, as in the absence of forensic
evidence it was invariably one person's word against another. And
if the accused was better connected to the IRA or Sinn Féin than
the accuser there was little prospect of receiving justice. A classic
case is that of Maria Cahill, grand-niece of revered IRA leader Joe
Cahill. Maria Cahill was a rising young star in Sinn Féin prior to
lodging a rape accusation with Sinn Féin against an IRA man. This
was the only form of redress Maria Cahill had. Getting the police
to investigate was totally out of the question, as this legitimised the
police, which went against the very essence of counter-societies.
How Sinn Féin and the IRA handled the matter was shambolic,
much to the disgust of the victim, and resulted in no significant
sanction against the accused. Moreover, the environment created

by the Provos prevented an early report to the police, which worked against the victim. That someone with the republican pedigree of Maria Cahill was treated this way epitomises why few victims ever came forward.

The IRA and Sinn Féin swept potentially damaging complaints against their members under the carpet or discredited the victim in order to discredit the allegation. At all cost they wanted to avoid a scandal and prevent a complaint becoming public knowledge. Given the Provos ruthlessness in controlling republican communities and Sinn Féin's skill at turning untruths into truths a complainant was unlikely to remonstrate, especially when the complaint is as personal as rape.

For the Provos and Sinn Féin there was no incentive to deal with sexual offences. They did not produce the same popularity dividend as straightforward crimes that most of the community witnessed, like 'joyriding,' a local name for driving a stolen car dangerously. Joyriding was tangible; something everyone could see and recognised as a nuisance whereas child abuse or rape was intangible and not openly talked about as a problem.

Besides crimes like assault that involved criminal injury claims there were other crimes where contacting the police was also unavoidable because of financial claims involving private insurance companies. Examples are road traffic accidents, criminal damage and burglary. In each, compensation is not paid out unless the police have been informed. Sinn Féin advised on what to say to the police in these situations.

Counter-societies were about insurgents controlling their support base, undermining the rule of law and legitimising IRA activity so that they could continue their terrorist campaign. This is what the Head of Special Branch expressed concern about in his 1970 annual report in the sense of the Provisionals controlling republican enclaves. The IRA's desire not to be seen as criminals is evident in the secret communiqué from 4th battalion IRA (Maze prison) to Sinn Féin HQ in Belfast in 1975:

The success or failure of this Brit strategy [criminalisation] will depend on our ability to adopt a strategy which will link us more closely with our base of support and that any attack on the Republican Movement will be seen clearly as an attack on the Nationalist people as a whole.

4th battalion, the IRA's think tank in the Maze, was counting on controlling republican ghettoes through counter-societies and attracting wider nationalist sympathy in order to undermine the criminalisation policy that defined a rule of law approach from the mid-1970s onward. The formal introduction of counter-societies coincided with a fundamental revision in IRA structure and strategy.

The sentiment in the communiqué was critical to the IRA's long war, using active and passive supports to dislocate the police from the minority community. Counter-societies implicated nationalists in the 'armed struggle,' obtained as a minimum their passive complicity, and reinforced the police as the enemy of Catholics and the IRA as the defenders of Catholics. The republican movement had superbly harnessed subversion and political militancy to accompany and support terrorism.

Not only does the IRA communiqué link counter-societies to the insurgency's determination to challenge the criminalisation policy, it also emphasises the importance of prisoners to the republican movement, which Special Branch identified as the Provisionals' greatest vulnerability. Illustrating what the police thought about counter-societies is an internal police briefing paper (1977):

The implementation of the system got under way in May 1976 ... offices were established at ___ [PSF Advice Centre] to receive complaints from the public regarding crime. Except in certain cases where compensation was involved the report of these alleged crimes was not passed to the police. In fact the public living in these areas are persuaded to sever contact with the police under veiled threats of touting. A deliberate campaign of speeches against the police and display of posters headed

"Smash the R.U.C." is an example of the attempts to force the people to relate to the Provisional Sinn Fein and P.I.R.A. in every day life.

Counter-societies legalised lawlessness and sustained the conditions for revolutionary forces to maintain control. This drew the republican community closer to the insurgency, which was the IRA's aim. If one recalls the IRA and Sinn Féin are two halves of an insurgency, and that this was not popularly supported, counter-societies ensured what little support the IRA/Sinn Féin had insulated them against widespread condemnation. To survive, the Provos depended on a small nucleus of unquestioning devotees to see them through their darkest days when heavily criticised for outrageous attacks.

An example is the Hannigan Report noting that the IRA attack on the La Mon Hotel (1978) in which 12 Protestants were burnt to death was unpopular with nationalists, causing some senior IRA men to question the new cell structure controlled by an exclusive elite. Conversely, such condemnation encouraged this exclusive elite, who viewed it as confirmation their tactics and strategy were working. The way a few hardliners dominated the republican movement, which in turn dominated the republican community, guaranteed that any negative discussions of this type were quickly shut down.

The IRA/Sinn Féin leadership had a callous disregard for innocent lives that only changed when this translated into a loss of support, usually because casualties were Catholics. The Hannigan Report rated the republican movement's leadership singly responsible for prolonging the conflict. Freed of these few leaders, the IRA would have been receptive to a peace deal in the mid-1970s. As it was, the IRA and Sinn Féin prospered from the ghettoisation of republican areas, which was in their interests to maintain. Former British Army Colonel, Tim Collins, describes counter-societies as a "spectrum of subversion." He views Sinn Féin Advice Centres as:

Alternate police stations where torture and murder were often planned. Criminality was simply part of their DNA. It was not that they did not see anything wrong with it, they did. Moreover, they took a perverse delight in holding everyone else to account and regarded the law and humanity itself as a public convenience they used at their will.

A small clique controlled the republican movement and corrupted the morals of their own community to hide the sectarian and brutal character of an IRA that systematically violated humanitarian and human rights laws, to progress the political agenda of Sinn Féin. Strategically, counter-societies served the selfish interests of the republican movement. Thinking about this in an irregular war context, Collins argues that "a broad base of criminal activity ranging from petty crime to murder" is essential for any insurgency.

Pursuing a normal police response was central to undermining counter-societies, of which intelligence and Special Branch was crucial. Casting the Provisionals as the villain and cause of perpetuating the conflict was a viewpoint the IRA's 4th battalion had strategised to undermine. Nationalists had been conditioned by Sinn Féin not to see the Provisionals as the main problem.

The rule of law threatened the IRA and was strongly resisted. IRA leaders were running scared of Special Branch. Counter-societies protected them, creating republican strongholds that licenced the IRA to do whatever they wanted, including murder, in the name of Irish freedom. The republican community did not see them as criminals. The same applied to the loyalist side.

Key to breaking the IRA's ideological and physical stranglehold on the republican community was SB facilitating the spread of normal policing. But as 4th battalion's communiqué shows, the IRA and Sinn Féin knew this and made it very difficult.

Most people were initially angry with the rebels, but the executions changed everything.

Chapter 5

Nothing New

Since the 12th century the English and then the British have had a presence in Ireland. And for almost as long there have been wars and rebellions that pitted Irish republicans (often with France or Spain as allies) against British forces and Irish unionists. In relatively recent times this shared history has been used to amplify division between Gael and Planter, Catholic and Protestant, anti-British ruler and pro-British ruler. From the mid-1800s Irish republicans have weaponised history for political gain by attaching it to contemporary grievances to justify violence. When they did this their main obstacle was a locally recruited police force stitched into the social fabric of Irish society. This was because the police publicly enforced the laws of the land on behalf of all citizens, and these laws clearly showed that Irish republican violence was unlawful.

In 1814, Sir Robert Peel through the Peace Preservation Act created the first organised police forces in Ireland. Predominantly this was the Irish Constabulary, a semi-military police force that successfully quelled a number of insurrections in the early 1800s. In 1867 the Irish Constabulary received a 'Royal' prefix from Queen

Victoria for putting down the Fenian Rising, a rebellion against British rule by a forerunner of the IRA - the Irish Republican Brotherhood. The harp, crown and shamrocks symbolised the Royal Irish Constabulary (RIC). Police actions in the Fenian Rising highlight the security qualities associated with the RIC. Fenians attacked isolated and smaller police stations. The rebellion was suppressed with ruthless efficiency. This was due to the police having infiltrated the Fenians with well-placed informers.

In the Fenian Rising the police won the intelligence war. The instability caused by secret organisations behind armed insurgency and public disorder gave way to a prolonged period of stability. Policing mirrored that of a peaceful society. Dealing with ordinary crime was routine. Ireland was at its most peaceful. A major factor in this was good police work.

Ending the social harmony between the police and community in 1919 was the IRA murder of Royal Irish Constabulary constables James McDonnell and Patrick O'Connell at Soloheadbeg. The Soloheadbeg ambush, in Tipperary, started the Anglo-Irish conflict (1919-22), also known as the War of Independence. It could also be described as the 1919-22 Republican Insurgency, because this is what it was – an irregular war. The killings were treated as murders, and widely regarded as such at the time. Both constables were Irish born Catholics and well liked by the locals. Constable McDonnell would regularly ask children how to spell rhododendron and then tell them the correct spelling. McDonnell (50) was from Mayo, a widower with four children. O'Connell (30) was a single man from Cork. They were soft targets. The IRA unit that ambushed them was disappointed in only having shot dead two constables. They had hoped to announce the start of the conflict with more killings. The day after the ambush martial law was declared.

Insurgency in Ireland around this time involved militant republicans confronting local police. IRA leader Michael Collins considered the police his greatest threat. The RIC stood between the IRA/Sinn Féin and their goals of an independent Ireland. Collins knew that the RIC was well integrated in the community and well respected. A young man was considered a success if he became a priest or police constable. Although an armed force, the police rarely carried guns. Along with the priest, constables carried out an informal leadership role in local communities. Police stations were called barracks. Those in the city resembled an army barracks and those in rural areas consisted of a large ordinary house. Pay was low and discipline strict. Poor pay was subsidised by the local community supplying dairy products, vegetables and bread as gifts. The most common forms of patrolling were doing the beat or riding a bicycle. Both made it easy for the public to meet and talk with constables. Everyone knew the local constable and he knew them.

A constable was not allowed to serve in his home county nor that of his wife. Neither could a constable marry until he had several years' service. Married and single quarters were in the barracks or a neighbouring house. By 1901 there were approximately 1,600 barracks throughout Ireland. This is what a 'permanent police presence' looked like in a divided society prone to conflict. Not only did this extensive network integrate the police with the people it was also an early warning system for trouble because the police had the pulse of local communities.

The RIC could deliver security policing as well as normal policing, or a combination of the two, in treating outbreaks of armed insurgency. Its capacity to perform dual roles set it apart from the unarmed British bobby police model in the rest of the UK. Another major difference, the RIC model was not dependent on policing by consent, as consent by a section of society in times of conflict is withheld. The British bobby or Westminster police model has no plan B when consent is not forthcoming.

Michael Collins could not afford to have this police/community harmony continue. To win the war the IRA and Sinn Féin had to smash the RIC – physically and ideologically. Collins set about branding the RIC as the enemy of the Irish people. He deliberately undermined the rule of law because the law treated IRA killings as murders and IRA activities as crimes. The IRA and Sinn Féin did not recognise the law because of the British presence in Ireland. They disagreed with the prevailing political situation and on the back of the 1916 Easter Rising had capitalised on widespread public outrage at the execution of the rebels (men like Patrick Pearce). At the elections Sinn Féin popularised militancy and anti-British feeling in a way that swept aside moderate Irish nationalists. The IRA/Sinn Féin was impatient for Irish independence. They favoured violence over politics. Killings progressed their political agenda. Such killings were justified in the eyes of republicans because they attacked an anti-British policy standing in the way of an independent Ireland.

Anyone claiming to be an Irish republican was 'licenced' to kill. This was the patriotic thing to do. Resisting it was local police who had sworn a solemn oath to uphold the law, of which killings of this type were legally defined as murders. Viewing republican violence as terrorism and therefore wrong was unpatriotic. To hold this view, as the police did, was to be labelled an enemy of Ireland. Central to indoctrinating the population to think this way was the IRA and Sinn Féin promoting the RIC as local intelligence gatherers propping up an illegal British occupation, and not a neutral police force upholding the rule of law.

Part of the IRA/Sinn Féin campaign to dislodge police from local communities was threatening businesses to boycott selling goods and services to the police. This economic and social ostracism of the police was accompanied by the intimidation of their families. As a result around 600 RIC men resigned from a force of approximately 9,500. The IRA had destroyed over 400 police stations in the first year of the conflict and murdered 117 RIC members. The result was to replace the police as the authority in these areas with IRA/Sinn Féin counter-societies. In keeping with insurgency precepts - control territory is to control communities.

Republican myths and nationalist zeal were used to taint a police force 80% Catholic as pro-British. Collins' main aim was to create a level of instability that forced the police to focus more on security thereby reducing the frequency of normal interactions with the public. What this looked like was fewer police doing the beat or riding bicycles in preference to patrolling in armoured cars and spending more time in newly fortified barracks. This was the IRA/Sinn Féin insurgency template in the 1900s that was replicated in the Troubles. Terrorism and propaganda was the preferred method of Irish republicans to pursue political goals.

The difficulty the RIC had prior to the Anglo-Irish Conflict was that it had been neglected by Westminster, which was responsible for its antiquated operational practices that proved ineffective in countering the emerging threat. The RIC had warned Dublin about the real prospect of unrest but was refused in its request for extra resources. This is remarkably similar to the RUC warning London about the same things in 1968. Despite London's lack of investment in the RIC and not intervening early enough, in the Anglo-Irish conflict the IRA was on the brink of military defeat prior to the negotiated treaty. Having survived an extensive terrorist and propaganda campaign the RIC eventually regrouped to lead the security effort. But by this time it was too late.

Army primacy and martial law meant military force. The immediate security response turned an initially unpopular insurgency into a popular insurgency; similar to how the executions of the leaders of the 1916 Easter Rising turned public opinion against the state. Britain was in a world war and interpreted the Rising as a treacherous act. Most people were initially angry with the rebels, but the executions changed everything. As with young British soldiers accused of cowardice on the Western Front, the rebels' ringleaders were quickly court-martialed and shot. No mercy was shown. It was a fateful mistake.

It was one thing for the British to treat their own soldiers harshly but to do the same with Irish civilians who had taken up arms in opposing British rule was calamitous. Put another way, punishing those in your family is fine but anyone else doing this is a real problem. If you were not an Irish nationalist you were not part of the family. You were an outsider. As a consequence of the executions Sinn Féin swept aside moderate nationalists at the polls on a mandate to end British rule in Ireland. The response to the Rising fatally undermined the legitimacy of the British to govern.

Buoyed by Britain's self-inflicted injuries republicans abandoned politics and embarked in another bout of violent insurgency.

In the Anglo-Irish conflict a member of the security forces was just as likely to be killed as an IRA man. In conflicts today an insurgent is at least four times more likely to be killed than a member of the security forces. To help the RIC the Black and Tans and Auxiliaries were created. These were paramilitary organisations comprised of former British soldiers recently returned from the horrors of the Somme, Passchendaele and Ypres. In particular, the Black and Tans were brutally intolerant of republican violence. The response was counterproductive, causing resentment in the population. This played into the hands of Collins. Losing the hearts and minds contest in a security context, a poor political strategy and incoherent overall strategy guaranteed an IRA victory.

For republicans the infamy of the Black and Tans is as bitter today as it was then. This is because past events are not examined in an objective, historical way but in a subjective, personal way. Treating history in this manner vindicates past IRA actions, which is why the past intrudes in the present. The DNA of militant republicanism is based on victimhood and a corrupted history that blames others. It is similar to al-Qaeda and Islamic State linking the crusades of the 11th century and the creation of Israel in the 1940s to the west's current presence and influence in Muslim countries. For extreme Islamists and militant republicans the conflict is never their fault. This is central to their fundamental ideology.

Republicans call the Anglo-Irish conflict the Tan War. The naming shows how Irish republicans post-conflict sought to solely blame the British. In the newly created Irish Free State in 1922 a one-sided narrative emerged that demonised the British approach while ignoring IRA brutalities. There was no balance. Early nation building saw anything that contested the nationalist narrative being airbrushed out. In the Soloheadbeg memorial the only missing names are the only people who lost their lives - constables McDonnell and O'Connell. Any controversy about missing names is not about the constables but who exactly was in the IRA unit that murdered them. Being in this 'IRA flying column' was to be a war hero, to have songs and poems praising their patriotism. In Dublin, a statute immortalises IRA leader Seán Russell, who collaborated with the Nazis. Men like Seán Russell represented Irish nationalist values deserving of remembrance. Men like James McDonnell and Patrick O'Connell did not.

McDonnell and O'Connell were not seen as victims but enemy forces deservedly killed. Post-conflict, murders of this kind were downgraded to lawful killings, with those responsible lionised as freedom fighters. Each year large crowds attend memorials like Soloheadbeg to commemorate the IRA action and remember the IRA men involved. It would take a century before the names of RIC officers killed by republican militants would appear on a government memorial in the Republic.

In 1914, crowds cheered Irishmen as they went off to fight in the British Army in the Great War. In 1919, they returned to a nation that did not want to know them. Because of their war service many could not get jobs and had to emigrate. The same applied to Irishmen who fought in British regiments against Hitler.

Appreciating Irish nationalism's perspective of history highlights the importance of Sinn Féin myth making. Following the Anglo-Irish conflict dirty war syndrome is where Sinn Féin wrapped layers of lies around half-truths to taint the British approach and distract from IRA activities. The Free State press published Sinn Féin's view. There was little opposition to this. After all, republicans had just thrown the British out of 26 of Ireland's 32 counties.

Spinning the 'bad British good IRA' headline was easy and the popular thing to do. Contradicting facts or counter-views were irrelevant and, in any event, not tolerated. Not until the 1970s and 1980s did a few critics of the IRA and Sinn Féin in the Republic of Ireland emerge, like Connor Cruise O'Brien. O'Brien claimed that republicanism had a proclivity for self-deception. That is, not only did physical-force republican ideology fool others as a matter of routine it also fooled its own followers. A necessary fiction was needed otherwise the IRA and Sinn Féin had to face a credible outlook that argues, what they did was wrong and could have been achieved by peaceful means. Deception soothed the social conscience of those who committed and supported killing or what would otherwise be called murder. O'Brien, however, represented a minority view.

Irish republicans had determined how a new Dublin government would portray the conflict. The Free State showed little respect for the cultural diversity of an Irish unionist minority. Anything remotely associated with the British was anti-Irish – Irish being defined as pro-nationalist and Catholic. The story written after the Anglo-Irish conflict was as precious to republicans as the conflict. Killing local police officers was not enough, discrediting them afterwards was just as important.

The Protestant population in the Free State rapidly reduced from 10% to 7% and to an eventual low of 3% over the long-term. Former RIC officers were threatened and forced to leave. The IRA/Sinn Féin stand accused of ethnically cleansing west Cork of Protestants during the Anglo-Irish conflict. It is a recent accusation by an award winning Canadian historian Peter Hart. Hart's research was met with indignation by academics (mostly Irish). The Canadian touched a raw nationalist nerve when he claimed the IRA had a sectarian underbelly and in having raised the prospect of IRA actions being crimes. This was an attack on nationalist icons and events that underpin the Republic of Ireland's national identity.

In disputing Hart's claims his critics point out that the IRA in west Cork had killed Protestants for collaborating with the RIC just in the same way they killed Catholics for the same thing. Protestants were not killed because they were Protestants but because they were informers. But what could a small Protestant community know about a secret organisation made up almost entirely of Catholics? Regardless of motive, an organisation almost exclusively Catholic in a predominantly Catholic country was murdering Protestant civilians. It is naïve to believe that there was no sectarian element within the IRA/Sinn Féin. And it is equally naive not to reasonably suspect that this manifested in a short bout of ethnic cleansing against a small minority community in west Cork viewed as pro-British. Sectarianism of this kind is also in keeping with how insurgent networks like the IRA/Sinn Féin operate.

What signal did treating the murders of Protestants in west Cork as the legitimate killings of collaborators send out to Irish Protestants in a Catholic-based nation? What signal did this send to Protestants in Northern Ireland? In the aftermath of the conflict in the Free State, Irish Protestant culture was subtly suppressed. For the Protestant community that was left, this undoubtedly discouraged them from raising grievances that portrayed the IRA in a bad light. There was no benefit for any political party (or the Catholic Church) to criticise what was seen by many as a valiant and honourable IRA that brought independence to most of Ireland.

Relative to the Troubles, the Free State (later to become the Republic of Ireland) was a cold house for Protestants. This went largely unreported as the Protestant community was a small minority and did not publicise its grievances. The few Protestants who remained kept their heads down and assimilated into the Free State without complaint. A Catholic community was also trapped in Northern Ireland. The difference being, this was a significant minority and contained republicans accustomed to complaining and using violence. This meant that the majority community in power in each nation looked anxiously across the border at the other. Politically, mistrust between the two made future violence by militant republicans in Northern Ireland inevitable.

The IRA and Sinn Féin did not secure independence for the entire island of Ireland in the Anglo-Irish Treaty signed by the IRA leader Michael Collins and others in 1921. This caused a bitter split within republicanism. Sinn Féin leader Eamon de Valera blamed Michael Collins for negotiating a treaty that failed to gain independence for all of Ireland and retained too many connections with Britain. In the first Free State election in 1922 the pro-treaty side won the majority of votes. The result, however, did not avert a brief but bloody Irish Civil War (1922-3). On one side was Collins (pro-treaty) and on the other his former friend and comrade De Valera (anti-treaty). De Valera argued that the pro-treaty forces and the Provisional government led by Collins was a military junta doing Britain's bidding.

In contrast, the Free State government claimed it was democratically elected and carrying out the will of the people. Ironically, it was a repeat of the same political arguments in the Anglo-Irish conflict with Collins' pro-treaty forces replacing the Royal Irish Constabulary.

The Civil War split the IRA. Anti-treaty forces conducted an IRA style guerrilla campaign against pro-treaty Free State forces. Collins was assassinated in 1922. In Northern Ireland, the Free State forces secretly armed the Northern IRA to attack unionists. Even though the Free State forces prevailed, De Valera eventually became Irish Premier, accepting the treaty he had started a conflict by opposing. Having gained power, De Valera accepted the legitimacy of the Free State. With the formation of the Irish Republic in 1937 (a more independent entity than the Free State with no affiliation to Britain) the reasons for fighting the civil war had been settled. The exception was Sinn Féin.

The internecine conflict left a bitter legacy still felt in Irish politics to this day. The descendants of Collins' pro-treaty forces (Fine Gael) and De Valera's anti-treaty irregulars (Fianna Fáil) have been the two largest political parties in the Republic, dominating the political landscape since partition. Not until the 1950s was violence eradicated from Irish politics. A militant strain in republicanism, however, survived in the shape of a breakaway and unpopular IRA and Sinn Féin. This dissident faction continued to promote and use violence as a political instrument, its efforts focused on ending British rule in Northern Ireland. One can therefore see why policing in Northern Ireland was so important.

Many observers have described the RIC as the finest constabulary in the world. The RUC was its update, inheriting the Royal prefix. Even though the harp, crown and shamrocks symbolised the RUC Irish nationalists concentrated on the crown, a symbol they historically loathed. From the outset, the name of Northern Ireland's new police force and its symbols were a source of grievance for nationalists and something they longed to change.

The RIC and RUC had much in common, particularly a capacity to perform normal policing and security duties. This is the paradox of policing a divided society, especially during armed conflict and has proved the source of most criticism of the RUC. That is, striking a balance between normal policing and security policing. Nationalist leaders consistently accused the RUC of not being normal enough without acknowledging they were partly to blame by having refused to fully support the police in the first place. Similarly, insurgents make a concerted effort to ensure policing is not normal, as Collins' IRA evidences.

The political controversy over the creation of the Royal Ulster Constabulary in 1922 stemmed largely from its religious composition. While many RIC men disagreed with the Black and Tan/Auxiliary approach they were also happy to have them. For the RIC, the Black and Tans and Auxiliaries were both a curse and a cure. Conversely, some RIC men, out of fear or sympathy, or a mixture of both, helped the IRA, which posed problems for a new unionist administration in Belfast. At the same time nationalists in Northern Ireland were equally dismissive of the Ulster Special Constabulary (USC) element, seeing it is a milder version of the Black and Tans. The USC, commonly called the B Specials, was comprised mostly of part-time members. Its main function was to support the regular police on security duties, especially in times of an insurgency.

The RUC's birth symbolises the dilemma that persisted until its disbandment – its politicisation. Perhaps because of the threat posed by the Free State, unionists promoted the RUC as a unionist-controlled instrument. Catholic representation in the RUC peaked at 21% in 1923, falling to 10% by the outbreak of the Troubles and to 8% by the time the RUC was turned into the Police Service of Northern Ireland in 2001. Over this period Northern Ireland was approximately 65% Protestant and 35% Catholic.

The first minister for home affairs, Richard Dawson Bates, manipulated the structure and control of the RUC. Authors, such as

Chris Ryder, describe Bates as a bigot. His influence in determining what the RUC looked like was unfortunate. He abandoned the RIC's template of the police being religiously representative of the community. This was a regressive step. It presented the RUC as an unattractive force to the Catholic minority. Bates did the RUC and both communities a huge disservice. As a result, unionists felt an attachment to the RUC and nationalists did not, hence it was far less popular with nationalists than the RIC.

Soon after partition the IRA embarked on what is called the border campaign (1956-62). This was quickly put down by the mobilisation of 500 RUC Reserve and 1,500 USC along the border. But more important was the political resolve of Dublin. Irish Premier John Costello and then Eamon De Valera introduced tough legal measures. To place suspects before the courts Dublin worked hard to improve cross-border security co-operation, especially between police intelligence departments. Dublin was concerned that IRA violence challenged the authority of the Irish Republic. Having just endured several decades of violence political leaders in Dublin across the two main parties were intolerant of IRA activities.

A unionist Stormont was also anxious about IRA violence causing a reaction with loyalists, which was avoided by co-operating with Dublin to contain the IRA. Worth re-emphasising is that governments in Dublin and Belfast saw the IRA as the main threat. Both introduced internment (detention without trial). Consequently the IRA could not use the Irish Republic as a safe haven or the border as a strategic asset. A common political will and effective cross-border security quickly defeated the IRA. The same political harmony was missing in the late 1960s and early 1970s.

The recent history of Ireland, when examined objectively and with irregular war principles in mind, provides a fascinating insight into the Troubles, particularly how militant Irish republicanism behaves in times of conflict. From an intelligence perspective, in the Anglo-Irish conflict Michael Collins won the intelligence war. On 'Bloody Sunday' (21 November 1920) the

IRA killed 12 British intelligence officers in Dublin. It virtually crippled the state's intelligence effort. Collins had a network of spies in Dublin castle and further afield. Chief of these was David Neligan, a senior officer in the Dublin Metropolitan Police.

After the conflict Neligan became the first head of the Garda Special Branch. Collins considered a well-placed spy in the right place a "pearl beyond price." Republicans were acutely aware that an effective intelligence effort relied on well-placed informers. This is why the IRA/Sinn Féin feared the RIC because intelligence (Special Branch) was key to its operational effectiveness. Although the RIC/RUC is semi-military it is not a light infantry regiment and cannot withstand a sustained period of intensive violence, such as the initial 12-months of the Anglo-Irish conflict. There is a limit to how much violence it can take. Collins knew this. His overall strategy dampened the effectiveness of Special Branch by provoking a destructive military-based response rather than a non-destructive rule of law approach.

A legacy of the Anglo-Irish conflict and Civil War is that men like Neligan witnessed the worst side of republicanism. It was a dark and dirty side that they lamented. They viewed this aspect as communally divisive and a stain on traditional republican ideals, a retributive abomination incapable of letting bygones be bygones. Neligan did not have to wait long to see just how dark and dirty republicanism could get in the shape of the Provisionals. Or, as a former SB detective puts it:

Republicanism in the south moved on, but not in the north. Up here they're trapped in a time warp. It's toxic.

At the heart of Special Branch is intelligence.
But what is intelligence?

Chapter 6

British Made in Ireland

For over a century in Ireland, republicans routinely used insurgency to affect political change. Dealing with an insurgent threat and all it entailed was beyond the operational capacity of an ordinary police force. Something extraordinary was needed. What worked in policing England, Scotland or Wales and provided a good baseline of public safety in tackling ordinary crime was unsuited to Ireland's frequent bouts of insurrection. The unarmed British bobby style of policing would have been wiped out with ridiculous ease. Republicans aimed to make Ireland unpoliceable and therefore ungovernable. If Ireland was to remain part of the UK, republicans wanted to make sure it was under conditions of military rule. The Royal Irish Constabulary changed all that, epitomising how policing in Ireland had adapted to the republican menace. Ireland could be policed and the rule of law upheld even in times of armed insurgency. Policing a conflict is the graduate level of policing.

The main reason behind the RIC's effectiveness was Special Branch, arguably the world's first police intelligence model. Special

Branch guided and advised uniform commanders and senior CID detectives about the security situation so they and frontline police were well informed and directed in their everyday duties. Formalising intelligence that was community-based made policing smarter. It gave the police a vital edge over insurgents.

Special Branch was the heartbeat of the Royal Irish Constabulary. Much to the dismay of republicans this made Ireland policeable, taking away any cheaply won notion about republican insurgency being a product of popular dissent that could arise at any time of its own accord. Having the military in control fed this fantasy. Militants are magnificent myth-makers. Dispelling the fiction in this instance is the fact that militant republicanism was an unpopular fringe. They were extremists whose method of operation was to stoke up ethnic tension to provoke civil unrest in order to subvert the political and legal processes of a democracy. The instability this caused allowed them to start an irregular war. Ultimately, their aim was to politically profit from an insurgency. Which is why policing in Ireland was so important. The police, if properly resourced and supported, could contain the threat an insurgency posed and prevent it from escalating to a level of intensity that would require the military to take control. The police was the best means the state had to stop republicans fully exploiting their most prized asset – insurgency.

The RIC conveyed to the people it served and the outside world that the democratic machinery was at work and any attack against the state was subverting this. In other words, republican violence was not a legitimate act of political protest but crime. Policing was unapologetic and unequivocal. What the IRA did in the Anglo-Irish conflict at a time Home Rule draft legislation was on the statute books was unlawful. Whether it was killing police officers, Protestants in west Cork, executing prisoners or suspected informers, these were murders, shameful crimes and not glorious acts. The same applies to republicans in a dissident IRA who sought to overthrow the newly formed and democratically elected Free State government. From a police perspective, killings by De Valera's Irregulars against Collins' legitimate state forces in the civil war were also murders. It is simple black and white thinking that cuts through political, and academic, arguments that prefer to interpret premeditated killings of this kind in shades of grey. Unlike the IRA brand of republicanism, there is an ageless consistency and integrity in a philosophy based purely on upholding the rule of law in a democracy.

Out of necessity Irish policing was intelligence-led and central to security successes against republican insurgencies. As with Darwin's theory of evolution, it was not about the strongest surviving (the RIC was not that large and the military side of its credentials not that intrusive) but those who adapt to change the quickest. Special Branch was the policing change that adapted best to IRA terrorism and Sinn Féin propaganda. Without intelligence police officers would have been easily murdered. In such a situation quite quickly you run out of police and are left with no police force capable of countering an insurgency. Policing in any significant form is extinct. Which is what happened in Iraq and Afghanistan. If the police cannot protect themselves they cannot protect the people. If there are no police there is no rule of law. This is exactly what insurgent networks like the IRA/Sinn Féin want.

Special Branch was the natural antidote to the IRA. After all, the IRA created it. The RIC and its SB were British made in Ireland. Special Branch prioritised protection over detection, a change in emphasis rather than principle. Protecting life was the main priority. To this end, intelligence was more important than evidence, due to evidence being in scarce supply as a result of IRA and Sinn Féin tactics. It was a situation brought about by nationalists passively or actively supporting the IRA, and withholding support for the police. Evidence was still important and crucial to securing prosecutions but the practical reality was that it was very difficult to come by without intelligence. If intelligence dries up so do the evidential opportunities it creates. Fewer terrorists go to prison.

In an irregular war Special Branch was the policing answer, not only for Ireland and latterly Northern Ireland but also in parts of the Commonwealth prone to conflict. Since the mid-1800s the British had exported the RIC police model to Asia, the Middle

East and Africa with great success, such as Special Branch defeating communist insurgents in the Malaya Emergency in the 1940s and 1950s. The basic template has endured in most of these places. But the export was not limited to hostile areas. Rugged lands and expansive wildernesses that needed an armed police presence also proved receptive. Examples are the North West Mounted Police (predecessor of the Royal Canadian Mounted Police) and Royal Newfoundland Constabulary. For all the appeal of its image, the unarmed British bobby police system was seldom exported, and certainly not to countries prone to conflict. This was classic British counterinsurgency, a rule of law approach that had local police fronting the security effort. It was about empowering the locals to gather intelligence and look after security based on the well-worn principle that they did this far better than the military or foreigners.

Today Special Branch is still a main feature in places like Singapore, India, Bangladesh, Thailand, Malaysia and Jordan. But it is largely a thing of the past in the UK. The enduring nature of Special Branch in these places illustrates just how amenable they were to the introduction of the RIC police model. The RIC's semi-military makeup was a main attraction, a tougher form of law enforcement to the British bobby. The tough no-nonsense character better suited these cultures. Many liked the military aspect and were less sensitive of liberal sensibilities than the west. Almost certainly, these views still stand.

SB and the RIC police model was central to what was a package, with SB at the heart of how policing operated. SB was also used as a standalone police intelligence model in a way that it was not the central component. This format suited forces in England, Scotland and Wales but differed from the Irish version, with London's Metropolitan Police Special Branch perhaps the closest. Many SBs in GB were very small, a few officers working at points of entry/exit to the UK (harbours/airports) to monitor people entering and leaving. The harbour/airport was their main area of responsibility. SB's across the UK were also networked with each other, allowing information to be exchanged and points of contact to be established. From an RUC perspective the relationship with SB's in London and Strathclyde were excellent and regularly used due to both having a strong connection with Irish terrorism (republican and loyalist).

Similar to the RIC, Special Branch in London's Metropolitan Police was created in response to Irish republicanism when the Fenian bombing campaign of 1881-5 brought terrorism into England. London's Special Branch was originally called Special Irish Branch in recognition of this. Unsurprisingly, given that Ireland was part of the UK and with the possibility to join one UK police force from another, former RIC men featured prominently at Scotland Yard. English officers saw them as different, a view that remained fixed during the Troubles. SB detectives in London saw their RUC counterparts as more robust in how they policed. Following partition RIC officers also took up new policing jobs overseas in many other nations. Most had been forced to flee Ireland. Their services were highly sought after, primarily because of an intimacy of policing a troubled area few other westerners had that struck a familiar chord with their hosts.

Special Branch is a police intelligence model that enabled a police force, and not the military, to defeat an insurgency. It was designed for a crisis like the Troubles, providing the means and know-how to defeat the Provisionals. As a concept Special Branch was conceived as a secret intelligence agency running a network of spies to protect the state against subversives. Reflecting the RIC, it was dual purpose, coping equally well in conflict and peacetime conditions, a version of the latter being used in the UK. It had chameleon qualities. In times of stability it reduced in size and merged into the background, maintaining a discreet and limited over-watch of subversives. A strong CID dominated, typical of investigative-led policing in the west. This was the case prior to the Troubles and is also the case afterward. In times of conflict it grew in size and strength and dominated the policing response.

For a rule of law approach in a conflict Special Branch was what the British employed. It is the type of police intelligence model coalition forces in Iraq and Afghanistan should have used but did not. Instead, modern policing systems and practices designed for peacetime situations were used with disastrous results. These are the tragic consequences of selecting unsuited policing approaches in a conflict, a glimpse of what would have happened in Northern Ireland if Special Branch had not been given the security lead.

The difficulty of the SB model is that it has to protect its secrets while integrating with mainstream policing, particularly during conflict. This is largely because its role was primarily laid down by MI5. To a large extent SB detectives are MI5's foot soldiers, although in a conflict this is less so. In the Troubles SB had a larger operational footprint than MI5 and came under the central command of a Chief Constable who had more on his plate than just intelligence. SB's in England, Scotland and Wales did not have this supremacy. Also, the same as soldiers think differently to police officers, especially regarding intelligence in a conflict context, SB detectives think differently to spooks (MI5).

Special Branch dealt with Top Secret intelligence and national security. Its officers signed the Official Secrets Act (1911), legislation that treated any hint of disclosure as a criminal offence. This legal obligation was unique to Special Branch and appeared in no other facet of policing. As such, there was a limit to how far SB could integrate with normal police systems and practices. In the RIC and RUC, Special Branch was better integrated than its UK counterparts because it was the centrepiece of the police model. In England, Scotland and Wales, SB did not have the same central position.

In GB the unarmed British bobby style of policing is based on consent and is investigative-led. The public support the police. A strong CID dominates wherein intelligence is a supporting function. But in the Troubles a minority nationalist community withheld consent for the police, forcing policing to be intelligence-led, which equated to a dominant Special Branch. While an inversion of policing a peaceful society and what many call 'normal' policing, it is the norm for a conflict. Due to SB's dominance, the RUC had to better integrate Special Branch with the wider police family. The improved integration and ability of

SB to dominate is the major difference between the Irish version and the GB version.

After WW2, Sir Arthur Young (RUC Chief Constable 1969-1970) and Sir Ken Newman (RUC Chief Constable 1976-1980) policed Palestine, Malaya and Kenya. Both men had a practical understanding of how Special Branch operated in an insurgency prior to Northern Ireland and extensive experience of policing in England. Young and Newman were the top cops of their day and possessed ideal CVs to determine what policing approach was needed for the Troubles. They understood both the value of Special Branch and the limitations of normal policing in a conflict. From first-hand experience they knew what worked and what did not. Separating SB from CID in order to have SB dominating was standard practice in an irregular war. Coincidentally, separating SB from CID was also deemed best practice in UK throughout the 1970s to 1990s until the arrival of SB's replacement - the National Intelligence Model. Young, Newman and some of the world's top experts on intelligence and security all understood that this was the correct course of action.

Establishing a strong Special Branch was not about introducing anything new, but of reaffirming that this was a wise choice based on previous conflicts. When all else had been tried and failed - Army primacy and a series of investigative-led initiatives - it gave an intelligence-led approach the solid platform it needed to progress. From the outset the right policing approach was prescribed, albeit unannounced and not fully implemented straightaway. In the intelligence war this early decision was strategic gold dust. Special Branch had come full circle, required to prove itself once again in its own backyard.

Often overlooked because it is so obvious is that, at the heart of Special Branch is intelligence. But what is intelligence? As originally defined in ancient times by Chinese military leader Sun Tzu, intelligence is about being armed with foreknowledge of the enemy. Spies in the enemy's camp brought back news of the enemy. For Sun Tzu it was crucial that only a few people should know about secret intelligence - the 'need to know' principle. In the

6th century BC the penalty for speaking about secret intelligence before the appropriate time was death to the person who disclosed it and anyone who repeated the same.

During WW2 Churchill famously said to Stalin about the impending D-Day landings, "In wartime, the truth is so precious that she should always be attended by a bodyguard of lies." To which Stalin replied, "This is what we call military cunning." The sentiment conveys the importance of keeping secrets secret and sources safe. Intelligence remains crucial to counterinsurgency and the Global War on Terror. For an irregular war the US Army and Marine Corps Counterinsurgency Field Manual states: "Effective, accurate and timely intelligence is essential."

Foreknowledge, secrecy, accuracy, effectiveness, source protection, need to know and timeliness are the classic definitional ingredients of intelligence. Intelligence is a military concept in a war context. This is its classic form and how Special Branch understood it. Intrigue, danger, deception, guile and risk are also part of the equation. Commonly taken for granted, quality intelligence is extremely hard to get.

On the other hand, in normal policing in the west intelligence is defined as processed information. This modern definition is dramatically different to the traditional definition. It is an important distinction. In a conflict defining intelligence is not the same as in peacetime. One is high risk and the other low risk. The risk appetite in a conflict is far greater. Most police services today in the west are risk averse. Knowing about a serious crime before it happens poses many challenges. What to do and what not to do. Modern after-the-fact intelligence is less problematic. The police cannot be blamed for preventing something they did not know about. But if it appears they did, regardless of how tenuous the link, huge problems arise - career ending stuff. Modern intelligence is safe and easily managed. For a non-conflict environment it does not need to be anything else.

Currently in the west the National Intelligence Model (NIM) and intelligence-led policing are in vogue. They are one and the same. Intelligence-led policing is a catchy term that speaks sophistication. NIM is a business model, a managerial philosophy. Supermarket chains and commercial companies employ NIM-type thinking. This helps them to analyse and interpret data, aids their decision-making and informs overall strategy. Whether analysing crime patterns for burglaries in a rural town or the best place to position potatoes in a store to increase sales, the same principles apply. All UK police services formulate their enforcement and preventative strategies based on NIM. As such, NIM was designed as a top-down process driven by intelligence requirements. Senior managers dictate what is required and should be reported on and form working groups and committees accordingly. At its worst NIM is a talk-shop. Plenty is discussed but little is done.

NIM took intelligence from its traditional users like the CIA, MI5 and SB and gave it to a wider audience - intelligence for beginners. Popularising intelligence, however, has diluted it. NIM can be described more accurately as an information model that markets information-led policing. NIM brings benefits to modern UK policing and policing in the west in general, and there is no doubting its popularity. But it is foolhardy to believe that it is the same as practices, systems and procedures used by dedicated intelligence agencies in a conflict. Chiefly, Special Branch is bottom-up. Constables on the beat know what the policing problems are from talking to people in the local community. In turn, they talk to SB detectives in their station. Local Special Branch assesses this information alongside other information they have gathered. They then feed this upwards, advising the local uniform and Special Branch commanders on a daily basis. In broad terms, operational police at the tactical level tell their commanders what the policing problems are and not the other way around. It is community-based. Intelligence-led policing in a conflict is a survival mechanism, not a business model.

A crucial benefit of being a ground-up model like Special Branch is that, in an irregular war, there is no frontline. Terrorists can appear anywhere. Information feeds in from the ground and percolates upward. It does not cascade downward. Top-down models like NIM turn into clunky bureaucratic messes, slowing down the decision-making process. This sits badly with a high pace conflict environment. Top-down processes are also susceptible to being manipulated by the managers who control them, particularly in presenting crime statistics based on detections. The policing priority is detection. Prevention is still important, but it is an abstract difficult to quantify and get across to the public in a sound-bite or headline.

A profound difficulty with NIM is that it tries to turn intelligence into a science so that it is easier managed. But intelligence cannot be made scientific; it is as much art as science. The arty part often produces the best results and makes the rest work. Nowhere is this more so than in a conflict. But it is business models and managerial philosophies that are in style, pervasive in all areas of government. Modernity detests the abstract. The abstract is hard to measure, track, manage, oversee, analyse, review, regulate or take credit for. Transparency, the antithesis of secrecy, is also fashionable. Which, along with modernity's dislike of the intangible, is mainly why Special Branch in the UK was replaced by NIM at the turn of the 21st century. As the UK sleepwalked into a politically correct era under Prime Minister Tony Blair's New Labour, Special Branch ticked few boxes. Its number was up.

What makes Special Branch suited for a conflict makes it unsuited for peacetime policing today. The reverse is true of NIM. Even with the most basic element - intelligence - one can see that what is regarded as normal in an armed conflict is dramatically different from that of a peaceful environment. Whilst timely pro-active intelligence is the key priority in an irregular war it is not in a peacetime context.

Less contentious are the qualities of intelligence. It is not fact but a version of the truth. Fact is a legal term. Truth is a moral term. Intelligence is flawed information that will always have unknowns. It comes with a margin of uncertainty. Time degrades its value. At one end intelligence is lies, rumour or innuendo and at the other completely honest and accurate. But even the best intelligence only tells part of the story. You never get the full picture. Dealing with intelligence in a conflict is a formidable undertaking. The right choices are not always made or obvious. Covering or predicting all eventualities is impossible. Things get missed. In the UK intelligence is not evidence capable of securing a criminal conviction. It is evidence, however, of the effectiveness or ineffectiveness of the agency that produced it. To secure criminal prosecutions intelligence guides to where evidence is. Intelligence cannot magically mutate into evidence.

Insurgency in Ireland by republicans caused the creation of Special Branch, a unique police intelligence model handling the traditional definition of intelligence with all its challenges and nuances. Its weakness is an inability to sit comfortably within legal systems with all their requirements for transparency and disclosure while simultaneously protecting secret methodologies, secret sources and practitioners in order to keep them as viable resources.

Intelligence by its very nature is a product of secrecy. Those against whom intelligence is directed should be mystified about its origins. Special Branch left terrorists bewildered by its diversity of intelligence sources (human, technical etc). Other crucial principles are the circle of knowledge being kept small and 'need to know' principle strong. All these rely on secrecy, the single most important component of intelligence. Once secrecy is weakened intelligence loses its strength and value and an intelligence agency's effectiveness recedes. No secrecy no intelligence.

In a conflict, demands on Special Branch require it to keep producing premium intelligence of the sort useable in pro-active operations. In a modern peacetime setting legal and political systems demand ever more layers of external scrutiny, micro accountability and disclosure. It is hard to see how these can be reconciled in any meaningful way without secrecy and the main intelligence principles suffering. Which is a major reason why current police intelligence models are of limited value in an irregular war. The point has been reached where there are no secrets any longer because trust, as a concept, is virtually absent in or between agencies of the state and the public. To compensate, political and legal systems have overdosed on accountability and transparency. This has radically increased bureaucracy and re-diverted limited resources in the shape of more back-office staff to satisfy demand. Perhaps the best example of this in the public service sector is the National Health Service (NHS).

Today the NHS has as many staff not looking after patients as there are looking after patients. Administrators and managers will soon outnumber doctors and nurses. It is an imbalance previously unthinkable. The NHS typifies how a steady diet of political correctness has caused bureaucratic obesity. A mountain of rules, regulations, policy and associate oversight bodies have bloated public services and slowed them to a snail's pace. Fear of litigation and criticism determines most practice and procedures, not practitioners. When criticised, chief executives in charge of Health Trusts use statistics to defend their position, just as police chiefs employ crime statistics for the same purpose. The consequences of being weighed down and slowed down this way in a conflict would be catastrophic.

The genesis of the RUC Special Branch left it uniquely placed to deal with the tumult of the Troubles. Both it and the RUC had a strong counterinsurgency pedigree. Intelligence-led policing in the Troubles was very different to other parts of the UK. Policing a conflict is nothing like policing a peacetime environment. Recognising this is vital to understanding Special Branch, and with it the intelligence war it waged against the IRA. Put another way, there is no example of an investigative-led approach being effective in an irregular war. Which is why it failed in the Troubles. It is therefore naïve to think that a Senior Investigating Officer can benefit from an intelligence-led approach that is succeeding and at the same time dictate how intelligence is exploited without detracting from what had made it succeed in the first place. In a conflict intelligence does not always work in combination with investigations. Not every evidential opportunity can be grasped. Picking and choosing is not an option. It is a delicate eco system. Tamper with one part and the rest suffers. Everything is interconnected. These are the basics.

Deploying Special Branch against the IRA (and loyalist terrorist organisations) was the best way to protect the public and end the Troubles. It was a rule of law approach capable of going toe-to-toe with the Provisionals. A strong Special Branch, however, was always destined to upset nationalists, left wing socialists and bleeding heart liberals. But it was also the last thing the IRA/Sinn Féin wanted, as good a reason as any to justify its use.

Agents in illegal republican terrorist organisations saved at least 16,500 lives.

Chapter 7

Agents & Handlers

Approximately 60% of all intelligence gathered in the Troubles was from people giving information or what SB called agents. Of the rest, approximately 20% was technical (telephone intercepts and eavesdropping on buildings/ vehicles of known terrorists), 15% surveillance and the last 5% almost evenly split between framework operations (routine police and Army patrols that interacted with the public) and open sources (local newspapers, community/parish bulletins). When we talk about intelligence diversity that left the IRA guessing after a setback, this is it.

The recent history of policing conflict in Ireland shows that agents were central to Special Branch operations, whether in the Fenian Rising in the 1800s or in the IRA border campaign 100 years later. It is therefore unsurprising that they were central to policing the Troubles. Agents are the mainstay of a dedicated intelligence agency. Against an insurgency it is a highly effective tactic. US General David Petraeus states that this remains the case. It is what SB was built for and excelled at.

Ancient Chinese warlord Sun Tzu famously said: "Nothing

is more demoralising to the enemy than realising that people inside their organisation are providing information to the other side." Agents provided detailed information on terrorist organisations. A system was used to categorise them, with those who were members of terrorist organisations, or what can be called well-placed agents, the smallest category. SB also had relationships with people who were not agents, people below the radar of terrorist organisations and the security forces because they were usually middle class professionals with no connection whatsoever with terrorism. They were uniquely placed to assist with discreet inquiries and requests, such as an employer providing details about his staff or the owner/occupier of a building allowing a covert camera in it to monitor a specific location. Unlike agents, they were not paid a monthly retainer or rewarded for results. A small gift at Christmas or the occasional gratuity was it. Money was not a motivating factor. They were decent people who abhorred terrorism and supported the rule of law.

Former SB detectives reckon an IRA green-booked agent (a common term for a fully fledged IRA member) saved around 37 lives per year but were a tiny portion of the agent stable. The SB/agent relationship was secret and invariably long-term. Although for a well-placed agent it could be a short shift. Being an integral part of a terrorist cell routinely engaged in murder plots and the deadly fallout when these went wrong was a perilous existence. But it is extremely difficult, albeit not impossible, for someone to know the secrets of a terrorist organisation without being in it. What all these people did was potentially fatal. For the IRA and loyalist terrorist organisations anyone they believed were 'helping' SB in anyway was a certainty to be shot dead.

Well-placed agents carried the greatest risk but also the greatest reward, producing the majority of quality and life saving intelligence. All types of agent provided information on the IRA that ranged from identifying a suspect's address to giving details on an impending attack. While a Regional Head of SB would be aware of his own agent stable he was unaware of others. Only a select handful in SB knew what its network of agents looked like in its totality.

The true identity of agents and other members of the public who helped the police was jealously guarded on a strict 'need to know' basis. Even using the word agent in conversation was off limits. Under no circumstances were real names mentioned. Which is ultimately what terrorist organisations wanted to know. How desperate they were (and still are) to find out is illustrated by the IRA breaking into SB's main Belfast office in 2002, four years after the conflict ended. The risk of being an agent did not end with the Troubles.

Conversely, in the traditional crime context was an 'informant,' someone giving occasional information to CID in a short-term as-and-when confidential relationship. Informants were not categorised. Their information was on ordinary crime, usually after-the-event and mostly from loose talk. The risk of being exposed was seldom life threatening. They were a minor aid in an investigative strategy.

In an ideal world people are not afraid to come forward and testify against offenders in open court and are willing to do so because they support the rule of law. But Northern Ireland circa 1969 to 1998 was far from ideal, so the opposite applied. How people could give information to the police without anyone else knowing was a big issue. Agents are completely different to informants and also to what the public and most police believe when thinking of this subject. When one knows how SB defined intelligence and the context the security forces were operating in, the agent concept makes sense. The difference between agent and informant mirrors the difference between intelligence-led policing and investigative-led policing. Understanding this is crucial to understanding SB.

Agents in illegal republican terrorist organisations saved at least 16, 500 lives in the Troubles. A former SB detective chief superintendent assesses that 15 well-placed agents were active at any one time in the IRA (1:33 ratio when based on an IRA of 500). On a yearly basis, considering a well-placed agent on average saved 37 lives per year, this equates to 555, which over 30 years is 16,650 lives. This excludes other types of agents and 40% of the intelligence effort against the IRA. It also completely excludes loyalist terrorist organisations.

Agents were a force multiplier, inducing paranoia in the IRA and loyalist terrorist organisations that prevented many attacks. Sixteen and a half thousand is not an inflated estimate. In numbers it shows the IRA's true intent and what underpinned an 85% prevention rate. Agents were preventing murders almost as fast as the Provos were planning them.

Provo ideology portrays agents as sub-human, naturally enough given that they had to find ways to justify their sectarian terror campaign. It compelled republicans to say nothing about IRA killings because in their eyes they were not murders but legitimate acts and those who direct, plan and did the killing deserve protection. To fit in you had to be seen to toe the party line. Not to conform raised suspicion. But there were dissenters. Agents were the resistance movement within, the sole and silent voice of sanity in a regime intoxicated by a rancid ideology. Most saw IRA killings as a needless waste of life designed to advance the hidden agenda of republican leaders and not the movement. Quite a few were sickened by those in the IRA who enjoyed killing. Many realised the 'armed struggle' was a charade and recognised its sectarian character.

But to whisper any of this was treachery, and treachery was punishable by death. The IRA went to extraordinary lengths to condition republicans into believing that the deaths of civilians at their hands was the fault of her majesty's government. The most extraordinary length was the creation of an internal security team personally controlled by the Provisional Army Council to hunt and kill 'touts.' As a matter of policy insurgent leaders were quick to turn IRA guns on their own community. It was important for the IRA to demonise agents to shut down any debate within the republican community about the morality of IRA killings. This is why 'touting' was prioritised as the main threat and treated with utter contempt and ruthlessness.

The only viable outlet an IRA member had of stopping

IRA murders was by providing information in secret to the state, predominantly the police. Special Branch was set up for this purpose. For quite a few insurgents, seeing a victim's family on television, the uncensored reality of the IRA's handiwork and the depravity of some of their comrades was not what they had signed up for.

Telling police about murders, as a good thing to do, would have ruined the illusion the IRA and Sinn Féin had constructed. The Provos' existence depended on having indoctrinated 'volunteers' and cushioned the social conscience of republican communities against any notion that the IRA was bad. Agents were reviled as immoral money grabbers or gullible fools exploited by manipulative Special Branch masters. For an agent, finance was a motivator, as was self-protection, in the face of a sense that sooner or later they would be caught. But in most cases it was decency. In any event, the financial incentive, although not insignificant in some cases, was nowhere near enough to compensate for the risks. In agreeing to be an agent a person risked losing everything – their life, family, friends, identity, reputation and community.

A well-placed agent faced a dilemma at every stage in their terrorist lifetime, from the factors that idealistically motivated them to join a terrorist organisation, and the propaganda or social pressures that propelled or seduced them to take up arms. To become an agent was a life-changing choice. It meant constant psychological stress in a double life of being the perfect terrorist while working against their associates and the organisation. An unguarded moment could be fatal. The strains in family life this caused were immense.

Whilst possessing an Irish patriot's spirit they also had a strong moral conscience and were not pressured into working for SB, but having got there by personal decision-making and motivated by higher objectives and a courage lacking in many in their communities. Men like Sean O'Callaghan, Kevin Fulton, Martin McGartland and Raymond Gilmour illustrate this. They self-disclosed as agents through the books they wrote, although the government and intelligence agencies have neither confirmed nor denied this. Recruiting an agent was about gaining trust, putting an arm around a shoulder and listening, and not a fist in the face and shouting. Of course, the Provisionals could not let this get out. Hence, torturing confessions out of suspected agents (usually followed by execution) to propagandise the 'bad Brit bad tout' message.

Former SB detectives claim they managed agents who were not the most malevolent figures. The whole idea was that a green-booked agent was the least worst. Redeeming qualities set them apart from the hardliners. Only those who CID had no chance of prosecuting were selected. SB did not recruit the hard-men of the IRA but those who could put the hard-men behind bars. Which also applies to loyalist terrorist organisations. The difficulty, however, is that once the media spin stories about someone they believe is an agent, sensationalising his terrorist role is the headline. In reading this most people are shocked. They struggle to understand why on earth would the police use someone as distasteful as this? Surely the police should be putting people like this in prison and not talking to them?

But if one accepts the premise that agents are the most effective means of countering terrorism and protecting life in an irregular war, and also that Northern Ireland's terrorist train was well and truly rolling, the question is: how does this person the press have highlighted compare to the rest in that terrorist cell? He might look like an IRA hard man, but in contrast to the rest he is not. Unless you know who the rest are how can you fairly judge?

Regardless of not being a central player every green-booked member was continually involved in conspiracies to murder and therefore a murder suspect. It is impossible to be anything else in a network with an ideology that promotes murder as a legitimate act. Terrorists planned murder as frequently as ordinary people planned dinner. Because of sheer volume, distinguishing between the speculative and substantive was a constant problem. Another dilemma for SB was the 'unknowns' - terrorist crimes an agent has committed, is committing or planning to commit.

Infrequent face-to-face short meetings in dangerous places

worked against reducing the unknowns, as did an inability to conduct proper research and reviews. One former SB officer points out: "You didn't have a lot of time with them." To be precise, usually one hurried meeting every few weeks to download 14 to 21 days of information. The constancy of threat was also a factor in what another officer describes: "The pace was hectic. Stuff was coming in all the time." The Warner Report in 1996 (leading MI5 figure reviewing SB) recognised how SB met agents was not ideal and in marked contrast to the Army and MI5. Warner notes that this was imposed on SB due to its limited resources and higher workload in comparison to the other intelligence agencies. Handlers were run ragged with no respite. It was impossible to know or deal with everything.

The world of the handler was a high-pressure environment. Not only had they and their colleagues to deal with their own family and work pressures but the pressure of dealing with all the daily concerns of the agent. They were the only person the agent could fully trust and talk to about their innermost fears and anxieties. Communication with an agent was notoriously problematic, as were the vagaries of what was said and the self-preservation factors that motivated agents to hold back on information that if disclosed and then used or misused would increase the risk of their discovery and death. This pressure was greatest for pre-emptive information or planned action of which few in the terrorist organisation were aware.

Handlers were the smartest of street-wise cops. They knew every nook and cranny of their patch, who lived where and who drove what. They knew the family trees of suspects better than their own. All of this and covert field-craft was their survival mechanism. To raise any suspicion in areas where they were hate figures risked a hostile crowd gathering around the car or a terrorist attack. And there was not enough backup to fend these off. Not until the late 1980s did most high risk meetings of this type get substantial armed backup as SB's resources increased.

In meeting an agent the handler had to blend in and scan the area at the same time as listening to what the agent was saying.

The main struggle was accurately interpreting what the agent said and how to manage the agent's participation in a way that protects him and yet identifies and protects the intended victim. For the handler 'phoning a friend' was not an option. There was no panic but calmness based on experience that produced sound guidance. For an imminent attack the main priority was to slow it down, either through the agent's influence or security forces activities. This was done through initial handler guidance, a quick and short-term fix that bought time for SB to devise a more permanent solution to deny terrorists achieving their goal. Time was of the essence. From meeting the agent and getting back to base with the information was all happening within a few hours. Meeting agents was a fast problem-solving dynamic riddled with risk.

Only in a lull in violence was there an opportunity to get an agent to a less hostile area to have a relaxed conversation. Even then, the risk of a well-known IRA man being seen by an off duty police officer near a known SB detective in a quiet town was a concern. The higher the agent's profile the higher this risk. SB was not only concerned about terrorist organisations exposing an agent but also their own side.

An agent's self-defence mechanism is not telling everything they know. Also, seldom do they know everything. This was emphasised in SB training material and foremost in the minds of handlers. Agents are skilled liars. They have to be. Their memory recall mixes lies with facts to become their truth in a process that instinctively filters what they say before they say it. For a handler, deciphering fact from fiction, lies from truth, as well as figuring out what has been omitted, is a constant. Building trust is what kept lies and omissions to a tolerable level. Everything that makes a good agent makes a poor witness.

Handlers were trained never to trust an agent, doubt what they say and never think of them as a friend. You need to be emotionally detached, too close and you lose objectivity. But where the life of the agent and handler often depended on each other, such as when meeting in a dark alleyway in west Belfast, the human factor and its flaws cannot be totally eliminated.

Well-placed agents think differently to normal people. In everyday life they are constantly calculating and recalculating what they can and cannot say. For conversations that revolve around conspiracies to murder, once they are included in the plot there is no opt out. With stakes this high, they cannot look too interested or disinterested. Either attracts adverse attention.

In the event of a security success, a reverse audit of who knew what took place. The risk of being exposed was reduced if there were plausible explanations of how the police knew that did not solely point to them. Having diverse intelligence sources greatly assisted in this respect, as did the agent being pre-armed with a menu of explanations, such as blaming IRA sloppiness and not SB excellence. In the worse case – suspicion solely directed at him – never, ever admit to being an agent. To do so guaranteed a horrible end.

Every time a piece of information a well-placed agent provided was acted on that stifled the intent of the IRA unit involved increased the risk to them. This is another dilemma. To continue getting valuable information he has to involve himself to some degree in successful operations. To this end he needs to be two or three steps ahead of his co-conspirators to anticipate his role. The nerve-shredding tension and personal risks this involves are unimaginable, a sample offered by a retired SB detective who states:

In one incident he was grabbed at the last minute. He'd no chance to tell us. Within minutes he was in a safe house being briefed on a car bomb attack. Someone was needed to drive the scout car, pickup car and actual car bomb. He ended up driving the car bomb. His job was to park it at a certain spot and flick the switch, so to speak. Anyway, within minutes they were on the road and at the spot. Everything worked sweet as a nut. He parked it up and casually got into the pickup car. But he deliberately didn't flick the switch so the bomb couldn't go off. The IRA phoned it in and the security operation made the TV. Had the bomb exploded as planned the area would not have been cleared in time. There'd have been massive casualties. He was grilled about why it didn't but stuck to his story and swore blind that he flicked the switch, and they believed him. But they weren't that annoyed, putting it down to a faulty timer or detonator. In their books it was a success - they made the headlines, everyone got there and back safely.

For the IRA, success did not hinge on a kill. In protecting life this well-placed agent committed crimes of conspiracy to murder and illegal possession of explosives. Should he be prosecuted? In knowing what he did, are the handlers guilty of assisting offenders? What if he had managed to tell his handlers in a hurried 30-second phone call? If they go along with his plan, are they guilty of conspiracy to murder? What should CID, who are investigating the incident as attempted murder, be told? What is the evidence against him? Will more people be saved with him remaining in place or not?

All the difficulty in the case outlined begins with the first decision, to go or not to go. The handlers had him schooled about options, one of which he took. Others produced the same outcome. These are positive steps to protect life based on past terrorist behaviour and what previously worked to counter it. You cannot cover every eventuality, just the main and reasonable ones. To complicate matters, his OC may have been testing him because of suspicions he was 'touting,' which was a common Provo tactic. Talk of an attack was fiction and staged in order to see his reaction. Rarely was anything straightforward with the IRA.

If he did not go he faced an IRA inquiry with probable execution or an overnight flit from Northern Ireland in a resettlement scheme courtesy of her majesty's government. But the threat has not gone away. People are still at risk but SB no longer has someone on the inside. This was the ebb and flow of the intelligence war.

All of the aforementioned permutations are by no means exhaustive. The scenario is only one of many, each of them different. Further variables are the agent's position, activeness of the IRA cell and operational environment. The scenario shows that protecting the life of a well-placed agent and prospective victim/s is a real-time balancing act where to varying degrees many things cannot be identified, controlled or predicted. It is a balancing act SB rarely fell down on. Critics, however, do not see it this way. They accuse SB of allowing murders to take place to protect agents. They rationalise that maintaining an agent's position within the IRA was more valuable than the life lost or the life lost was of no consequence. It is called SB 'playing God,' an allegation the police found offensive and strenuously denied when accused of having sacrificed three uniform police officers to protect an agent in a 1982 so called 'shoot-to-kill' incident. An offshoot of the allegation is that in running command figures in the IRA (and loyalist terror groups) SB was directing terrorism. SB on the other hand claim that an agent in a command position protected more lives from being in that position than would have been the case otherwise. To be clear on this, no agent, no matter how well placed and irrespective of status or potential, had a licence to kill, and nowhere is 'playing God' prescribed in SB policy or training material or represented by former officers.

The entire reason for agents was to stop murders. The vast majority of the time they succeeded. But it was not fool-proof. Everyone could not be saved. Based on the information known at the time, agents were people assessed to be making an honest effort to protect life. Did some agents and SB detectives fall short in this respect? It would be foolish to think they did not. There is a major difference, however, between genuinely trying to protect life and coming up short, and making a conscious decision that someone dies. The latter constitutes murder, which goes against everything an SB detective was trained, told and sworn to do. The net effect of agents was more lives were saved than lost, a vital point the selective moralising of the 'playing God' chorus ignores.

The biggest dilemma was legal. A Home Office circular 97/1969 (12 May 1969) contained guidelines that catered for informants reporting on burglaries and not agents reporting on terrorist murders, an investigative-led approach by CID and not an intelligence-led approach by SB. The de Silva Report (2012) into the loyalist murder of Patrick Finucane in 1989 reviewed this aspect, acknowledging that the Home Office guidelines were designed for ordinary crime. They were of no use in the Troubles. Guidelines of this kind usually are founded in a statute law but these originated from the deliberations of a committee of GB-based police chiefs that predated the Troubles. As the guidelines were not legally binding the RUC formed the view that they could not be fully adapted for a conflict context. The reasoning was that a well-placed agent and the police agency managing him could not comply with such guidelines in any meaningful way and still have the agent providing information on the terrorist organisation of which he is part. To comply would have put the public in jeopardy.

The SB model and its core function came without legal instructions. The criminal justice system was also unkindly disposed. Throughout the Troubles no legal body, international human rights-based organisation, law or national guidelines had any clue about how to legally manage agents. Yet at the same time they commend this approach. Nowhere in an irregular war is a legal framework and guidance needed more than for well-placed agents. This is as relevant today as it was in 1969.

British Army Colonel Robin Evelegh in the early 1970s identified these legal shortcomings. He expressed his concerns in a book, arguing that a lack of law hampered security, especially in intelligence. Another is retired Head of Special Branch, assistant chief constable Raymond White. He claims the police consistently raised this issue with Westminster but it was simply too difficult to do. Evelegh and White had identified that having no statute law for agents and covert policing in general invited contrary legal arguments at a later date. These would contest the actions of police at the time. They predicted that lawyers would allege, on behalf of their clients, that things should have been done differently. As when what was done failed to prevent a certain outcome, such as a terrorist murder. No law or guidelines and intelligence based on foreknowledge made this inevitable. Evelegh and White knew that this left the police vulnerable to retrospective accusations. They also raised concern that the criminal justice system worked against prosecutions resulting from covert operations. As Raymond White says:

We'd have much preferred a law on the statute books specific to agents from which we could have drafted guidance. Not having these made our job more difficult. As it was we had to do without. We'd no other option.

White says he raised the legal issue with Prime Margaret Minister Thatcher, but she was unable to help. According to White, her view was to: "Get on with it and don't get caught as what you're doing is working well." White's view is that the Prime Minister was not implying that SB was doing anything unlawful or that she condoned unlawful activity. To clarify 'don't get caught', White explains that this refers to the approach not attracting attention from which legal arguments disputing what was done would result. Thatcher's thinking was wishful. White, on the other hand, knew the police would be ensnared in legal and political controversy once the conflict ended. Yet, not to employ the tactic would cost more lives.

With no statute law the police used the Common Law principle and fundamental policing principle of protecting life. Although looser than statute law it evidences the integrity of recruiting and running agents (and any covert operation) was manifestly lawful and ethical because its purpose was always to protect life. If life was lost it was not by intent or malice aforethought.

The covert world only has so many strings to its bow. For it to be effective it needs to be protected for all our sakes and not left open to forensic scrutiny each time a terrorist is put before the courts. This is the dilemma for the criminal justice system in any democracy facing terrorism. SB needed better legal support in unraveling the Gordian intelligence knot. In putting 20,000 before the courts for Troubles-related crimes, the police was doing something right. The trick for any democracy is to create the parameters for the intelligence world and then have the populace trust the oversight agencies and the courts to police the system in confidence on their behalf. You cannot have transparency and secrecy at the same time.

For the first time ever an irregular war was happening in a liberal democracy. Laws and the legislative framework came under the spotlight as never before. No civilised nation faced with the same threat would have done anything different. It was not the police who profited most from the legal deficiency but its critics.

Agents are the heartbeat and soul of an effective intelligence effort. They come in many guises, a distinction often missed even within the police world. And they are fundamentally different to an informant in an ordinary crime context who comes together with others in a loose alliance to carry out a one-off criminal enterprise and then dissolves back to his everyday routine. The agent existing within a terrorist cell has a totally different set of pressures and relationships. He is subject to discipline of the severest kind and cannot pick and choose the activities in which he is engaged. His life depends on his ability to appear to be the perfect terrorist. All this dictates the information flow he can provide. His handling produces unique pressures not readily appreciated. Handlers were not clairvoyants but ordinary people doing an extraordinary job to the best of their ability. Limited understanding of an agent's role has led to perceptions of full knowledge of events yet to occur. The rules governing the handling of an informant and agent are poles apart. One size does not fit all. To adopt this approach, as the Home Office guidelines did, is a recipe for mismanagement of a valuable resource.

Individuals who became agents and others who helped SB are the real heroes of the Troubles. Many are alive today because of them. They had the courage to help the police catch killers and stop murders when most of their community did not. Hence their communities vilify them. The information they provided could not have been gathered any other way. Their actions showed that there were people in the republican community, including Provos, who disagreed with 'armed struggle' and were prepared to help the police. They put their trust in a stranger to handle matters in a way that did not endanger their already precarious existence. Who would want to be that stranger? Who would want to be an agent?

Having well-placed agents in an organisation that is committed to destroying you saves more lives than not having them and radically improves your chances of success or survival. Agents were the decisive factor in the intelligence war. Eventually surveillance, armed response and tactical co-ordination were added in what was a revolutionary new format, a potent combination that would be instrumental in forcing the Provisionals to capitulate.

The causes were eminently predictable
preventable.

Chapter 8

Barbed Wire and Bayonets

The cause of the Troubles was a combination of political ineptitude by unionists and nationalists, London and Dublin that gave republicans an excuse to re-brand a new IRA. None of the political protagonists, who ought to have known better, emerges untainted. The main culprit, however, was unionism. As a former SB detective notes: "Something was wrong, and no matter what way you look at it the bulk of that something was a privileged old unionist elite." Since partition, unionist single party rule at the Stormont parliament had discriminated against a Catholic minority. Unionist narrow-mindedness went unchecked for decades aided and abetted by Westminster's disinterest in Northern Ireland's affairs. Unionists demonstrated that they could not be trusted on their own to govern or serve all the people fairly.

Railing against this, middle class Catholics who had benefitted from improved living standards created inflated expectations on political reforms. They started anti-government protests via a supposedly non-sectarian Northern Ireland Civil Rights Association (NICRA). Even though this was meant to be cross-community it attracted almost exclusively nationalist

113

groups. The civil rights movement was the Trojan horse militant republicans had longed for, guaranteeing violent confrontations between working class Catholics and the police. Civil rights protests amplified ethnic division rather than political, legal, economic or social sentiments capable of bringing together both communities. An embryonic Provisional IRA infiltrated and then weaponised the civil rights movement. This is what intimidated unionists, not an irrational fear given republicanism's historic preference for insurgency. Dublin, unsurprisingly, sided with northern nationalists in a partisan partnership and was ambivalent or uncaring about unionist concerns. Political battle lines had been drawn in simple sectarian orange and green sides, a familiar scene that should have sounded alarm bells. It was totally in keeping with how irregular wars start.

Dublin supporting northern nationalists was similar to the unionist/London alliance. British Prime Ministers and Irish Taoiseachs backed their side. From the outset two political opposites emerged, eroding the middle ground of compromise and moderation and with it any chance of a peaceful settlement. Militants prospered from primitive politics that had proved unwilling or incapable of changing entrenched constituency mindsets that voted according to ethnicity. Politics north and south, east and west had spectacularly failed the people of Northern Ireland, particularly the working class. Out of this political paralysis stepped the Provisionals.

While genuine social and political grievances did exist, they were not as severe as nationalists claim and minor when taken in a wider context. And they certainly were not worth starting an irregular war over. The racial discrimination black Americans were suffering at the same time was far worse yet did not lead to a Troubles equivalent in the US. Illustrating that nationalist grievances, on their own, were insufficient to start a conflict. Comprehensive reforms to remedy discriminatory practices, which black Americans would have been delighted by, had been quickly drafted by Northern Ireland's reforming unionist Prime Minster Captain Terence O'Neill. But by this time it was too late.

O'Neill would pay for the sins of his predecessors. After 50 years of Protestant misrule Catholics had lost patience. There was to be no peaceful solution. Civil disorder resulted in sectarian violence. Getting people out on the streets, as nationalists did, was destined to end one way - badly. The militant republican genie was out of the bottle. Realising this, in 1968 O'Neill famously declared in a televised broadcast that, "Northern Ireland is at the crossroads."

Hampered by his own hardliners O'Neill interpreted civil rights marches as a threat as opposed to an unthreatening initiative for reform. Most of the population wanted decisive action to restore order in the face of unprecedented levels of sustained violence. These factors and the increasingly sinister character of a civil rights movement dominated by nationalists and steered by republicans, influenced O'Neill's decision. It was a decision that brought the police into the equation. Nationalist intransigence had followed unionist belligerence. Neither, seemingly, recognised their flaws or how these alienated the other side and the overall destabilising effect on society. Good neighbourliness was in short supply.

Dublin's contribution in the lead-in to the Troubles was poor and probably the worst of all the political protagonists in the long run. Dublin's sympathy for fellow nationalists in the north was no longer balanced by fear of IRA violence in the south. This had been the case in the IRA border campaign seven years earlier. Freed of this concern the Republic's main political parties appeased roughneck relatives in the wider nationalist family. Unifying Ireland attracted popular support and tied in with Articles 2 and 3 of the constitution. It was therefore unconstitutional for Fianna Fáil or Fine Gael to argue against the traditional headline aim of the IRA. Painful wounds of the civil war, not yet healed, were soothed by aspirations of a united Ireland. This and how the Republic had vilified the British approach in Ireland and glorified Collins' IRA benefited the emerging Provisionals.

Sympathy for the IRA in the north played out well in the south. After all, it was Northern Ireland and not the Republic of Ireland that was in danger. Predictably, therefore, Dublin did not consider cross-border security co-operation, particularly between

SB's, a priority. The reverse, it co-operated with burgeoning insurgents. The 'arms trial' that accused government ministers Charles Haughey and Neil Blaney of arming northern republican militants in mid-1969 to defend Catholics against Protestant attacks indicates where Dublin's allegiances and strategic interests sat.

The Republic's stance encouraged republican militants in the north, showing them that its territory could be used as a safe haven and the border a strategic asset for any terrorist campaign in Northern Ireland. Without this it is unlikely the Provisionals would have got off the ground, and if they did, it would not have been for long. Dublin's minimalist security approach was crucial to starting and prolonging the Troubles. Its treatment of a Protestant minority since partition and overtly Catholic ethos did nothing to allay unionist concerns in the north. What developed between the Irish government and the IRA was a tacit, 'you leave us alone and we'll leave you alone' pact. For most unionists the Republic's government was anti-Protestant and pro-IRA, a view diehard unionist Ian Paisley exploited, which undermined reforming unionist leaders like O'Neill.

Ultimately, O'Neill's plea for calm was ignored as civil protests intensified. What he urged in 1968 was the last chance to avoid a conflict. And it is not that his appeals fell on deaf ears. Militant republicans were listening. But a conflict is exactly what they wanted, unwittingly assisted by a vindictive strain in nationalism that also looked to bring Northern Ireland to the brink. The worsening situation saw O'Neill replaced by James Chichester-Clark, who fared no better.

The street violence of civil rights protests gave birth to the insurgency, which is when the police became a central protagonist. By over-reacting to protests the police became part of the problem as opposed to the solution, increasing Catholic resentment of them that played into the hands of republicans. Key events were the Battle of the Bogside in August 1969 during an Apprentice Boys march in Londonderry that erupted into violence. Catholics barricaded their areas in no-go zones, establishing Free Derry.

B-Specials who tried to enter were attacked. The violence spilled over into Belfast, resulting in the burning of Bombay Street, a Catholic area with similar no-go zones.

During street disorder in 1969 the police were responsible for killing eight Catholics, the most tragic of which was nine-year old Patrick Rooney, hit by a stray police bullet. These deaths, sectarian rioting and no-go zones left working class Catholics feeling vulnerable. They viewed the police and loyalists as the perpetrators. The debate within republicanism had Cathal Goulding (moderate) arguing that the British Army and police had to protect Catholics whilst Billy McMillen (militant) looked towards the IRA. Militants like McMillen noted the IRA could not defend nationalist areas from loyalist violence. Neither had republicanism an adequate outlet to politically articulate their viewpoint. Gerry Adams would soon fill this void. For emerging Provos, overcoming the political and military impotency they felt was predicated on undermining the police and promoting themselves as the protectors of Catholics. They created the problem to profit from the perception of solving it.

The Cameron Report (1969) into the civil disorder triggered the Hunt Report (1969) that examined the police in Northern Ireland. The Scarman Tribunal (1972) was another. These inquiries identified the disenfranchisement and grievances of Catholics, the influence of republican militants in civil rights protests and the unacceptable aspects of the police response as the causes of public unrest. Catholic animosity was directed at the B-Specials not the RUC. The upshot was that the Ulster Defence Regiment (UDR) replaced the B-Specials. Unionists saw this as a sop to nationalists and nationalists viewed the UDR as no different to its predecessor.

During civil disorder nationalists (as opposed to republicans) had waged a propaganda war to discredit the police. Specific to the Battle of the Bogside, police officers noted the violence was very different from anything previous. It was more vicious and organised. Nationalist hotheads set out to get the police to over-react and the police fell into the trap. Most nationalists wanted a crisis. Without, it would appear, properly understanding the full ramifications of what this would entail (insurgency), which the briefest reading of Irish history would have shown.

The IRA and Sinn Féin were behind lots of riots because they, unlike nationalists, knew what events were leading to. They had to keep the violence churning in order to stoke up sectarian tension. Mistakes by the state would do the rest. For emerging Provos everything was falling into place as planned and the state was not only incapable of stopping it but assisted. Which is why, even though the start is the most vulnerable time for it, an insurgency is seldom defeated in its start-up phase.

The Hunt Report found that there was no provision for mainland police forces to support the RUC in order to help quell widespread rioting. The police was chronically under-resourced in numbers and material. It was 3,000 strong at this time and the government at Stormont did not listen to earlier appeals in 1968 warning it was too small to cope with widespread public disorder. Which mirrors similar appeals by the RIC prior to the Anglo-Irish conflict. Westminster only acted in Ireland once a crisis had started. The irony being, this encourages a crisis. At 3% of the UK population and with bouts of civil disorder not uncommon Westminster was uninterested in Northern Ireland's internal problems. Other political and economic issues that affected votes on the UK mainland were the priority.

The police were dealing regularly with protests of 15,000 people over weekends and most weekdays with around 700 officers, and accumulating casualties in the process. Violence of this kind was far in excess of anything a western police force had ever faced, both in severity and frequency. A third of all police officers suffered injuries, which the press failed to report, preferring stories about police attacking demonstrators. Few journalists understood what was happening and therefore failed to report on where everything was leading.

To give a proper sense of the RUC under-resourcing, a single episode of public disorder in London over several days in August 2011 involving far fewer rioters and much less violence attracted an initial police response of 6,000 officers that increased to 16,000. The culmination of relentless disorder managed by extremists in both communities and pitiful police resources drove the police to exhaustion, which was the objective of militant republicans and nationalists. For them, portraying to the outside world that Northern Ireland was unpoliceable, a failed state, was a main objective. Regardless of the intent of others, from a police perspective, an unprofessional response had alienated nationalists.

During this period the police had represented to government that extreme loyalists were not differentiating between civil rights protestors and the IRA, a situation they believed the IRA would take advantage of. It was the sectarian reaction militant republicans had provoked and sought to benefit from. The government ignored the guidance, another part of which was requesting that British troops garrisoned in Ulster should act in support of the police, as occurred during riots in 1966. The whole idea was to keep the police in control and have the Army in support. Even though the police had made mistakes they were less likely to repeat these than the Army and had a superior understanding of what was actually happening and why.

Many blame the head of the RUC, Inspector General Anthony Peacocke, for poor judgement in underestimating the threat and believing the police could deal with it unaided. Deploying troops sooner to support the police would have been an effective measure, which Peacocke failed to see. He was forced to resign. As it was, militant republicans and nationalists got what they wanted. Prime Minister Harold Wilson's Labour government in 1969 appointed Lt-General Sir Ian Freeland as Director of Operations with supreme responsibility for ensuring law and order. The Army and not the police were now in charge. Arguably, it was the biggest strategic mistake by the state of the entire conflict. The barbered wire and bayonets of soldiers was new to most of the population and astonished them.

Soldiers used as the means of restoring civil order rarely works out well, especially in Ireland. Moreover, it went against classic British counterinsurgency principles. Budding Provos could not believe their luck. Catholic euphoria in 1969 in Belfast that greeted British troops was reminiscent of the Shia in 2003 greeting Coalition Forces in Baghdad. Both were false dawns and short-lived. In dealing with public disorder nationalist opinion of the Army soon soured. Similar to the police, the Army was tainted as anti-Catholic.

In this period Special Branch was particularly overstretched. A former officer states one detective constable was in charge of Donegal Pass police area (which covered the university, a hotbed of radicalism) and that he was "run off his feet." He states, "We were scattered very thinly." Another explains that they monitored three distinct threats - communism (including radical socialism), republicanism and loyalism. He states, "We had three desks at HQ - Red [communism], Republican and Loyalist - that received and assessed intelligence from frontline SB officers." He describes the peacetime character of Special Branch:

> ____ was the Head of Special Branch when I joined it in 1958. ... He came from the Republic of Ireland. During WW2 ____ was in Springfield Road. He would have been the model of a top Branch man. I think the IRA shot him during the war. He was the original guy, running agents, doing his own surveillance and things like that. He was a Protestant married to a Catholic. ... Back then we would have speculated about who his main agent was, as you never knew who anyone else was running. ... He knew everyone and everyone knew him. ... What you wanted to do was know what they were doing at all times. You weren't working incognito. When we walked down the road people would stop and talk to us. ... My own private car sat parked outside Springfield Road. It never got a scratch on it but they all knew me. I would sign passport applications for IRA men. They knew me better than other police. ...
>
> ... Also of interest were the activities of the Communist Party. The number of card-carrying members of the Communist Party in Belfast was quite high ...

Special Branch was very small; no more than 100 officers and not all gathering intelligence. Duties were performed in plain clothes. We carried out any surveillance ourselves. We also were usually part of the team to do the search or arrest, which meant we briefed and organised the uniform. Even though I was in Special Branch I answered to a Detective Chief Inspector in CID and also the County Inspector. We were dealing with political and foreign citizens. Uniform was kept abreast of what you were doing but not the specifics. It was a stupid man who didn't keep his District Inspector [senior uniform officer] informed about what was happening. There was a degree of confidentiality and trust involved.

It is easy to forget that this was the era of the Cuban Missile Crisis, Iron Curtain and Cold War. Special Branch was not exclusively dedicated to suppressing Catholic dissent or numerically capable of doing so.

As a general character trait the officer illustrates the 'need to know' principle was strong and that SB recruited and managed agents as well as conducting surveillance. These were the two elements of covert policing that SB could perform autonomously, albeit surveillance was ancillary to the core 'agents' business.

A certain amount of gentlemanly respect existed between SB and the IRA prior to the schism within republicanism in 1969. This explains an overt style of covert policing in plain clothes that brought officers into close contact with the community, particularly those suspected of subversion. The 1957 Surveillance guidelines refers to this tactic as 'Restrictive Surveillance' in explaining:

Restrictive Surveillance is the term used when a person is being kept under observation, and it does not matter if he becomes aware of such observation. The object of restrictive surveillance is to deter, hinder or prevent a suspect engaging in subversive activity; the suspect is allowed to realise that he is under observation, and that consequently he must mind his behaviour.

Many covert procedures were in need of urgent change.

Organisationally, however, SB's integrated framework throughout the force was sound. This is significant given the strategic importance of maintaining a permanent police presence. On this, former SB officers point out that closing police stations in Londonderry was a mistake as this allowed the Provos to move in and establish a firm base after events of 1968 and 1969 had alienated the Catholic community. Prior to this police/community relations in these areas were good. Due to an economic decision SB had been prised out of key hotspots. And due to a political decision, developing SB was delayed by Army primacy.

A rapidly deteriorating security situation of which Londonderry was a critical factor witnessed Sir Arthur Young replacing Peacocke in becoming the first RUC Chief Constable in October 1969. His tenure ended in November 1970. Young was a complicated figure. He was a physical link with previous counterinsurgencies in Malaya and Kenya. His approach in Northern Ireland was idealistic. Somewhat naïvely, Young unsuccessfully attempted to disarm the Malayan Police during the Malayan Emergency. He seemed to believe that Malaya was the same policing proposition as England, replicating this with the RUC. His philosophy was that the British bobby style of policing would prevail. Nationalist leaders in the SDLP shared Young's outlook.

Most criticism of the RUC is about it not being normal enough, normal being based on the Young/SDLP thesis. This philosophy, while admirable, was questionable in the political tumult and civil unrest of the late 1960s and subsequent Troubles. Young appears to have been influenced by SDLP leaders and their socialist ideals. Perhaps this is why he was Westminster's choice, as Labour shared the same socialist philosophy as the SDLP. The thrust of inquiries by Cameron, Hunt and Scarman was to make the police more acceptable to nationalists through 'normal policing', which is what Young and the SDLP also advocated. Consequently the RUC was disarmed in November 1970 in standardising it with the rest of the UK. Although it had been operating unarmed in recent years anyway, a feature of the police model in peacetime. In

1971 the decision was rescinded due to worsening violence. Young, the SDLP and three inquiries had forgotten one very important factor - insurgency. The paradox of all this is that what nationalists applauded (Army primacy) and requested (normal policing) was mutually exclusive. You cannot have both.

Young overlooked basic counterinsurgency principles, heading a force emasculated by Army primacy thereby preventing a rule of law approach. Yet police primacy and a rapid expansion of police numbers were crucial to what Young did in Malaya. Young, however, much admired by nationalists, established the foundations for a strong SB that nationalists despised. He commissioned a review by Commander Cunningham (New Scotland Yard) of SB in November 1969 and May 1970. A main recommendation was that SB personnel should be responsible only to the Head of SB. This complied with national practice and did away with CID or uniform exercising operational control over SB. Coincidentally; it also copied the separation of intelligence and investigative departments (an irregular war principle) central to a successful counterinsurgency in the Malaya Emergency.

Separation protected intelligence-gathering efforts and systems the product of which was shared with mainstream policing. Thus, the RUC complied with the most recent best practice in both a counterinsurgency and normal policing context. One gets a sense that Young had hedged his bets, quietly putting down a foundation for Special Branch just in case his normal policing initiative failed. Associated with Cunningham's review was the civilian head of SB registry at New Scotland Yard re-organising the RUC SB registry (secret library) with the aim of improving record keeping and the intelligence flow. MI5 also played an important advisory role in helping to develop SB. A former SB officer states that MI5 was superb in providing expertise in "technical and support fields," part of which was the appointment of an MI5 Officer as Security Liaison Officer and Army Director of Intelligence.

Looking at what caused the Troubles, politics had done little to narrow the gap of a divided society and plenty to widen it. Two political sides evolved based on ethnicity. It was not the sides, however, that were the main problem but the divisions within them. They felt compelled to accommodate their extreme fringe that propelled each on a collision course with the other. Although it was a mix of political failings that caused the political chaos, the initial impetus that triggered this was unionist misrule. Political self-interest took precedence over peace. In the absence of a normally functioning political system the police filled the void. This put them in an impossible position. They did not have the resources or training to cope with violent protests and menacing sectarian undercurrent that was the prelude to an insurgency. For sure, unionists, nationalists, Dublin, London and the police made mistakes but none wanted to start an irregular war. Militant republicans did. Without them there would have been no conflict. Causes of the Troubles are important to analyse, but it was people and not causes who took up arms to overthrow a democracy.

The political knee-jerk to initial police failings and nationalist demands resulted in Army primacy, a strategic mistake and one still difficult to fathom. Everything militant republicans, who would eventually form the Provisionals, were doing was aimed to discredit and get rid of the police. Replacing the police with the Army therefore made no sense. The state had lost its most effective instrument – the rule of law. Special Branch was sidelined. Other than Young commissioning a review of SB and MI5 appointing a senior figure to co-ordinate police and Army intelligence, there was no substantial effort to get a strong SB up and running as the immediate priority. In the intelligence war the Provisionals were given a head start.

Westminster placed too much stock in nationalist opinion that contained fanciful theories about policing a conflict. Against a republican insurgency the British bobby style of policing nationalists wanted was never going to work, a crucial fact the Hunt Report failed to grasp. The only policing option that would work is what nationalists and Westminster had contrived to get rid of. It is possible Young knew this but was politically obligated to play along. What was needed is not what happened. This tends to be the norm for irregular wars. The lessons learned from earlier conflicts had been well and truly lost.

More than any aspect of the Troubles, examining it from an irregular war perspective frustratingly shows that the causes were eminently predictable and preventable. There is no easier and better opportunity to defeat an insurgency than at the start. Yet the west consistently fails in this regard.

From the outset Special Branch advised the government against internment.

Chapter 9

Shock and Awe

In July 1971 a terrorist incident took place almost every hour. For a place the size of Yorkshire and with less than half the population, where homes were left unlocked and murder was a novelty, the frequency and type of violence bewildered and frightened. Who was responsible? How could it be stopped? These were questions people asked. In the first 20 months of the Troubles, republicans committed the majority of violence and 95% of all murders, mostly by a turf war between two IRA factions competing to dominate the streets of Belfast and Londonderry. Compelled to respond, in August 1971, the government introduced internment. A former SB detective states:

We had reported on what we were being told, and you must remember that this was nationalists and republicans we were getting this from. We were not fully prepared and it was too one-sided. Yes, we all knew the Provos were now the major threat and the Officials were still there, or thereabouts, but it was really important to also deal with the loyalists, even though it was a much smaller threat, and more importantly to show nationalists that we were dealing with it.

Despite internment not being deemed discrimination by Europe, it sent out a bad signal to nationalists. The first loyalists were not interned until February 1973. Up to then, all detainees were Catholics. From the outset Special Branch advised the government against internment. A disturbing incident influencing the decision in March 1971 was the abduction and execution of three Royal Highland Fusiliers - John McCaig (17), Joseph McCaig (18) and Dougald McCaughey (23).

These were the first soldiers killed off-duty, soft targets snared in an IRA trap in a city bar by people they had thought were friendly. They were taken from Belfast's bright lights and bustle to a dark and lonely mountain lane, lined up and shot in the head. John and Joseph were teenage brothers. Their killers knew this. For most of the ordeal the infectious idealism of youth would have given all of them hope of being set free. Perhaps, not until the final moments did the awful reality of what was to happen sink in. Even contemplating their mental torment today is uncomfortable.

Tens of thousands gathered in Belfast to condemn the murders, to no avail. The Provos did not need to be popular to exist. They just needed to be tolerated. An irregular war forces people to pick sides and no amount of prevarication is enough to hide this. Elements within nationalism one would have expected to unconditionally condemn IRA killings resorted to generalised condemnation, equating murders by illegal terrorists groups to lawful killings by the security forces. It is warped thinking seeded in prejudice, ignorance and self-interest. Moderates blurring moral boundaries benefit extremists.

The incident shows why the Officials were swiftly swept aside. It was not in them to stoop to such depravity. Falling to this level is what gave the Provos the edge and appealed to nationalists. The slaying of the defenceless soldiers did what it was meant to. It shocked London, horrified wider society, antagonised a loyalist community that adored the British Army and appealed to republican hardliners. Insurgents prosper off chaos, fear and division. The IRA murdered to sectarianise the conflict, which relied on provoking a loyalist reaction. The Fusiliers incident was part of this strategy, a brazen insult personal to London, of significance because it marks a turning point in the British approach. The state's patience of IRA violence was near exhausted. The murders of David Walker (30) by an IRA sniper followed a few days later by that of Richard Barton (24) by three IRA gunmen, may have been the straws that broke the camel's back. Walker and Barton were British soldiers. Both murders took place in nationalist west Belfast weeks before internment.

Good policing in a divided society is community-based, an early warning system to alert government of serious trouble in the assumption government would respond. This did not happen. Half a century of normality meant the police force was too small to cope with a new IRA menace. In pre-empting what was to unfold, requests for extra resources were made. These were refused and guidance on how to tackle the threat dismissed. SB predicted an upward trend in republican violence would persist and cause a backlash from loyalists, exactly what the Provisionals wanted. Northern Ireland's new Prime Minister Brian Faulkner knew this and the crisis the country was in, but few in Westminster shared his concern. He believed the British government's tolerance of republican militants encouraged violence. Tougher action was needed.

It seems Westminster had ignored the Provos having declared war on the Northern Ireland state and insatiable appetite for killing, in the forlorn hope they would go away. The main decision-makers were ambivalent or did not grasp the gravity of the situation, much to Faulkner's frustration. Britain had abandoned Ulster.

By the time the soldiers' barbaric executions woke Westminster out of its slumber it was too late. A crisis had long turned into an irregular war. Unprecedented levels of violence prevented the normal functioning of civic society, placing Faulkner in an impossible position. For the majority of the population (who were law-abiding) something had to be done. Internment - detention of terrorist suspects without trial - was that something. Its purpose was to protect life and restore order by taking terrorists off the streets. The depraved minds that murdered the Fusiliers must be locked up. The priority was to prevent a loyalist backlash by curtailing republican violence, deterring nationalists from supporting the IRA and placating hard-line unionist calls for tougher action.

A difficulty in implementing internment was that Army primacy had created a confused chain of command. The MOD and Home Office blamed each other for the introduction of harsh interrogations. The techniques followed a government study by Bowen (1966) into RAF air crews subjected to mock captures by the enemy. They were held for several days and put through various stress situations (that the study did not consider torture) to see if they would break. At the start of internment the same techniques were piloted on 14 detainees rated the IRA's "hard-core" by Faulkner. They have since become known as the 'hooded men,' after one of the techniques.

SB detectives, due to their local knowledge, conducted the interrogations under the Army's supervision. This contravened SB's knowledge and empathy approach. It was a bad professional misjudgement and SB's lowest moment of the conflict. Nationalists exaggerated events in portraying unionists as anti-Catholic to the world. General Petraeus describes such claims as "non-bio degradable." In Iraq, his experience was that, communities resentful of the US presence judged his troops' actions by the worst excesses of a few in unfairly misrepresenting events. This gifted insurgents an opportunity to taint the US as anti-Muslim to a global audience.

Championing nationalist 'torture' claims, the Republic brought the UK to the European Court of Human Rights in Strasbourg in 1978. The court ruled against torture but found the techniques inhuman and degrading treatment. Westminster was dismayed at the unusual step of one state taking another to court. The British and unionists saw Dublin's actions as sympathetic to terrorists. They had good grounds to be annoyed. The Republic was the IRA's safe haven. And on extradition it interpreted terrorism as a political act and not a crime, contravening the

European Convention of the Suppression of Terrorism (1977), which the Republic put off signing for 13 years. One of the terrorists responsible for the Fusiliers murders, fearing he would be prosecuted for the crime, took shelter in the Republic knowing he would not be handed over to a British court. The Republic's stance on extradition resembles that of a developing nation more than a civilised democracy.

Everyone on the British side admitted harsh interrogations were wrong and apologised. The practice was immediately stopped and measures put in place to prevent any repeat. Police policy that had always prohibited maltreatment of prisoners was reinforced and Army bases replaced by new police holding centres to interview terrorist suspects. There was no change of approach in the Republic. The IRA continued to operate freely in the south, Dublin failing to countenance how this underpinned an IRA terrorist campaign in the north. The Republic ignored unionist claims of IRA cross-border units ethnically cleansing border Protestants. Dublin highlighted British failings while ignoring its own. It was a suspicious inconsistency that disturbed and disappointed victims of IRA terrorism.

Such was the tense atmosphere in the months before internment that the Taoiseach on the 9th December 1970 told the Dáil he was prepared to introduce internment in the Republic. As it turned out Dublin did not need to. The Provisionals did not pose the risk in the 26 counties they had anticipated. There is no question, however, that if faced with a portion of what its neighbour was suffering, the Dáil would have introduced internment in a heartbeat.

In an environment where there was no threat from IRA activities and minimal security risk from the Troubles overall, no government of the Republic was going to enforce a security measure that would be viewed as anti-IRA and pro-British. In the Troubles, constitutional nationalists found it hard to see the IRA as criminals. This was not the case in the IRA border campaign (1956-62). Dublin interned IRA men, and in doing so played a crucial part in preventing a loyalist reaction. Good cross-border security co-operation, especially between SBs, quickly defeated the IRA and averted a messy sectarian conflict. Eight years later, it is inconceivable that Dublin did not know this.

Turning a blind eye to the IRA in its territory gave Dublin political leverage over London. The prospect of improved security could be bargained for political concessions on Northern Ireland's internal affairs. And if the IRA won, as some respected observers believed, by proxy this delivered on the Republic's constitutional claim of unifying Ireland. An insurgency in the north achieving its headline aim would have been politically popular in the south. While both options benefited Dublin, they also benefited the Provos. A conflict in Northern Ireland was not entirely inconvenient for the Republic of Ireland.

Instead of restoring order, internment provoked disorder. Terrorism rose by 40% and deaths trebled, with the IRA still the main protagonist. Most of all, the dreaded loyalist backlash happened. Northern Ireland was gripped by sectarian conflict, the exact thing the Provos had worked tirelessly to achieve. Nationalists who dared to point this out, like SDLP leader Gerry Fitt, were savaged by the IRA's political Rottweiler - Sinn Féin. Fitt saw through the IRA and was unafraid to put the responsibility for increased violence and sectarian killings firmly on them. SB reports show the republican movement accused him of "collusion with the British" in the same sentence as blaming the murders of Catholics on "professional killers in the British Army and Special Branch" colluding with loyalists. Voices like his were soon drowned out. Sinn Féin weaponising 'collusion' to discredit opponents was immeasurably strengthened by a sectarian Troubles.

In a rule of law approach a drawback of internment was the political status it gave to detainees. This was a huge boost for the IRA. Detainees were portrayed as POWs, constructing a false legitimacy of terrorists being soldiers of a bona fide army. Despite internment ending in 1975, Sinn Féin forever thereafter used the political status label to mask IRA terrorists being criminals and the fabled 'armed struggle' a fraud. Another drawback, the Republic's approach to security contributed to its territory becoming the

IRA's strategic base and a resort for republican outlaws. This made it extremely difficult for the RUC to arrest the most prolific offenders.

Of SB, it had known enough to accurately outline the overall threat but lacked detail beyond this. Intelligence was outdated and would take time to update. These shortcomings were communicated to Stormont and the Army in arguing against internment. Politics, however, took priority. The timing suited British Prime Minister Edward Heath. Faulkner would take the heat if things went wrong before Westminster took over through direct rule. Internment played out well in GB, showing voters Westminster was taking action against the killers of British soldiers.

Compounding internment's controversial start, 14 Catholic civilians were shot dead by the Army during an anti-internment protest in Londonderry on what has become known as Bloody Sunday (Jan 1972). Londonderry's police commander Frank Lagan (a Catholic), having been advised by SB, warned the Army against their plan. He recommended a non-confrontational approach, as community tensions were high. His advice was rejected. Adding to nationalist feelings of injustice was the Widgery Tribunal (1972) that exonerated the Army.

Bloody Sunday radicalised many nationalists, removing the last remnants of goodwill for the police and pushing them toward the IRA side. The Republic recalled its Ambassador from London, the UK Embassy in Dublin was burnt down, Labour divided the House of Commons in a fractious emergency debate and direct rule from Westminster was imposed in March 1972. All of this was music to the IRA's ears. For Provo leaders there was no incentive to stop. They marveled at their own shock and awe strategy. These were young, hardline northerners who struggled to hide their bigotry and whose hatred of the 'Brits' was matched by their capacity to kill 'Brits.'

In an attempt to solve the political impasse the first Secretary of State of Northern Ireland, William Whitelaw, held secret talks with the insurgent leadership. During a short ceasefire they demanded British withdrawal by 1975 and an amnesty for all prisoners. It was one of three 'talks' in the early 1970s. All failed due to unrealistic IRA demands. Insurgent leaders were uninterested in peace, which Whitelaw came to realise. The IRA's response was 'Bloody Friday' (July 1972) when 20 bombs devastated Belfast, killing seven civilians, two soldiers and injuring hundreds. The IRA was buoyant. In their eyes, they were winning. Internment's shambolic introduction and the 'Prods' having been pulled in gave them no reason to think otherwise.

The great irony with internment is, for sure it was badly implemented and fuelled further violence, but as time went on security successes increased. Even though SB was against internment, and not withstanding the stain of harsh interrogations, they made the most of it. Accurate intelligence increased monthly. Internment was not the unmitigated disaster republican mythmakers portrayed. An SB document reads:

> As a result of arrests and arms seizures the effectiveness of the IRA, especially in the Belfast area where the security forces have so far concentrated their efforts, has been seriously reduced. The removal from circulation of 600-700 members is creating increasing problems for the IRA in terms of both morale and key personnel. While losses have been made good to a limited extent the damage caused is evidenced by the fact that the officers in some companies have had to be replaced two or three times over, and that volunteers are now reluctant to come forward.

The document also shows a threefold increase in seizures in the seven months prior to internment and the same period afterwards. The higher figures are approximately 3,500 lbs of explosives and 520 firearms. Making adjustments for population size, in the UK mainland this equates to 140,000 lbs of explosives and 20,800 firearms. In bombs and guns, terrorism's instruments of death, one sees security's effectiveness and, more importantly, the intent of the opponent and scale of the challenge.

By 1974 half the IRA was in custody and its leadership refuged in the Republic. IRA buoyancy had been deflated.

Most arrests were outside of internment, terrorists processed through the normal criminal justice system. Despite its ham-fisted introduction, had internment lasted for another six months the IRA was finished. Internment brought the IRA to the brink of defeat. It robbed the insurgency of its best leaders, brightest thinkers and precious munitions. The IRA put this down to SB recruiting detainees as agents.

Given the insurgency was not popularly supported and the friction between two IRA groups, the Provos were right to be concerned about their arch enemy. Lots of information damaging to the Provisionals was gathered from disaffected republicans who did not see the Provos as the 'great green hope' but sectarian thugs peddling pain and misery. In the intelligence war, internment gave SB a crucial leg-up. The SB annual report (1971) is instructive on this count: "During the year Special Branch personnel were highly successful in obtaining information, which greatly assisted to defeat the I.R.A. [Officials]." The Officials turned into the Workers Party. The Provisionals knew that SB aimed to do this with them.

Politics is where internment had lasting damage. Sinn Féin socially conditioned nationalists across Ireland into blaming the police (particularly SB) for internment's worst features. This is evident with the SDLP in the Sunningdale power-sharing experiment in 1973-74 when Northern Ireland came close to a stable government. Still smarting from internment and Bloody Sunday, the SDLP campaigned strongly for a new police force. Sunningdale failed, not purely for this reason, but because of an unbridgeable gap between nationalism and unionism, in which an SDLP closely aligned with Sinn Féin on the policing issue was a huge factor. The inability of moderates from both sides to co-operate paralysed local politics. This played into the hands of extremists and placed enormous additional pressures on the police.

Going outside the normal processes of the law, as internment did, gave terrorists a semblance of respectability they ill-deserved and made it harder to stigmatise them as criminals. Long-term there were security benefits, especially for intelligence, but at a political cost. This was internment's dilemma. Internment exposes Dublin's duplicity and shows why the SDLP became serial critics of the police. The blemish of harsh interrogations would not be forgotten or forgiven. For nationalists, SB was the big bad wolf. Battle lines had been drawn, sides had been chosen. With a few exceptions, the nationalist family conformed to the republican movement's definition of terrorism. This excluded acts like the extra-judicial execution of three young British soldiers.

For the IRA to sustain a long war, Protestants must kill Catholics. The Troubles had to be sectarianised. The IRA needed to provoke a loyalist reaction without it being obvious they did. An inept introduction of internment is what they had hoped for. SB knew this. As Merlyn Rees, Northern Ireland Secretary of State, said: "the police had been against detention from the beginning. It had been imposed on them."

SB intimately understood the Provos hidden agenda and next moves. Few others on the security side did. Had SB led on security, internment probably would still have happened. Intolerable levels of violence needed a tough response. It would, however, have been smarter. Incredibly, in spite of internment's faults, at the hands of their nemesis and greatest worry the Provos came perilously close to collapse. Internment made the IRA wiser and stronger and a sectarian conflict made them harder to defeat. For SB to properly get at them, police primacy was needed. The Army, however, would have something to say about that.

The intelligence machinery to beat an insurgency was very different to anything before it.

Chapter 10

Knowledge and Empathy

In 1972, violence and the threat of violence shrouded Londonderry like a heavy mist. Peter Gilgunn (26) and David Montgomery (20) were two police officers murdered by an IRA gun team on the 27th January 1972. Richard Ham (20), a soldier in the Royal Artillery was shot dead by an IRA sniper on the 29th December 1971. Both incidents were the most recent fatalities in Londonderry prior to an illegal protest march by nationalists in what became known as Bloody Sunday.

Young British soldiers had been thrown into a ferocious bloodbath, the sectarian complexity of which was beyond the comprehension of most. Every day they met people who wanted them dead. Kids threw stones at them and adults threw insults. Walls were covered with 'Brits out' and 'Victory to the IRA.' Republican areas were thick with hatred. To comfort a soldier dying in the street was a rarity. Celebrating his death was not. Seeing colleagues murdered and maimed was routine. The British Army took a hammering and it is testament to their restraint and professionalism that there was only one Bloody Sunday. The start of an insurgency is always the most turbulent. 1972 was the

Troubles high watermark for killings.

For soldiers the expectation of being hit was constant. A burning building could be an ambush or a 'civil rights' protest a chance to riot, with snipers secreted in the crowd. A car oddly parked or curtains fluttering at an open window raised suspicion. No kids playing in the street or disturbed ground on a roadside verge were signs of danger. Some young soldiers were physically sick with fear as they put on their kit before leaving base. There was a chance they would not return in one piece, or at all. It was unnerving for soldiers to patrol a place where people spoke English and take cover from gunfire behind houses the same as many grew up in. These were troops trained for a conventional war on foreign soil. They were unprepared for an IRA dirty war on British turf. It was a steep learning curve.

The Army prevented Ulster from unravelling. The main beneficiary of this was the police, particularly Special Branch. During internment soldiers provided enough stability to allow a small Special Branch to make in-roads into the IRA. Internment ended in 1975 because politics intruded in the shape of a government report. Detention without trial had over-strained the sensitivities of a liberal democracy. And by default, so did Army primacy. The benefit of ending internment was that this did away with political status for prisoners. The criminal law was now the main counterterrorism weapon and the best agency to exploit this was the police.

The difficulty in 1975 was that the Army was in charge and a rift had developed between them and SB around interrogation tactics and how to gather information. Even though Amnesty International claimed maltreatment of terrorist suspects persisted, it recognised the harshest aspects were discontinued. On this issue SB was demoralised by criticism of it in government reports and reluctant to take part in interviews at the Army's behest thereafter. The Army saw SB as weak and a reason for it to continue to lead on intelligence.

Free from the Army's influence SB went back to what it did best and the Provos felt the heat. A secret document found on an IRA leader in 1973 warned of SB's intelligence-gathering methods. Another in 1972 from "Long Kesh Concentration Camp to Derry Brigade staff, Oglaigh na hEireann, Derry City" had alerted 'volunteers' to the same thing. The IRA did not see prisoner abuse as an SB tactic. The concern was of SB's knowledge and empathy methods. The leadership could not let it get out that tough IRA men could be turned by a conversation with a 'Branch' man.

SB held the view that only by understanding the wider political, social and economic issues could IRA violence be ended. As one retired officer put it, "You'd need to be made of stone not to feel for a young Catholic in Derry or west Belfast back then. Like, they weren't getting much of a chance." The empathetic approach meant that any opportunity SB had to talk to a republican increased the chances of them being listened to. Many local uniform and CID officers interpreted this unorthodoxy as sympathising with republicans. Unsurprisingly, the Provisionals feared this more than any other security initiative and strove to shut down any interactions of this kind. Or, in the words of a former SB officer, "The last thing they wanted was one of us talking to one of them."

A landmark date in policing is 1972. It is when the Stormont government fell, and with it, an unhealthy unionist influence over the police. It is widely accepted that this was the start of professionalising the police, training them for what was needed in an irregular war. Increased professionalism, however, did not translate into SDLP support. No matter how effective or even-handed the police, the SDLP would not publicly give them credit. But behind closed doors was a different story. A retired senior officer calls this "back-stage and front-stage faces." In private, SDLP politicians got on well with police commanders and praised them for good policing, such as stopping loyalist parades entering nationalist areas.

An aspect of the RUC police model is how well SB was integrated for the purpose of servicing frontline police. The guidance on a non-confrontational approach given to the uniform police commander in Londonderry prior to Bloody Sunday is an example. The police code, containing official policies and practices, shows SB is "located at strategic points throughout the Force area," and its purpose and function is the "collection, collation, processing and recording of intelligence relating to the security of the State." The code shows SB detectives are directly responsible to the Head of SB but are also required to liaise with local police commanders and keep them regularly informed of security matters affecting their respective areas. The code formalised earlier official reports recommending local police (uniform and CID) are not to have operational control over SB. Instead, SB closely liaises with them. Although separate from local police SB sat alongside them. It was a smart structure, as was the regional setup.

Northern Ireland was territorially divided into three police regions (Belfast, North and South), each commanded by a uniform assistant chief constable. A region had four to six divisions. According to the police code the regional concept was engineered to: "achieve maximum co-ordination in the divisions, the most efficient use of manpower and resources, liaison with the Army and local liaison committees and in border areas with the Garda Siochana."

A Regional Head of Special Branch (RHSB) was a powerful man. His most important local relationship was with the regional assistant chief constable – his local boss. He regularly met and briefed his equivalents in uniform, CID, Army, Military Intelligence and MI5. A healthy degree of regional autonomy gave SB excellent flexibility, tempered by the regions feeding into a small HQ in Belfast (desk system, registry and administration). The Head of SB (HSB) was an assistant chief constable located at HQ. He answered to the Chief Constable and was the real boss of the three RHSBs. The Head of SB was the Chief's senior intelligence adviser, and like his Regional Heads, liaised with his equivalents in the police family, military and MI5. SB was under the same central command as the rest of the force. SB's smart structure was vital to maintaining a permanent police presence at frontline sites, essential in depriving the insurgency of territory. The police was a ground-up, tactically driven organisation. Outside of structure and command, giving a glimpse into SB's ethos and its people, a former officer states:

The unwritten thing never talked about was the fact that Catholic officers were treated differently. The vast majority of detective sergeants and inspectors in west Belfast, Derry, Newry and other staunch nationalist areas were Catholics. Not only did this go down well with the locals, but also the Garda and Catholic Church were much happier dealing with what they considered one of their own, which meant better relationships, or at least as good as could be expected. Nobody objected to it or saw it as discriminatory in any way. We saw it as a pragmatic use, and the best use, of very limited resources. All told, the mix of religion within Special Branch, especially at senior levels, created a healthy balance. It was a great strength of the Branch. The Branch was in no way bigoted, and this was one of the reasons why. Not that this mattered to the republican propaganda machine that made out we were.

Normally the highest any Branch man could get would be Deputy Head of SB. You could not go further. There was a glass ceiling. Heads were purposely filled from uniform or CID ranks. It was not a force within a force.

The reasoning for an outsider as HSB was he could be objective, conduct reviews of policies and procedures, and rectify bad practice influenced by incestuous thinking. There was one exception to the 'glass ceiling' rule, because the 'Catholic' rule trumped it. As much as 21% of SB personnel were Catholic. It was more representative of society than any other policing or security agency. This tends to bear out 30% of SB fatalities being Catholic.

Even within the police very few understood SB's organisational makeup and ethos, a failing particularly pronounced in the military. The IRA had a better handle on this than most in the security forces. In the early 1970s, Colonel Robin Evelegh noted: "The police, for all the abuse flung at them, were in general extraordinarily brave, hard-working and fair." Other Army commanders did not share his view. They did not trust SB, persuading the Chief of General Staff (1971-3) Michael Carver that some in SB were linked to loyalists and SB overall was incompetent. Fresh-faced military intelligence officers smartly dressed in tweed jackets, corduroys and brogues tended to see events in simplistic Catholic versus Protestant terms, misinterpreting anti-IRA as anti-Catholic. At this early juncture the Army had a limited understanding of the province, its people, culture, the police and the threat. Ulster humour and rough cop banter were lost on soldiers. SB's approach was different to the Army's, which unsettled many well-mannered young men just out of Sandhurst and seasoned officers alike.

In having gained control of intelligence, the military did not want to relinquish this. Intelligence is knowledge and knowledge is power. Carver's natural instinct was for police primacy and a strong SB. But he convinced himself that this irregular war was different. What happened in previous conflicts did not apply. This was the Army saying it could gather intelligence better than local police, a mindset that went against over 100 years of experience. Military Intelligence misguidedly believed it could beat SB in recruiting and running agents.

By 1973, SB was the best option, and even more so in 1975 once internment ended. At 100 detectives it did not have the operational capacity to fully take on the IRA and loyalist terror groups, but it should have been listened to more. And, given the IRA's obsession with discrediting SB, the Army should have known this. Army primacy also worked against the few nationalists, like Gerry Fitt and Paddy Devlin, whose back stage and front stage faces were the same.

Control of many republican areas had been lost and would take time to win back. There was no quick fix, which the Army and London did not grasp. Things like brokering agreements on 'no-go' areas were bad decisions. Allowing republicans to build barricades created a bigger problem when it came to dismantling them. Decisions of this kind dismissed police advice, which undermined the rule of law. Showing how in practical terms, the

Special Branch annual report 1970 reads:

Our main problems lay in Belfast and to a lesser extent in Londonderry. In the early part of the year we were physically excluded as a Branch from the 'No-Go' areas by agreements in one form or another between the Army and Local Defence Committees. While we ignored these where we could we did so at our personal peril and our contacts within were reduced to negligible proportions. Eventually these 'understandings' were erased and we got down again to the task of re-establishing our penetrations.

The Army implemented measures that cut off SB from the local community making it harder to gather information. Although SB was not centre stage and despite such drawbacks it produced security successes, good advice and correctly diagnosed the problem when few did. SB also formulated an accurate mission: defeat the IRA and you end the conflict, as loyalist violence is reactionary. SB knew the IRA was beatable but it would take time to convince others how this would be done.

In 1974, SB correctly predicted internment would end and the IRA would radically restructure into a small, cellular organisation with a strong connection to the Republic of Ireland and a permanent leadership that would not get their hands dirty. The Provos would be harder to beat. After internment the criminal justice system would determine intelligence practices. An SB document states:

Under the law in Northern Ireland as in England it is necessary for the purpose of a criminal conviction to produce legally admissible evidence, which is capable of proving a criminal charge beyond reasonable doubt. This is a fundamental safeguard in ordinary times, but in times of civil disorder an entirely new problem arises. Civil and military intelligence about the activities of an armed conspiracy such as the IRA cannot be freely used as evidence in the courts without exposing and therefore risking the loss of the sources from which the information was obtained. If this happens the intelligence system itself breaks down and without it the most effective means available to destroy the conspiracy.

Uniquely for an irregular war, 'beyond reasonable doubt,' the evidential standard in a liberal democracy for thieves and rapists was used for terrorists. In the eyes of the law they were all criminals. Non-jury Diplock courts were used for terrorist trials. Juries would have been too easily intimated. The Republic had a similar arrangement. Naturally, terrorist organisations kicked up a fuss, supported by civil liberty groups. By and large, however, non-jury courts were fair and are still in place (north and south) today.

Abysmal murder clearance rates illustrate the challenge the new rule of law approach faced. The Chief Constable's annual report (1972) shows 1970 had a 35.7% murder clearance rate and 8.9% in 1971. The worst was for border Protestants murdered by insurgents - 8%. A 65% - 90% clearance rate is the norm in the west. Normal policing was struggling and this had to change. The police regaining primacy in 1977 was designed to do this. The Army had borne the brunt of the IRA attack, establishing a less hostile environment for the police to take over. Next up was sleuths not spooks - CID and traditional investigative-led policing aimed at improving the murder clearance rate. Detecting crime was the priority.

The Army had been given its chance. A beefed-up CID now had theirs. Investigative tactics used against gangsters in England would be used against terrorists in Northern Ireland. But British squeamishness over internment had not been lost on the IRA. Anytime they were under pressure from a security measure, Sinn Féin was put to work on prompting a government inquiry to end it.

For the moment, SB would continue to be subordinate. This gave it time to build on its basic structure and develop under MI5 guidance in readiness for taking over the security lead. The Army's limited understanding of SB that, effectively, distanced it from SB, was a surprising departure from classic British counterinsurgency. Military Intelligence would cling onto a small agent-running capability. This, however, would be overshadowed by innovations by Army special forces on surveillance and armed response working closely with, and managed by, SB. Regional Heads of SB and not Brigadiers would be the major power players. The intelligence machinery to beat an insurgency would be very different to anything before it.

Shoehorning what worked in a peacetime setting into an irregular war did not work.

Chapter 11

Super Sleuths and Supergrasses

Seven years of Army primacy (1969-76) had made the insurgency an Army problem. In the context of implementing a rule of law approach Northern Ireland Secretary of State Merlyn Rees knew this needed to change. He realised the police in a security role were not as effective as they could be, their response to the Ulster Workers Council strike in 1974 called by unionists opposed to the Sunningdale Agreement being a prime example. Loyalist terrorist organisations blocked roads to stop people going to work and murdered 39 civilians, most in bomb attacks in Dublin and Monaghan. The police relied too much on the Army for security. Rees saw this as a fault. In his view the police had to be in charge of security if it was to improve.

In 1976 Rees convened a ministerial committee chaired by John Bourn (NIO). This included assistant chief constable John Hermon and an Army Brigadier in what is known as the Way Ahead or Bourn Report. The aim was to increase stability and restore normality through police primacy, specifically by making the police more acceptable to the minority community. The insurgency was treated as a law and order problem. The

Bourn Report increased the size of the police, introduced specialist investigation teams and improved criminal intelligence processes. Rees had introduced a rule of law approach that criminalised the insurgency and loyalist terrorist organisations in a much more visible way than was the case before.

Police primacy demilitarised the security response, which was the main priority. In the process, however, it further militarised the police as they took on more security duties from the Army. In approximate terms, a result of police primacy was a steady reduction by 50% in the Army's manpower over the next two decades from a peak of 30,000 in 1972 to 15,000 in 1998 and a threefold increase in police numbers from 3,000 to 13,000 in the same period. This reduced British Army fatalities by 90%, from an average of 50 per year to five per year. Police primacy characterises what became known as the Internal Security Solution, of which Ulsterisation and normalisation were key features. The Internal Security Solution distanced the conflict from the English voting public, highlighted the sectarian nature of IRA violence and illustrated to both communities the failure of domestic politics.

A similar committee to Bourn produced the Report of the Working Group to Consider Progress on Security Policy (1978), or Hannigan Report. The Hannigan Report is probably the most significant strategic document of the Troubles. Hannigan (another senior NIO official) collected political, police and military views in a report that recognised political inertia had created an over-reliance on security. To make up for this it prioritised "community sensitivity" in tackling the insurgency because the "PIRA are the main obstacle" to peace and there must be a sustained effort "to bring about their defeat." This reinforced the mission of Special Branch. It reads:

> *Within the present policy the police aim is to pursue, within the law, a high level of attrition against PIRA and simultaneously move towards creating an atmosphere of normality and confidence in the community. The removal of the gunman and bomber through the normal process of law is essential to long*

term success. This report has laid great stress on the need to gain support of the community as a whole for the security forces and law and order. The paramilitary groups, especially in Belfast and Londonderry, are also concerned with maintaining their influence on the population. … Good community relations lie at the heart of our proposals to advance the acceptability of the RUC in all areas of Northern Ireland. The RUC have already laid the foundations for progress and consolidation in this field with the strengthening of their Community Relations Branch.

The Hannigan Report identified that increasing stability through normal policing threatened the IRA's position and, with that, increased the certainty of ending the conflict. A main barrier to achieving this was the border had become a major security liability due to politically inert Anglo-Irish relations. Isolated terrorist attacks in the Republic by loyalists were insufficient to raise the Republic's security profile. An IRA with a free hand in the Republic smacked of a foreign policy where they were the Republic's proxy army, defending its citizens by countering the loyalist threat at its source and confining it to the north. Whatever the case, the Republic's security abstinence meant that maintaining a permanent police presence in Northern Ireland's most hostile areas took a deadly toll. A former member of the Parachute Regiment, who later joined Special Branch, recounts these difficulties in south Armagh in 1976:

James Borucki was killed in Crossmaglen five days before the end of our tour, a vulnerable time. He was 19. We were sent out to clear a heli pad, Borucki was beside a bicycle. I was beside him when it went off. It was radio controlled. I think the firing point was the chapel. They made off south.

By the mid-1970s cross-border IRA units had replaced Belfast IRA as the greatest threat. That the Republic refused to accept this does little to counter claims it was content for the IRA to operate with impunity in its jurisdiction. In the first five years of the Troubles in south Armagh, in what became known as bandit country, the ratio of killing was almost 60:1. That is, 60 security force members (mostly soldiers) and one IRA man (killed by his own side). Former officers who worked there relate that attacks were either mounted from the Republic or insurgents escaped to the Republic afterwards. Very rarely did former SB officers see security on the southern side of the border.

Dublin's approach extended to not allowing 'hot pursuit' for a short distance into the Republic, a common practice today across Europe. Instead, Dublin insisted that the border was not the issue, claiming the RUC and Army should be able to contain the situation regardless of the border, and not being able to do so demonstrated incompetence. Following internment and roughly coinciding with police primacy in 1977 was prosecuting terrorist offenders through crime squads. SB played a supporting role. A large Crime department (CID in broad terms) dominated. A robust investigative-led approach used against organised crime in England was being road tested against the IRA and loyalist terrorist organisations under a new Chief Constable, Ken Newman. Newman was a respected and innovative leader. An Englishman, he was an RAF WW2 veteran who had been a police officer in Palestine's conflict prior to joining the London Metropolitan Police.

Crime squads had SB providing intelligence briefings on suspects in support of crime squad detectives doing the interviews. To implement this the Bourn Report recommended a new system of SB sharing intelligence with crime squads and CID in general.

The aim of the crime squads concept was to arrest a terrorist suspect and shock him into confessing by revelations about his criminal activity. SB intelligence provided the revelations. Crime squads contained many of CID's best detectives, super sleuths. Interviews were conducted in new police holding centres. Beyond reasonable doubt was the legal benchmark, which was unprecedented in an irregular war. The police had to produce evidence that stood a reasonable chance of securing a prosecution for a criminal offence, similar to the rest of the UK. For crime squads the evidence was usually just the confession.

Specific to SB's role, an internal SB directive titled, Procedures Relating to Arrest, Interviewing and Interrogation of Terrorist Suspects, 26 July 1976, shows that the main objective of an arrest was to secure a criminal prosecution. It reads:

> *The primary aim should be to remove terrorists by charging them, where this is possible. This aspect, therefore, lies more in the province of CID and uniform personnel involved. ... Special Branch should be kept informed of anything arising during interviews, which may be of intelligence value to the Security Forces. No operational action should follow, however, without consultation and agreement on whether such a course is available in the circumstances. ...*

> *Most persons arrested are, therefore, first to be questioned with a view to criminal charges being brought; but those against whom charges cannot be brought may be considered persons who should be interrogated for intelligence purposes.*

SB could only conduct an interview if crime squad detectives judged there was no likelihood of a prosecution. The curriculum of a Special Branch training course (22-24 September 1976) included a 45-minute class on "Interrogation, Interviewing and Documentation." The officer who undertook this event claims the lesson concerned looking for motivational triggers as part of a background study on the suspect and how these could be exploited through a knowledge and empathy technique. This entailed minor disclosures about the suspect's activities as a means of instilling a belief in the suspect that the interviewer knew more than they actually did. Another former officer describes an interview:

> *We had a totally different way than CID. They were after admissions, charging and convicting the guy they were interviewing. Short-term stuff. That wasn't our game. We were not under the same pressure to get results, you know, convictions. Not in that sense anyway. ... We were trying to befriend him, get on his good side or at least get him thinking about us as*

people, people who showed an interest in him. We were trying to start a relationship, continue the discussion outside and that's something you can't do if you start off with threats. You need trust, and you don't get that by beating or threatening people. Remember, I had to meet this guy on my own in a dark corner of the city. My life was in his hands. As I said, it was a totally different attitude to the CID lads.

Interviews by detectives in an investigative-led approach are completely different to interviews by detectives in an intelligence-led approach. The former is about detection and the latter prevention. Allegations of prisoner abuse were linked to obtaining an admission of guilt in a statement. As an example, former IRA member Eamon Collins claimed CID detectives beat him in trying to get him to confess to the murder of nine police officers in a mortar attack on Newry police station in 1985. Even though the IRA knew SB was not the central player Sinn Féin sustained the 'SB torturers' claim. The Hannigan Report explains why:

It is apparent that PIRA have problems on the manpower side. The main difficulty has been the fear of security force action and in particular worry about informers among their own ranks. Senior and middle level leaders have shown themselves sensitive to the risk of being arrested or killed and during 1978 this has made it difficult to restart and sustain their operations. There is also a shortage of dynamic leadership in certain areas. While the Provisional Army Council contain a number of dedicated men, some of them highly capable, the situation on the ground in Northern Ireland is less satisfactory for PIRA.

Even though the IRA was suffering badly at the hands of crime squads, SB fixated them. This is probably because there was a way to get rid of crime squads. Section 6 of the Northern Ireland (Emergency Provisions) Act 1973, in loose terms, states that any confession will be inadmissible unless the police satisfy the court the accused was not subjected to torture, inhuman or degrading treatment. By complaining of maltreatment a suspect immediately prepared their defence. The Act lays the burden of proof with the Crown. The police had to prove beyond reasonable doubt that they did not obtain a confession by coercion. Section 6 allowed for a retrospective complaint, a major factor given that, non-marking injuries and threats constituted degrading treatment. Against accomplished republican propagandists the burden of proof proved impossible to discharge. Crime squads were undone by accusations of prisoner abuse.

As one former SB detective describes it, "Complaints stopped not because crime squads changed their interviewing techniques but because they stopped taking admission statements." Another notes, "The Provos excelled in allegations that were forensically invisible." Many complaints required only a verbal accusation. Self-inflicted injuries were common. Being charged correlated to making a complaint in the same way not being charged correlated to not making one. Fraudulent complaints were part of republicanism's compensation culture and investigating them had the added bonus of removing precious police resources from frontline posts, as the IRA was well aware.

This is not to justify rough interviewing methods or commend uncorroborated confessions, but to point out that the IRA and Sinn Féin were adept at exploiting the law. Without doubt some terrorist suspects were slapped about to get them to confess. Usually, however, they were not. They did not need to be. Understanding the IRA helps to explain why. Some 'volunteers' could not live with what they had done. An example is a woman who confessed to murder. She was advised to claim she was assaulted, even though those advising knew she was not, as this would get her off. But she did not want off. Her conscience did not allow it. Her integrity is in stark contrast to those who advised her.

The details of the case are in an SB document called; Allegations of brutality, torture and ill-treatment, against the Royal Ulster Constabulary – Background Brief re-visit of Amnesty International (probably written in late 1977). In short, most complaints were false, any genuine injuries were superficial and almost all those interviewed were the right people. Nationalists would not have missed the last point. Communities under insurgent control know who the killers among them are. Proving it beyond reasonable doubt is the problem.

Robust interviews of murder suspects typify investigative-led policing in this era. To give an idea of the type of injury, an accused was acquitted of the IRA murder of constable Linda Baggley in Londonderry in 1976 because of a bruised nose and lip. She was 19. Her father William (43), also a police officer, had been murdered by the IRA in the same area two years previous. In the rest of the UK the police got away with tough interviewing. There was no real public outcry, whereas in Northern Ireland this was never going to be the case. The suspect was part of an insurgent network. The world's most proficient propaganda machine was fighting his or her corner. Terrorist suspects were detained for three to seven days. This outraged civil liberty groups, especially Amnesty International. After 7/7 terrorist suspects can be detained for 28 days under the Terrorism Act.

True to form the government launched an inquiry into crime squads - the Bennett Report (1979). Bennett recognised there was stricter legislative demands on the RUC than other UK police forces. Yet Bennett included recommendations that imposed a higher benchmark on them than the rest of the UK. This was the downside of a criminalisation policy. Confessions were uncorroborated because of a 'say nothing to the police' mindset and forensically-aware terrorists. Acutely aware of how Sinn Féin propaganda operated, Newman and Northern Ireland Secretary of State Roy Mason, who replaced Rees, had serious misgivings about criticism of crime squads from respectable quarters, like Amnesty International and certain journalists.

According to SB reports, even though the IRA had procured sufficient munitions for a prolonged campaign the conviction rate by crime squads was causing a loss of Catholic support. Being stigmatised as criminals was demoralising the IRA. In broad terms, crime squads had reduced levels of violence by 70%. Fewer insurgent attacks were happening and the IRA was now heavily dependent on using the Republic as a safe haven. Almost half of all active IRA terrorists were in prison. This was the outworking of Mason's tough approach. Once again, the IRA was staring at defeat. To survive, Sinn Féin had to undermine crime squads. This was achieved by secretly teaming up with loyalist terror groups.

The Hannigan Report shows that the UDA, UVF and RHC (Red Hand Commandos) were also suffering. The RHC was a particularly vicious sub-group of the UVF. Although worried by crime squads extracting a confession, as with the IRA, they were more worried about SB recruiting one of their members as an agent and saw the intelligence aspect as their greatest threat. The Hannigan Report shows that; good intelligence-led police work had hardened loyalist attitudes against the police, particularly Special Branch. Loyalist terrorist organisations were suffering worse than the IRA from security successes against them. The Amnesty International paper reads:

The UDA in particular know that they cannot go too far in this direction [anti-RUC propaganda campaign] in case they alienate the Loyalist population. In their statements in public they have shown a certain circumspection by stating that they are not anti-RUC in general but just opposed to an 'elitist' hard core of Special Branch Detectives, based mainly at Castlereagh.

The paper shows the UDA collaborated with the IRA to publicise police brutality. Both contrived to get a Catholic doctor to represent a Protestant prisoner, believing this would carry greater credibility and gain more public sympathy, especially from liberal quarters. Opposite terror factions with most to gain from ending a successful security initiative worked together in secret to discredit it. Republicans were teaching the loyalists classic republican propaganda. Crime squads and SB were tainted as torturers, and police holding centres tainted as torture chambers. Seven years of Sinn Féin propaganda had conditioned nationalists and respectable third parties, including some journalists, into believing this.

The police holding centre was a lucrative location for SB

to recruit IRA members as agents. The Bennett Report (1979) put a stop to this, removing any expectation of privacy in an interview. By the early 1980s, former SB detectives relate it was virtually impossible to recruit a terrorist suspect as an agent in a holding centre due to intrusive monitoring by uniform police and CCTV. This worked against the 'need to know' and 'small circle of knowledge' principles. One describes how the new regime affected operations:

> *During an interview nobody else needed to know if the person was recruited. The whole point was that they didn't. Doing this under the scrutiny of outsiders was impossible. You could quickly pop in just to get your face seen as part of a longer recruitment strategy but you couldn't pitch them properly. To be honest, it didn't really upset us that much but it closed down any success the crime squads were getting. We got out and about but crime squads couldn't as they relied on planned arrests.*

Although the police holding centre was a good venue to recruit agents because it was safe, losing it as a recruitment location was not a major drawback. Recruitment also happened elsewhere. There were endless places to make a recruitment pitch. Also, 'walk ins' was an unplanned aspect wherein a terrorist came into a police station and asked to speak to 'the Branch.'

Collating the views of former SB detectives produces three points about crime squads from an IRA perspective: 1) arrests/seizures caused 'tout hunts' and the standing down of ASUs and at times battalions; 2) the IRA rid itself of weaker members; and 3) increased acceptability of the police threatened the IRA 'defender' label and their local support-base. None of the three relates to prisoner abuse. This is a large part of why Ken Newman and Roy Mason were disturbed by Amnesty International's report into allegations of maltreatment (1978).

Both men saw criticism by Amnesty International as naivety of the situation and an unwarranted attack on an effective security effort that was saving life. They saw Sinn Féin pulling Amnesty's strings. Mason lists a series of atrocities prior to and after Amnesty International's nine-day visit, including the murder of a UDR soldier, William Gordon (41) and his daughter Lesley (10) by insurgents. He was annoyed why Amnesty International was uninterested in their human rights or exposing those who violated them. Newman was concerned at criticism having increased the risk to life of his officers. Mason and Newman were particularly dismayed at Amnesty International having ignored Sinn Féin propagandising erroneous complaints against its enthusiasm to repeat these.

Significantly, the Bennett Report states no officers were prosecuted as a result of any allegation, an observation strengthened in importance by the recommendation that the existing police system for investigating complaints against its officers should remain in place. One is confident the police complaints system would have been replaced had there been serious misgivings about the behaviour of its officers.

As it was the Bennett Report ended crime squads. Demonstrating the impact of this loss is the Chief Constable's annual report (1990), which shows that 1,308 people were charged with terrorist crimes in 1977 but less than half of this were charged by 1983 when Bennett's recommendations kicked in. Similar to internment, although crime squads had inflicted a devastating blow on every terrorist group, this was not enough to ensure it continued. Losing it was a serious setback to the security effort.

Replacing crime squads was the supergrass system in 1981 (formerly known as converted terrorists) that followed the same Law on Accomplice Evidence as England. Another security response based on normal policing was being trialled in an irregular war. The Chief Constable's annual report (1982) summarises it:

The origin lies in a combination of recognition by the public of the true nature and futility of terrorism and growing disillusionment within the ranks of the paramilitary organisations themselves. This led to increased assistance being given to the police. Extensive intelligence was assembled as a result of which very many persons were arrested, arms and explosives seized, acts of terrorism prevented and lives saved. It is clearly beyond question that the community as a whole has benefited immeasurably from this development. It was however identified by loyalist and republican terrorist organisations as posing a fundamental threat to their continued existence. Every means was employed by them in an effort to frustrate this healthy trend. These means included criminal conspiracy, intimidation, threats of death and various attempts to influence the public through the media, and undermine the judicial process and pervert the course of justice.

The supergrass system was not fully compatible with an intelligence-led approach because it encouraged existing and prospective agents to become a supergrass. Notwithstanding, the supergrass system severely curtailed the operational capabilities of all terrorist organisations. A paper called Supergrasses, June 1983, examines the concept. It describes the supergrass as a "super informer," as distinct from a 'super agent,' highlighting the concept had worked well in England prior to it being introduced in Northern Ireland. It was also used successfully in Italy against the Red Brigades and is similar to how the FBI dismantled the Mafia. Immunity from prosecution and surviving the suspicions of his organisation are the main motivational factors for a supergrass.

The Chief Constable's annual report (1983) states that the initiative had reduced the murder rate in one area of Belfast by 73% and an "overall reduction of 61% in terrorist crime." During its first three years more than 300 terrorists were charged, clearing nearly 1,000 serious terrorist crimes, according to the paper. Many insurgents went voluntarily on-the-run in the Republic, enhancing the IRA's cross-border component. The paper states the successes boosted the morale of "hard pressed" crime detectives and the force overall and that it sent terrorist leaders into a whirlpool of not knowing where the next mole would surface and wreak havoc. The jubilance was short-lived. Similar to confessions there was routinely no corroborating evidence. After a series of adverse legal rulings that undermined the credibility of the supergrass as a witness the initiative collapsed.

Raymond Gilmour and Eamon Collins were supergrasses. Gilmour is a self-disclosed SB agent who testified as a supergrass during which members of his family were abducted to prevent him doing so. Collins turned because he was wracked with guilt about his terrorist past and the IRA murders of some of his neighbours and work colleagues. Under pressure from his community and guaranteed his safety by the IRA Collins recanted. While part of the supergrass programme, he witnessed the IRA conspiring with loyalists to undermine the initiative. Collins shows that each used the conspiracy to gain intelligence on the other, resulting in later murders. Collins was never forgiven for his betrayal and despite the IRA's indemnity was viciously murdered by republicans in 1999. Again, opposite terrorist organisations secretly collaborated to undermine a security initiative that was harming their ability to conduct terrorist activity. It is another example of the IRA/Sinn Féin leadership prioritising their own goals to the detriment of those they professed to protect.

Under Newman's leadership the police used investigative-led procedures common to the rest of the UK. There was a concerted effort to be as normal as possible. But shoehorning what worked in a regular peacetime setting into an irregular war did not work. With the greatest will in the world, crime squads and the supergrass system against something as slick as the IRA and Sinn Féin were always destined to fail. In the process, however, they raised the profile of the criminalisation policy. It drew the IRA into a situation they did not want to be in, defending their actions in criminal courts under public scrutiny. Strategically, this is hugely significant. Forcing insurgents to engage and therefore recognise the criminal justice system was the biggest contribution to ending the conflict these security approaches made.

• The terrorist community secretly worked together to bring about the downfall of both investigative-led initiatives. Yet, even though crime squads and the supergrass system were under Crime department they made republican and loyalist terrorist organisations anxious about SB recruiting their members as agents.

These were the opening salvos of the intelligence war. The advantage still lay with the Provisionals, Sinn Féin having continued to excel in exploiting the sensitivities of a liberal democracy. But this would soon change. Adored by his men and highly intelligent, Newman had the foresight to invest heavily in SB as soon as he took office. The same as Young, Newman was obligated to try normal investigative-led approaches. Politically, going straight to a strong SB was a non-starter. It had to be incremental. The end destination, however, was inevitable. SB tentatively took over when it was clear that crime squads would finish, coinciding with the start of the supergrass system. When it was clear the supergrass system was also failing SB ascendency was assured. If the IRA was to be defeated by a criminal justice approach, having exhausted every other option, there was no choice other than SB.

A main lesson from the first decade of the Troubles is that the state cannot afford to release pressure on an insurgency because it rapidly recovers from setbacks. And inquiries like Gardiner (1975) that ended internment and Bennett (1979) that ended crime squads relieved pressure on the Provisionals. They stopped security initiatives on the cusp of defeating the IRA. Like internment, crime squads and supergrasses fell foul of Sinn Féin propagandists agitating London's liberal sensitivities. Despite Sinn Féin's best efforts, there would be no similar reprieve once Special Branch took over.

Newman brought us out of the dark ages.

Chapter 12

Without Fear or Favour

Looking at how Special Branch was developing in the shadow of larger security initiatives in the first decade of the Troubles reveals its influence on the overall counterinsurgency strategy. In modern terms US General David Petraeus calls this a Whole of Government strategy. It is where politics (soft power) and security (hard power) move together to defeat an insurgency. Peace would be achieved by transforming the Provisionals into a democratic political party.

Merlyn Rees initially conceived a Whole of Government strategy in the Bourn Report (1974), further bolstered by his successor Roy Mason in the Hannigan Report (1976). Both believed that political and economic stability was dependent on effective security to defeat an insurgency in much the same way General Petraeus reached the same conclusion 30 years later with similar situations in Iraq and Afghanistan. Of the Whole of Government strategy the Internal Security Solution was the security component. Criminalising an insurgency under police primacy and decreasing Army 'boots on the ground' was the British way.

In the late 1970s the political stewardship of Roy Mason set the tone. He believed 'special category' status for republican and loyalist prisoners had been a disaster. In his view, IRA activists were terrorist criminals and not prisoners of war or in anyway equal to those charged with upholding the rule of law. He wanted IRA men caught by the police and punished as criminals, not as politicals. Sinn Féin labelled Mason a Nazi. Mason made no apologies for hounding the IRA, but also understood that this was not enough. The economy was creating a tenth of jobs per year it did before the Troubles. Nearly 100 government-sponsored firms had folded, almost 20 factories had been destroyed and not replaced, and unemployment was just under 12%. Politics and economics had to develop alongside effective security.

Mason proposed a plan in late 1977 to re-boot a devolved government, which the SDLP rejected, seeing it as favouring unionists. Mason was politically hamstrung because Labour had no overall strategy on Northern Ireland. Not until Margaret Thatcher became Prime Minister in 1979 did a coherent Whole of Government strategy emerge. Thatcher based this on SB's mission, writing in her memoires:

The IRA are the core of the terrorist problem; their counterparts on the Protestant side would probably disappear if the IRA could be beaten.

Even though the SDLP disagreed with Mason's approach they admired his impartiality. Mason regarded the IRA as the main threat but was also alive to loyalist violence and saw some unionist leaders capable of provoking a sectarian civil war through their extreme rhetoric. Mason's memoires show that he believed unionist politician Ian Paisley inflamed the security situation by preying on Protestant fears of republican violence and suspicions of Dublin. On the nationalist side, the same could be said of Charles Haughey (Taoiseach 1979-81, 1982-82 and 1987-92). This hampered moderates on both sides contributing to a North/South solution.

Fianna Fáil was increasingly influenced by the SDLP who felt demoralised by the fall of Sunningdale and made little effort to improve cross-border security. For all local political parties Sunningdale was a missed opportunity to gain executive power and have a meaningful influence on what was happening, as opposed to helplessly watching from the sidelines. Paddy Devlin laments that some in the SDLP were too cosy with Haughey hard-liners. Ultimately, the SDLP's dislike of Labour's management of Northern Ireland caused it to vote against the government, ushering in the Conservatives. Airey Neave, a staunch critic of the IRA and close friend and mentor of Margaret Thatcher, was to replace Mason.

Neave was a war hero, the first British Army officer to escape from Colditz in 1942. He also served in the Nuremberg war crimes tribunals. Neave knew the IRA was nothing like a legitimate army and would loudly expose them as such. The IRA feared this and also that Neave would use the SAS against them more effectively than was the case up to then. He was murdered in Westminster by the INLA in March 1979. But this did not stop the British special forces playing an important role or dent the criminalisation policy. If anything, it made them stronger by convincing a new Prime Minister of their worth.

Within months of Neave's murder and taking occupancy of 10 Downing Street Thatcher was angered by Dublin's lacklustre security approach over two separate IRA attacks on the same day in August 1979. In Sligo, the IRA murdered Lord Louis Mountbatten (79), his grandson Nicholas Knatchbull (14), local boy Paul Maxwell (15) and Baroness Doreen Bradbourne (82), and in Warrenpoint they murdered 18 soldiers in a cross-border bomb attack. Thatcher's first Anglo-Irish summit showed her that Haughey had no plan for Northern Ireland. After both incidents Army commanders pressed the Prime Minister for a return of Army primacy, seeing the police incapable of providing security. Chief Constable Newman advised her otherwise. Under intense political pressure, Prime Minster Thatcher did what the IRA didn't want her to do - keeping the police in charge and the criminalisation policy intact. Prime Minister Thatcher was not for turning.

Stigmatising Provos as criminals peaked in the 1981 hunger strikes when republican prisoners were refused political status. Widespread rioting ensued, orchestrated by the IRA and Sinn Féin. Thatcher replaced Mason as republicanism's pin-up hate figure, blamed for the hunger strikers deaths. The IRA tried to murder her in 1984's Brighton bomb that killed five of her colleagues and injured many more. In taking office Thatcher had also put in motion steps to increase the special forces' role in an enlarged Special Branch. Neave would have been proud of his protégé, even more so when considering she mirrored SB's mission - ending the Troubles hinged on defeating the IRA. This would be done by: 1) nationalists rejecting the IRA and supporting constitutional institutions; 2) the IRA being deprived of international support – Irish-America and Libya; and 3) carefully managing Anglo-Irish relations.

Thatcher's premiership started by prioritising security and making concessions to the Republic to progress this. Dublin's security approach left plenty of room for improvement. At the same time she looked to form a devolved government acceptable to unionists and nationalists and opened a secret backchannel with the IRA. This was the Whole of Government strategy. The Provisionals were being pushed by security and pulled by politics toward peace.

By the end of the 1970s the criminalisation policy had the Provisionals at a strategic impasse. Prime Minister Thatcher knew this. So did most republicans but they could not admit it. A decade of violence had achieved nothing. The insurgency was drifting to politics, illustrating that the majority of IRA members and their supporters had not fully thought through the consequences of starting an irregular war in the first place. But having come this far the insurgent leadership needed time to figure out how to salvage a terrorist campaign that they knew would fail to achieve its headline aims into a success story that delivered some political gains.

Solving this problem increased in urgency the more normal policing returned to hostile areas, which was crucial to growing the Catholic community's confidence in the police. The Hannigan Report shows that the police wanted to be unaccompanied by soldiers in as many places as possible.

Framework operations and covert operations were the two categories of security force activity. Routine patrols by police and soldiers were to suppress the movements of terrorists and their munitions and obtain contact intelligence (information given by the public in face-to-face encounters). It was also to reassure the majority of law-abiding citizens. The overall aim was to maintain a permanent police presence and expand policing into areas where a full police service was not provided. A former SB detective relates his experience of this:

When I was in south Armagh everything was done by helicopter and you went nowhere without a full briefing, a multiple [12 soldiers], body armour and a rifle. In Bangor it was completely different. Tunics, no body armour or long weapons and you could serve a summons on your own. They were completely different worlds.

The mechanics of implementation meant operational decisions had to balance normalising policing against protecting officers, the most important aspect of which was intelligence guiding on the threat and risks. In developing intelligence, since the early 1970s Chief Constables commissioned top intelligence experts to review SB. At least seven reports were produced. All by senior MI5 people. These are:

Morton Report (1974): Review of Special Branch
Parker Report (1979): Intelligence Resources
Walker Report (1980): Interchange of Intelligence
Richards Report (1981): Co-ordination of Security
Cradock Report (1984): Development of SB at HQ
Deverell Report (1988): Analysis and Workload of SB
Warner Report (1996): Increased role of MI5

The seven reports conformed to the Whole of Government strategy and aided the implementation of the criminalisation policy. Looking at the titles (which have been summarised) broadly charts how SB evolved and the challenges this entailed. The first was by Jack Morton. Morton was originally a police officer in India in 1937, going on to hold senior posts up to his retirement in 1971, such as Deputy Director General of MI5. His international experience was extensive, working in places like Malaya and Iraq, as well as having been involved in successfully countering the 1956-62 IRA border campaign. Jack Morton was probably the top intelligence expert in the world regarding policing a conflict. In Malaya, he had Arthur Young split SB from CID to concentrate SB on counterinsurgency. In 1973 he came out of retirement to reorganise the RUC SB in an advisory mission for the government.

Morton typifies the impressive calibre of experts from MI5 who conducted reviews of SB. Morton undoubtedly influenced the introduction of police primacy. His report recommended SB separates from the larger CID and that it compartmentalises to accommodate different covert functions. Compartmentalising, as an operational concept, was a departure from SB detectives doing everything – handling agents, surveillance, co-ordination and armed response. How operational practices had changed are related by a former officer:

> We ran an operation against a top Provo unit in Myrtlefield Park in Belfast on the 10th May 1974. They were intercepting telephone calls made by the Army. Anyway, I organised the Det and then uniform to hit the house. They got the full team. Darkie [Brendan Hughes] was one of them. When he came out of the house he asked to speak to the Branch man. The uniform constable brought him over. We chatted for a few minutes. He said, "I'm glad it was you fuckers and not those Khaki bastards [Army]." Either way, he knew it was down to us but he couldn't figure out how. He asked, "How the fuck did you do it?" and congratulated us. ... I just smiled back.

Another states, "Myrtlefield Park was the first time we used police in this way." It was 'passive surveillance.' The watchers do not break cover but rely on an armed response team, in uniform, to do the reaction. A large arms cache and sensitive documents were recovered and leading IRA men imprisoned. Specialist police and Army teams had successfully worked together. It was a sign of things to come.

Popular accounts of Myrtlefield Park and similar incidents describe them as police undercover operations. It is crucial to know, however, that SB did not do undercover. Undercover is a tactic in an investigative-led approach where CID dominates. Police undercover operations involve a highly trained officer working his/her way into a crime gang under the guise of being a criminal and then evidencing his/her interactions in court. The undercover cop is the agent. Interestingly, the same case law applies to both. In the eyes of the law a well-placed agent and undercover cop are the same. That is somewhat detached from reality but in keeping with how the law struggles with the agent concept.

Undercover operations as a tactic were unsuited to the parochial intimacy of Northern Ireland and irregular war in general. An undercover operator would not last five minutes in a republican area, as the Army found out at great cost. Myrtlefield Park was SB co-ordinating surveillance and armed response based on pro-active intelligence it had gathered, which is totally different from an undercover operation. A former SB officer claims that, after such an operation a briefing took place with a CID officer who subsequently explained to the court, if asked, matters regarding information received that triggered the reaction. This process is still regularly used in many jurisdictions.

The CID detective was not told about the origins of the intelligence. The aim was to protect the source and keep SB officers out of court. It did not burden the CID detective with secrets that placed him or her in a difficult position in court. It also prevented inadvertent disclosure that could expose the source or sensitive methodologies, thereby preserving them for future use. The overarching aim was to protect life. Disclosure of certain details, however innocuous, could place someone's life at risk.

Although compartmentalising within the intelligence department complicated matters, it revolutionised the intelligence attack. Being caught red-handed, as those in Myrtlefield Park were, intimidated and demoralised the IRA.

Myrtlefield Park piloted new covert practices from which the Special Patrol Group (SPG) developed the Bronze Section in 1976. SB addressed its surveillance and armed response deficit by using the Bronze Section. The SPG and its Bronze Section however, were not part of SB. Former SB officers believe Bronze Section was effective but not as professional as the Det. Neither Bronze Section nor any SPG personnel underwent the rigorous selection and training of the Det, nor received training from British special forces. Former SB officers state that the SPG worried them as it occasionally collected its own intelligence and ran its own operations. The situation was not ideal. But there were only a few Det teams and they were working around the clock. And, as SB would soon find out, it took a long time to properly train a surveillance operator.

In a rapidly changing covert world intelligence-gathering was the one thing that changed least and at which SB excelled. The result was too much actionable intelligence and too few operators to action it. SB, therefore, out-sourced intelligence of this kind to the SPG; otherwise good opportunities to arrest terrorists and recover munitions would have been lost.

The Bronze Section and the Det were the early steps in compartmentalising covert specialisms – intelligence-gathering and surveillance being the first two disciplines catered for. The system being used to connect them was uncomplicated, described by one former officer as, "Basic hand-to-mouth stuff of getting a fifty [SB50] from SB to the Det and the Det acting on it." Accompanying the SB50 (intelligence report) was a 'target pack' of the suspect/s similar to the background file prepared for crime squads. That the Det had no parallel unit in the police was a failing. If the police were to successfully replace the Army they had to reach the same professional standards in surveillance and armed response. A former SB officer states:

In 1975 Brendan and me, [a detective sergeant and detective inspector] were commissioned by Flanagan [Chief Constable Jamie Flanagan] to write a paper about adding a surveillance unit to Special Branch. It ended up being called 'E' department simply because it was the next letter available. We already had 'A' to 'D' departments. We went to England and visited with the Box [MI5] and the Det to analyse what they had and adopt it for us. I sent in the report but he [Flanagan] sat on it. But when Newman came in [May 1976] it was a different story. He liked it. It slotted into his plan for the future. He wanted it set up yesterday. Some older SB officers said it would never work. ... For a number of reasons we named it E4A. ... Without Newman it would never have happened.

In 1976 'E' department was established. Its motto was, 'without fear or favour.' It was a revamped version of SB. The two labels referred to the same thing. For reasons of operational security it continued to be referred to as SB or 'the Branch' in order to hide how it was changing. The Malayan SB was also known as 'E' department. It was no coincidence. Something extra is needed in an irregular war beyond the four normal departments (Administration, Operations, Crime and Finance). The creation of E4A (dedicated surveillance teams) was a significant milestone in the development of SB. A former detective who experienced the transition states:

Newman brought us out of the dark ages. ... dedicated surveillance teams in Belfast and handlers sent across the water to courses in New Scotland Yard. We also had the MRF, which was the early Det, work along the border.

Under Newman, SB started to properly progress. In the early stages of SB taking over it is worth showing how SB shared intelligence with the rest of the force. The Wallace and Mountain Report in 1978 (a senior uniform police officer and MI5 officer) reviewed Divisional SB. It reads:

The maximum amount of intelligence available to SB from all sources is made available to CID to enable it to achieve the greatest number of charges against terrorist and subversive targets.

Wallace and Mountain emphasised that SB intelligence must be shared with CID in a manner that protects SB sources as, "Men's lives and delicate technical sources are at stake." Another is the Walker Report (1980). It shows SB intelligence was "easily assimilated by members of the RUC outside SB." The Parker Report (1979) similarly commends SB but criticises CID for failing to share information on terrorism with SB, further stating that SB record keeping was better than CID and recommending the identity of CID "informers" must be shared with SB as the latter "occupies the fundamental position in the intelligence attack on terrorist organisations." The CID issue led the RHSB South Region to write to the HSB on 11 Dec 1979:

By far the greatest difficulty is Divisional C.I.D. and Regional Crime Squad arrests. There have been a number of arrests by these groups, with little and sometimes no consultation with Special Branch, which has led to the arrest for interview of both Army and Special Branch Agents or Sources. This has arisen I believe on occasions when there was a suspicion that the persons concerned may have been helpful to the intelligence factions, and that by arresting for short-term gain they could possibly clear or get information regarding a crime, whereas our long-term gain must always be foremost in our minds.

SB accused CID of short sightedness and mischief concerning agents. The Walker Report deals with this, identifying SB's remit is subversive crime and CID's ordinary crime, and that the relationship between "SB and CID is close but sometimes uneasy." Walker overturns CID directives to recruit terrorist suspects as informers, as this detracts from CID's primary role and transgressed into an area they were neither trained nor funded to perform. Only SB should manage agents. Walker warned:

At a time when subversive organisations are reduced to a hard core of experienced activists, the result can be confusion and duplication of effort, and in extreme cases the loss of valuable agents. It was to overcome this problem that the Army agreed to declare their agents to SB at both HQ and Regional level.

Picking up on CID prioritising detection over prevention Walker advised CID that there is "usually more than one way of exploiting intelligence and the possibility of mounting covert operations rather than going directly for further arrests and interviews must always be considered." Walker felt compelled to make another important point:

Circumstances have produced in Northern Ireland an intelligence system which, as the result of the threat from subversive organisations and the need to devote a large proportion of RUC effort against this threat, is significantly different from that in Great Britain. In Great Britain intelligence of a Special Branch nature forms a small part of Police intelligence; there is not the same emphasis on subversive as opposed to ordinary crime.

The Walker Report shows that CID resisted the emergence of a strong SB but not to a degree that significantly impeded security. Military Intelligence also had a CID-type outlook. These were the practical challenges of moving from investigative-led policing to intelligence-led policing and Army primacy to police primacy. SB was highly rated for sharing its intelligence with the rest of the force.

SB's ascendency coincided with the introduction of a comprehensive Whole of Government strategy. All the elements of this strategy had been in place since the beginning but it was under Thatcher's premiership that they were properly harnessed. She understood that ending the conflict and forming an inclusive devolved government depended on defeating the IRA, defeat defined as the IRA prioritising the ballot box over the Armalite. The Anglo-Irish Agreement engineered by her and Taoiseach Garret Fitzgerald in 1985 was crucial, though the Republic persisted in refusing to recognise the IRA was using its territory as its major base of operations to plan and mount attacks in Northern Ireland. The Anglo-Irish Agreement demonstrated Dublin and London's political willingness to co-operate in ending the Troubles.

The dilemma for the IRA leadership was that the hatred and division of the extremist ideology they promoted to subvert a democratic system had, after ten years, created an IRA hardcore reluctant to give up violence. Not because they believed it would bring victory, although many believed it would. Rather, they were addicted to the power and social standing violence gave them. For many, violence was their life. They knew nothing else. Having sacrificed so much to unite Ireland, why give up now? Insurgent leaders had become entrapped by their own duplicity; unable to explain to members and supporters they deceived that turning into a respectable political party was always the aim. It was Thatcher's steely commitment to a criminalisation policy that made this transformation possible by forcing the IRA and Sinn Féin into thinking up the 'Armalite and ballot box' strategy.

If the IRA did not take a political route they would be defeated and obviously so. This would seriously undermine the political benefits the IRA accrued for its political partner. Then, the 'armed struggle' from a republican perspective really would have been a total waste. As it was, the galvanising effect of the hunger strikes facilitated Sinn Féin's creation of the 'Armalite and ballot box' catchphrase, conditioning republicans to the prospect that a united Ireland was not going to happen any time soon. The insurgent leadership was off the hook. It had got the minority community thinking about a post-conflict situation that still involved partition was not failure. True to type, they did this by blaming the 'Brits' for the conflict (which appealed to nationalists) and justifying the 'armed struggle' (which appealed to republicans). The message told passive and active IRA supporters that once the shooting stops, only Sinn Féin could deliver a united Ireland in a future date.

Behind the scenes talented and experienced people were making SB fit for purpose through 'E' department. 'E' department is inseparable from and was crucial to the Whole of Government strategy, guiding the regular security forces that the public knew and met daily and also the smaller covert element very few people ever saw. The criminalisation policy was steadily making the IRA unpopular with its small support base. By the time Prime Minister Thatcher left office in November 1990 the insurgent leadership was looking to get rid of the Armalite.

An elite police department had been formed.

Chapter 13

Quality not Quantity

Divisional SB located in offices in the larger police stations throughout the force and a small HQ in Belfast greatly benefited from MI5 guidance. This was how the traditional intelligence-gathering function progressed. Similarly, British Army special forces were instrumental in establishing SB's new executive arm – surveillance and armed response. The one element of the military not partnered up with its police counterpart was the Force Research Unit (FRU) in what the Army went on to call HUMINT (Human Intelligence).

Relations between the FRU and SB had not the same warmth as the others. A former SB detective claims his office was knocked back in its efforts to work with FRU staff in Bessbrook and Newry, two busy SB offices that covered Northern Ireland's 'Helmand' and closest to the insurgency's Dundalk capital. Dundalk probably contained more outlaws proportionate to the town's population than anywhere else in the world. It was the Republic's El Paso. The detective's experience echoes the wider sentiment of former SB officers about the FRU.

He states:

I'm not sure what the rest of the country was like but the FRU never really endeared themselves in South Region. It was hard to figure out why they wanted to approach some folk or what value it added. Usually a couple of them would come down once a week for a natter over a coffee. We'd great relationships with the Army. Most of us worked hand in glove with them in our uniform days and went through some very tough times together. We had the greatest respect and admiration for the soldiers. But the FRU guys were different. They were not like the rest. You always had the feeling they were trying to recruit you. Or you'd appear in one of their reports. There was always an angle.

The Army's lack of local knowledge was a major failing. Short tours of duty meant there was little time to establish good working relationships with the police. Some Army commanders found it difficult to grasp police primacy and the Northern Irish culture. The emergence of the FRU in 1980 may have rectified some of these shortcomings. Little, however, could be done about the fact that soldiers think differently to police officers. The briefest examination of Army intelligence documents reveals excellent attention to the mechanics of how an agent is met. In contrast to SB these were Spielberg productions, helicopters providing aerial surveillance, lots of personnel in the target area providing close cover and an Army unit close at hand as a Quick Reaction Force. The instructions given to the agent were less comprehensive, often revealing a lack of understanding of the criminal law and associate implications if certain courses of action were proposed or taken.

As one former SB officer noted: "The Army treated the Provos as the enemy in the military sense of the word." Unlike the police, the Army was slow to realise the legal hazards connected with a well-placed agent in a terrorist organisation. Soldiers were being exposed to legal risks they had no idea existed. There was little appreciation that, at a future date, their actions would be legally scrutinised. There was even less appreciation how republicanism historically behaved after a war.

Whilst the FRU contribution is not insignificant, it was small and not as effective as the Det or SAS. Unlike other specialist military units the FRU was a strained fit within the new 'E' department and a departure from classic British counterinsurgency. Experience in previous conflicts, and conflicts since, is that separate intelligence agencies turn into zealously guarded fiefdoms causing confusion and generally blunting the intelligence attack. Just by existing the FRU made it hard for SB. So why did the Army persist with running agents? A former FRU officer answers:

> *Firstly, the Army is set up to do this. It has all the organisational attributes to support HUMINT operations. In Northern Ireland the Army was able to recruit and run agents that Special Branch could not because the individuals concerned preferred to deal with the Army.*

Former SB officers are unconvinced. They believe that SB detectives originally from England with military service could have allayed these concerns. Another reason offered is that people became Army agents because they saw the police as sectarian. Stacked against the facts this is also unconvincing. The FRU only had a handful of agents of any worth who were mostly in Belfast. All of whom, in the opinion of former SB officers, would have been prepared to talk to SB. If a prospective agent wanted an English accent or a Catholic, SB had both.

The origins of the FRU are in the Military Reaction Force (MRF). In the early 1970s the MRF concocted an unhealthy mix of undercover, agents, surveillance and armed response. The MRF was the Army's substitute for SB. But it transgressed too many intelligence principles to succeed. Out of this emerged a strange type of agent called a 'Fred.' A Fred was a mix of undercover and agent, and an unmitigated disaster.

Undeterred, the Army insisted in keeping the agent aspect. In a time of police primacy what benefit did this bring? A big clue is a classified Army report that fell into the hands of the IRA in

1978 and ended up in Sinn Féin's main propaganda publication the Republican News. The report concluded that, it was impossible to defeat the IRA militarily, which became the headline in the national press, much to the delight of the IRA and Sinn Féin. This was at odds with the Whole of Government strategy and the secret victory it would produce. Senior MI5 figure Sir Brooks Richards regarded the assessment depressing wherein the Army believed it was "not winning and could conceivably lose." The report's author was General Glover, creator of the FRU. Appeals by Army commanders to the Prime Minister following the Warrenpoint incident in 1979 reinforced Glover's sentiment. The FRU was established in 1980 as, many believe, a concession to the Army.

In reacting to Warrenpoint what the Army also seem to have missed was Dublin's attitude on border security. The testimony of the RUC's Senior Investigating Officer in 2012 at the Smithwick Tribunal into IRA/Garda 'collusion' states: "Mr McLaughlin [Garda deputy commissioner] decreed the killings were a political crime and no assistance would be given to the RUC." He then goes on to testify that no assistance was given because the Taoiseach directed such. Glover's report showed a limited understanding of the border's significance and how this restricted security efforts in Northern Ireland. There was only so much a rule of law approach could achieve. But an element of the Army, if Glover's report is anything to go by, was not thinking rule of law but in Alpha male military versus military terms, an antiquated destructive approach that failed in other irregular wars and also previously failed in Ireland.

It is said that those in the Army who held this view believed it was a war but could not say this because of the criminalisation policy. Whatever the case, the FRU kept the Army at the forefront of the fight from an intelligence standpoint. HUMINT brought power and political leverage. It meant the Army was not totally reliant on SB. They could gather their own intelligence. Of the Army, cynics would say that the Troubles were an opportunity that could not be missed to test HUMINT for later wars, defending the realm against threats still to be identified. The FRU became an appendage of 14 Intelligence Company (Det). In the Richards Report (1981) one detects more than a hint that this was a mistake because the FRU competed with SB. After the Troubles HUMINT became a standard feature of a downsized Army.

According to Richards, after Warrenpoint Prime Minister Thatcher appointed a senior retired MI5 officer Sir Maurice Oldfield (attached to the Northern Ireland Office) on the 8th October 1979 in order to, "assist the Secretary of State for Northern Ireland in improving co-ordination and effectiveness of the fight against terrorism." The Army provoked MI5's intervention in the hope MI5 would side with them. This was not the case, and was never likely to be when considering reports by people like Jack Morton. Richards succeeded Oldfield. His report concluded:

I am satisfied that all concerned with security in the Province are now well seized both of the rightness of the policy they are implementing and of the need for close, effective and continuing co-ordination.

The Army wanted a stronger Director and Co-Ordinator of Intelligence (DCI) with executive authority over both the police and Army. The DCI was a Northern Ireland Office appointment and a key post for all the intelligence agencies. Again the Army was knocked back. Richards knew the historical precedence of the DCI function, especially its relevance to the Malayan Emergency, but does not regard it as suitable for Northern Ireland in its traditional form:

It has been used successfully in anti-terrorist campaigns overseas. However in those cases both the constitutional position and the security force structure were different. Moreover the existence of executive detention obviated the need to work through the normal processes of the law – intelligence was thus relatively more important than evidence. There are also other important factors. To be effective such a post would need to carry unquestioned authority over Police and Army personnel engaged in intelligence work. The consequent need to modify the authority of the Chief Constable over an integral part of his own Force would be a significant reversal of current Government policy. No less important, it could adversely affect the RUC's morale, especially that of SB whose work requires flair and initiative at all levels.

Harsher laws in Malaya meant it was obvious that intelligence was more important than evidence. In Northern Ireland this was less vivid because 'beyond reasonable doubt' was the legal benchmark. Nonetheless, the same prioritisation existed. To manage this MI5 considered SB better placed than the Army and was keen to preserve police independence. MI5 advocated strengthening SB and that the DCI deals with requests from the Army and police, offers advice and provides single service directives that both adhere to. By doing so the Parker Report argues the co-ordination and flow of intelligence is more effective:

The sharpness of the intelligence attack in Northern Ireland depends to a large extent on SB personnel who, in addition to their professional capability can bring to bear deep knowledge of the Northern Ireland scene, whether in respect of running Agents, maintaining surveillance or transcribing tapes from technical operations. … RUC Special Branch is a highly professional Agent handling organisation, which has consistently over the years produced most of the intelligence on which the SF [Security Forces] operate.

Helping to improve police/Army co-operation was the excellent personal relationship between the new Chief Constable, John Hermon, and new GOC, Lieutenant General Sir Richard Lawson, both appointed late in 1979. Politically, there were also benefits. Taoiseach Fitzgerald praised Hermon in presiding over a force that was impartial and non-political. Overall, things were moving well in the right direction, as the Parker Report (1979) records in showing that, SB and the Army exchanged intelligence "at the appropriate level." It notes the bulk of intelligence is from SB to the Army and that "a small proportion of SB intelligence requires such exceptionally careful protection that it cannot be passed without an unacceptable risk of the source being compromised." It also states, "SB never withhold intelligence if there is a danger of lives being lost." The Regional Head of SB for South Region in the same report that criticised CID and crime squads observed that the Army was complying with similar Walker-type instructions on disclosing the identities of their informers to SB.

One must remember that SB's relationships with the Army and CID were developing under the shadow of larger investigative-led security initiatives, which the IRA and Sinn Féin undermined. The Chief Constable's annual report 1981 reminds us what the IRA and Sinn Féin were doing to discredit the criminalisation policy:

> *Ten hunger strikers died, as did 67 other persons in the terrorist-orchestrated violence. Of these deaths, 15 were police officers, 15 soldiers and 37 civilians. … Many instances of riot and disorder occurred involving the use of explosives, rockets, firearms and petrol bombs in which the security forces would have been morally and legally justified to resorting to the use of firearms. It is a tribute to their restraint that they did not. Critics of the tactics of the security forces signally failed to suggest an acceptable or effective alternative. …… a vicious resurgence of the Republican murder and bombing campaign following on the ending of the hunger strike. Here the object was to foment a loyalist reaction and to achieve what the hunger strike had failed to bring about – widespread communal turmoil and strife.*

Killing 30 members of the security forces displays the harmony between the military and political blocs of the insurgency. Within 24-hours of the first hunger striker's death, Bobby Sands (27), constable Philip Ellis (33), a father of five, was murdered by insurgents. He was shot in the head at close range while policing an interface area in Belfast. The gunman hid behind children to shoot him. The next hunger striker to die was Francis Hughes (27), revered by republicans for having killed a dozen members of the security forces.

The violence and propaganda the hunger strikes produced were the IRA trying to get rid of the criminalisation policy, characterised by investigative-led approaches at that time. The difficulty for the insurgency was SB could also lead a criminalisation policy. Unknowingly, by undermining crime squads and supergrasses the IRA created the conditions for their SB nemesis to take control. Showing what was in store for the IRA is a paper titled The Early Years (2010) by a person writing about SB:

In the late 1970's there was still little or no co-ordination between the security forces to counter the terrorist campaign, by either overt or covert resources. The arrangements for the co-ordinating of units worked mainly as a result of the determination on the part of those involved, with no one group either receiving or processing all the intelligence, on which operations should have been based. This situation resulted in a disjointed approach towards the problems on the ground, and also produced the very real likelihood that differing Security Force agencies would mistake each other for terrorists, with deadly results.

There was no single Branch, police or Army, in charge of co-ordination. The Early Years paper shows that the Tasking and Co-ordination Group (TCG) in December 1978 rectified this. Authorisation by a senior police officer was required prior to undertaking any reactive covert operation, which was a step up from the co-ordination at Myrtlefield Park. Co-ordination was a new tactical feature of policing. TCG was designed to end the chaos of multiple covert agencies and ad hoc units doing their own thing. A former SB detective describes the issues resolved:

Too many agencies were working on the same target without any of them knowing. On one target, at a Hamburger stand on the street, the target was selling the hamburgers. When the target moved so did the entire queue! Blue on blue and duplicate taskings stopped overnight. As opposed to four agencies looking at the one target we had four agencies looking at four different targets.

The Richards Report commends the concept:

At a Regional level the introduction of the Tasking and Co-ordination Groups has been a major advance and has ensured that all useable intelligence is better exploited. The greatest success has been achieved in Belfast and I think that the experience gained there is now effectively applied elsewhere in the Province.

A former SB officer notes: "The Provos talked about luck. We didn't need luck. We had TCG." But what of SB's new E4A surveillance teams; how were they developing? A Specialist Operations Branch poster (2010) states:

E4A was initially part-funded and trained by the Security Service (MI5). … The initial team consisted of eight surveillance officers. … As successes against terrorist operations mounted daily, the recognition of this specialist type of work was seen to be cutting-edge in averting terrorist acts and carrying out arrest operations. The initial team in Belfast became two, … In 1980 South Region were allocated a dedicated surveillance team … A new Headquarters Team, … was created to concentrate on GHQ staff and Northern Command PIRA [1982].

And what about SB's problems with acquiring its own armed response teams? A report called, Accommodation for E4A, (22 May 1979) by ACC 'E' reads:

E4A is a purely surveillance unit which operates mainly in hostile areas and for security reasons its existence and modus operandi must remain secret; 2) While Bronze Section of the SPG is to be trained for semi surveillance activity it will remain essentially a reactive unit.

Surveillance (E4A) and co-ordination (TCG) were integrated into SB. Due to a shortage of manpower, workload and intensity of violence SB still relied on non-SB police units, particularly armed response. Specific to the Bronze Section, since the unit's inception

(Aug 1976) former members relate that there was no requirement to sign the Official Secrets Act (1911). Every officer who signed this had his or her attention drawn to Section 2 that focused on the penalties for wrongfully communicating secret information. Neither were officers in Bronze Section Develop Vetted (Top Secret security clearance). This was a UK requirement for anyone working in national security; hence it was unique to SB within a police context. Because these units worked on SB intelligence it placed their officers in positions where they could speculate on who the agent was or expose sensitive methodologies without breaching the Official Secrets Act or DV protocols.

The police leadership and SB regarded the level of operational security concerning non-SB personnel as unsatisfactory. Consequently, from 1979 Bronze Section members were required to sign the Official Secrets Act and undergo a DV. Further change occurred when Hermon disbanded the SPG in 1980 in favour of the Divisional Mobile Support Units (DMSUs) who undertook the same anti-terrorist role. The Bronze Section escaped being integrated into the DMSU initiative. Instead, it was formally transferred into SB where it became known as E4 Special Support Unit (E4 SSU), with some members with a talent for surveillance going into E4A (contingent on passing selection and initial training). A former Head of E4 points out that it was not a police version of the SAS or a copy of Bronze Section but a dedicated Quick Reaction Force to surveillance teams.

Case officers (former Divisional SB detectives) ran TCG, wherein there were also Det, SAS, Close Observation Platoon (COP), E4A and E4 SSU liaison officers. TCG in Belfast was the first, located at a secure site physically separated from other police. Other technical units associated with E4 were later added, but these were the main components of SB's executive arm, eventually replicated in the other Regional HQs. A reliance on the DMSU still existed. Having them perform a restricted role and careful disclosure of intelligence in briefing DMSU personnel mitigated the risk in a source protection context.

The evolutionary path continued the principle that Divisional

SB would not give evidence in court, which now also included surveillance operators. To do so risked exposing their identity and sensitive methodologies. The potential for compromise was considered too high a risk on a number of levels: physical threat posed by the IRA; small number of personnel engaged in this type of activity and the time/cost it would take to find and train suitable replacements; and the criticality of protecting sources (human and technical) and associate methodology. Therefore, it was the reactive aspect (E4 SSU) that would give evidence and become the public face of SB.

Covert operations began by Divisional SB submitting intelligence in an SB50 to their Regional Intelligence Unit, which linked into HQ. An example is, 'Intelligence indicates that the IRA intend to mount an attack against Crossmaglen police station in the next 74-hrs.' The intelligence debrief justified deploying resources. Minimal attention was paid to the intelligence grading. Rather, it was the source number that was important. Everyone in the decision-making chain knew who the good sources were – agent and technical. They were the ones that routinely delivered. And this, perhaps, is the clearest illustration of why defining intelligence is so important. In this situation it was all about timeliness, getting inside information about a terrorist attack before it happened. This is what every Divisional SB detective was trying to gather, the five star debrief that resulted in arrests, convictions and the recovery of munitions.

A decision would then be made if a reaction was feasible and what unit or combination of units (E4A, Det, SAS, E4 SSU) was the best tactical option. If a covert operation was commissioned the operational plan was presented to the RHSB wherein he considered any potential compromise to the source alongside public safety and wider protection of life issues prior to it being authorised. Outside of reactive operations the Regional Intelligence Unit also ensured that 'threat intelligence' was shared with the appropriate Divisional SB Office who in turn informed local police.

Quite often TCG operations required an area to be placed Out of Bounds (OOB). To do this TCG contacted the local Divisional SB office to seek the local police commander's authorisation. In the context of a covert operation the reason for placing an area OOB was to make sure no security forces other than those TCG controlled would be in it, thus eliminating the risk of 'blue-on-blue'. Outside of this, an area would go OOB because of suspicious activity or similar heightened threat against the security forces, the reason being it denied terrorists their target. Equally, threat intelligence could also entail increasing the security force presence. This was usually due to an assessment of the intelligence indicating an increased police profile would prevent an attack. Both responses were daily occurrences and worked well as a preventative measure in protecting life. A former SB officer describes an example:

A two-legged [agent] brought a gun to us. It was to be used as part of a 'come on' call. And it had to go back otherwise he was in big trouble. When the police responded they'd hit them. We had our hands on it, so it didn't work. The place was put Out of Bounds and the sections briefed about the threat of a 'come on.' But when the night crew came on someone in uniform forgot to brief them. They responded to a call in the middle of the Out of Bounds. The gun was used when they got out of the car. It didn't go off. Not the way we had planned it, but the main thing was nobody got hurt. We managed any fallout at our end.

The TCG and Regional Intelligence Unit exemplify the daily fusion between Divisional SB and its executive arm and the wider force. The difficulty was that systems, structures and procedures were still being bedded in. ACC 'E' in his Accommodation for E4A report (22 May 1979) focused on improving this through training, which put the wheels in motion to establish a dedicated training cadre designed to run courses in Northern Ireland. An early member of the cadre explains it comprised three different teams – E4A (surveillance), E4 SSU (armed response) and Divisional SB (agent handling).

The first team to emerge was E4A in 1980. Post-selection

E4A members had to successfully pass a 10-week course in London taken by M15 and Det personnel. Next was the E4 SSU team in 1980 and finally Divisional SB in 1983. The initial intake of E4 SSU, according to someone who took part, "undertook a six week course with the SAS in England. It was given a codename - Operation Catacomb One – and we were all sworn to secrecy." This was preceded by a 10-day assessment. Those who came across from the Bronze Section and had not undergone the E4A assessment and course had to pass the E4 SSU entrance tests. Not everyone passed. Anyone who failed was returned to uniform.

The 10-day selection was tough. Several former SAS troopers who joined the RUC and went through it to get into 'E' department rate it as just below the SAS selection. No other British police force and probably no other law enforcement agency in the world put their officers through anything similar. One former E4 SSU officer states:

It was day six, by which point we were physically and mentally exhausted. We'd little sleep; little food, cold showers, no heat and anytime we weren't running we were doing press-ups and sit-ups, sometimes in the Atlantic Ocean. And it was a rifle and full Bergen you were running with, up and down sand dunes that pulled the legs off you or night navigation through a forest. You were always wet. There was no let-up. Then it began. They [E4 SSU training team] started to test you in other ways when you were at your lowest ebb.

They devised a classroom scenario where a gunman had just shot dead the officer beside you. We were doing a rapid house entry. Having done this the gunman drops his rifle and puts his hands in the air. "What do you do?" they asked. All of us said we'd arrest him. But the trainers laughed. They said, "forget the course answer, what would you really do?" They got the same reply. Then they latched onto one of us who had a brother in the Police. They said, "the cop shot dead was your brother and this fucker smiled at you when he threw the rifle down. He knows you don't have the balls to shoot him. What are you going to do now?" The guy said: "Arrest him." But they came back. "Bollocks. Grow a set of balls. He's a terrorist. Nobody will ever know, there's only you and him in the room. Shoot the fucker. Is this not what you're here for? For God's sake are you a man! What are you going to do? Make a fucking decision will you. Come on, everyone else here is afraid to. Make the call. Pull the fucking trigger."

By this time they were screaming at him, right up close in his face. "I can't hear you, what are you going to do?" They kept at him. Finally he said, "Shoot him. I'd fucking shoot him." Everything went silent. You could have heard a pin drop. I'm thinking, is he right and am I wrong? To get into this unit is that what they do. You know, it was all clouded in secrecy, nobody outside of SB knew what they did or how they did it. So was this it? The silence lasted for a while. "End of exercise" they said calmly and softly, and walked out of the classroom. He failed.

The focus was on quality not quantity. A tough selection was the common gate of entry to all disciplines. The pass rate was 5%. An elite police department had been formed, along with the inevitable professional jealousies this created with some in the rest of the force. 'E' Department was a learning organisation. Candid debriefs or wash-ups took place after every operation. These were often hard hitting. But this is what the training instilled. If a surveillance operator blew his cover he spoke up, or someone else would. If suspects escaped in E4 SSU's reaction, fingers were pointed, but in an objective way.

Lessons learned were captured and best practice quickly absorbed, standardised and disseminated throughout the operational arm. They also learned from others. For instance, a SAS trooper in a covert operation at night fired a flare. Launching the flare identified his position, which an insurgent shot at, killing the trooper. Days after this everyone was briefed that the new SOP (which was integrated into the training) was to quickly move position immediately after having fired a flare. The training cadre had some of the best people. There was a steady turnover so trainers were operationally current. Three to four years in training was the norm.

The insignia for 'E' department is a flying eagle holding a tourniquet in its talons overlaid on an outline of Northern Ireland. Operation Tourniquet (loyalists) and operation Eagle (republicans) were successful covert operations that harnessed all the aspects of 'E' department - originated by Divisional SB intelligence, co-ordinated by TCG, E4A surveillance and E4 SSU reaction. Both resulted in convictions and the recovery of firearms and explosives. A former SB officer states:

We had an excellent working relationship with the Gardaí Special Branch. Great people. On one occasion we took an agent all the way down to the far South. He knew where an arms dump was and could take us to it. We went unarmed. There was nothing illegal about it. A Gardaí Special Branch car followed us … we found the dump. They didn't sit on it though. Recovered it within days. Much too quick. Got no arrests but a big haul of explosives. …

On another day we had two detective chief superintendents sent up from Dublin. They'd been told about another arms dump and briefed Haughey on it. He instructed them to sit on it this time. But the Garda lads didn't know how. Haughey then asked how do those boys up North do it? They came up to us and we showed them what to do. To be fair to them they did not have the same training or resources we had.

We had recently run a successful operation against loyalists and recovered quite a haul of guns and a few arrests [operation Tourniquet] … We used that as a case study. The Gardaí Special Branch lads really appreciated it. They saw we were active against both sides. We regularly met them on courses in

England. Special Branch to Special Branch the relationship was excellent. ... Just be sure not to bring the British Army to any meeting. They had no time for them.

Good personal relations between SBs did little to improve cross-border security. Politicians influencing police operations at the tactical level hindered the Garda.

SB's workload was immense but its resources small. A report by ACC 'E' (Oct 1979) gives the establishment of 'E' department at 308, 5% of the regular force. Almost 200 were Divisional SB, approximately 50 in E4A and the majority of the rest in HQ. Bronze Section had 20. Around 60 civilian support staff were at HQ (mostly in registry), with some also at regional HQs and Divisional offices. 'E' department was about a third the size of CID (crime branch). The military collective, commonly called the security group, was also bigger - five times the size. It had 1,500 soldiers engaged in intelligence work, according to the Parker Report, including the Det, FRU, SAS, Close Observation Platoons, transcribers/monitors for technical operations, support, administration, analysis, weapons intelligence, photography, computer-related duties and police liaison. One hundred and seventy seven were Det.

An example of Divisional SB resources is Bessbrook containing one detective sergeant and a detective constable to cover south Armagh. The Parker Report expressed concern about staffing levels, particularly at HQ. It states:

HQ is under such pressure to deal with paper requiring immediate processing that they have little or no time to analyse reports from all sources as a basis for guiding investigations.

The report also notes the surveillance capacity in Belfast was "insufficient to undertake long term investigation of terrorist groups in hard areas." Parker saw SB's workload as excessive and way beyond that of any other department.

Parker recommended E4A increase to 120 and the Bronze Section (soon to be E4 SSU) to 60, which would take at least several years if standards were to be maintained. Broadly speaking, to reach an operational standard it took at least six months to train an E4 SSU officer, 12-months for an E4A operator and 24-months for an agent handler. Parker recommended that E4A should operate in the relatively less hostile areas of the province as an apprenticeship until operationally proficient. He also recommended Divisional SB was doubled in strength. While Belfast had always commanded most attention since 1969, and would always require the bulk of resources to contain Belfast IRA, there was a clear determination to increase the operational capability in South Region. Given the fact that Anglo-Irish politics had produced no tangible security measures in the Republic this was not surprising. Surveillance in border areas would significantly boost the intelligence effort.

While a large degree of parity and camaraderie existed between police and Army surveillance and armed response units, the same was not true of intelligence-gathering. The FRU was not as well integrated into covert policing as the Det or SAS. For many former SB detectives, other than appeasing Army commanders and helping the Army devise a new unit for future conflicts, it is difficult to see what practical benefits the FRU brought. They see it as having caused tension and confusion where there should have been harmony and clarity. Soldiers recruiting civilians as agents in a rule of law approach is a contradiction of what a rule of law approach is about. It gives credence to the IRA claiming to be a legitimate army. The FRU and CID placed extra demands on SB from totally opposite angles. While not a major drawback, it was something SB could have done without.

In the process of taking the lead and coming out of the shadow of Army primacy and then investigative-led initiatives, there were helps and hindrances. CID and the FRU expressed a degree of resentment about a strong Special Branch. But this was not representative of the overall support given by both and minor when considering the rest of the security forces and the government were behind the initiative. To put things into perspective, senior police and Army command, the vast majority of British Army special forces and the full weight of MI5, Downing Street and the Northern Ireland Office were behind strengthening Special Branch in order that it would lead the security effort.

Within a few years of taking over and by the early 1980s, SB was central to the strategic and tactical co-ordination of the entire security apparatus. The arrangement better prepared SB against suffering the same fate as crime squads and supergrasses. In this regard it would not take long for SB's resilience to be tested.

In 1982 three covert operations in which E4 SSU shot dead five insurgents and one suspected insurgent would raise 'E' department's profile. 'Shoot-to-kill' and 'cover up' would be the headlines. Sinn Féin stoked sensationalism and provoked controversy to get rid of SB. After all, this is what it did best. Dark forces, sectarian death squads, state killers were all the stuff of a secret dirty war. Journalists had a field day. This was so much sexier than writing about suspects beaten into confessing or terrorists testifying. And the secrecy aspect gave a licence to wrap supposition around some loose facts. Endless columns were printed, books published, documentaries screened and reputations made. Perception turned into reality. Nationalists were outraged, Amnesty International horrified, Dublin appalled and Irish-America incandescent. Inquiries were called for. SB was a scandal. The security approach had to go. Not this time though.

The negative 'shoot-to-kill' and conspiracy headlines were predictable and would continue. But so would the arrests of IRA men and funerals of those most wedded to the gun. Headlines, however, bring little comfort to a grieving family or a wife whose husband is serving 25 years. The insurgent leadership was increasingly inventive in hiding their true intent. They were not yet ready to cash in their terrorist chips for political currency. In the late 1970s they still believed more political gains could be made. The pretence that the IRA was undefeatable was maintained. More people had to die. Had an accurate assessment of the insurgency fallen into IRA hands in 1978 it would not have seen the light of day.

Even in 1982 'E' department was still a tiny fraction of the security forces and much smaller than the agencies that led the security effort before it. Man for man it was just over half the size of the IRA. If one adds Sinn Féin it was outnumbered four to one. SB had yet to fully mature. Yet, there would be no relief for the IRA as SB transformed from an awkward teenager into a young adult. When on-the-runs came up north there would be no hiding place. The border would be taken out of the equation despite Dublin, as the 1982 incidents will show. Against a co-ordinated security effort, especially at the tactical level in covert operations, for the IRA there was not enough luck in Ireland to prevent their defeat.

The press were on Stalker's side.

Chapter 14

Red-Handed

By the late 1970s the IRA in Belfast had been irreparably weakened by SB and no longer capable of delivering what they regard as victory on their own. The focus of the insurgency shifted, as a review of SB by MI5 in the Richards Report (1981) shows:

> *There are now few parts of the province where the PIRA can operate with ease. This is reflected in a general movement of the incidence of terrorism towards the border areas and adjacent towns and away from Belfast in particular.*

The IRA was losing ground, and how this was panning out was the outworking of an effective security effort in Northern Ireland and an ineffective one in the Republic. Noting this Richards states: "Cross-border terrorism of the traditional type has proved more intractable, as the terrorist structure south of the border remains largely intact." He further points out how stability was being achieved:

> *Though it took time to perfect, the RUC's reaction to this changing situation was to develop, in collaboration with the*

Army, a sophisticated method of operation based on good intelligence and surveillance leading to the 'red-handed' capture of active terrorists.

Lack of Garda resources and a lack of political will in Dublin ensured the continuance of a lame security approach against the IRA in the Republic. Since the start of the Troubles no security measure in the Republic corresponded to that in Northern Ireland. An intelligence-led approach was to be no exception.

Garda SB was no 'E' department, but they still had well-placed agents and the operational capacity to put together something to catch perpetrators 'in the act.' Yet rarely did this happen. Proactive intelligence was never handed over. And it is unthinkable that the Garda had none. Clearly, there was a policy not to share. For many in SB, the Republic did not want to be associated with a potential situation where an IRA man was shot dead by British security forces. If the connect became public, the political fallout in Dublin would have been devastating. 'Shoot-to-kill' ensured there was no chance the status quo would change. Indeed, several covert operations in the mid-1990s along the border where the Garda had been informed suspiciously fizzled out into nothing. The result should have been the 'red-handed' capture of insurgents in possession of munitions.

In a cross-border context, in the intelligence war SB was very much on its own in fighting the IRA. This was a huge problem because the IRA was more reliant on cross-border units than ever. Part of this was a reluctance to use car bombs in the city, whereas large roadside bombs and heavy weapons were used in rural settings. The leadership wanted to reduce the number of civilians killed, although there was an acceptable level in this respect. The difficulty for SB, according to the Parker Report, was that the intelligence coverage through agents outside of Belfast was limited. In other words, there were not enough well-placed agents in border areas where the IRA was now most active.

The intelligence gained from surveillance and technical sources led to recruiting new agents. Secretly listening to a conversation between terrorists in a house, or an IRA man confiding to his wife, disclosed detail about them and others in the unit. Surveillance also threw up good stuff. If the target met a stranger, it was the stranger the surveillance team was directed to follow. The stranger was tracked to a car or house that could identify them. Surveillance operators would take photos, remotely operating covert cameras in their car in a 'drive past.' These were passed to Divisional SB for them to identify.

Sometimes the stranger was a 'clean skin,' someone who avoided republican haunts and did not fit the usual terrorist profile, a seemingly respectable member of society below the radar of local police. Some were the neighbours of police officers. At times it was a courier of secret communiqués or someone gathering intelligence for the IRA, such as a bank official handing over home addresses of police officers from having identified direct debits of police central pay branch.

For Divisional SB (who recruited agents and managed intelligence) this information was priceless. Imagine being the bank official who believed no-one knew about their clandestine activities. Then, one working day when having lunch in a café a man and woman politely excuse themselves and sat beside them. They seemed like a nice couple and started to chat. Then came the killer – "We know what you're at and this is who we are." Quite quickly the bank official would be asking, how did I get into this mess and how could I get out of it? It is the classic victim, persecutor, rescue triangle.

Alternatively, it might be better to keep the person under the radar, put a surveillance team on them and see where they lead. Who else did they meet? Perhaps the person had no redeeming qualities needed to be an agent. So there would be no recruitment pitch. Or perhaps it may suit to have them arrested and search their house and office. Not because there was any real chance of a prosecution but that it should prevent their future activities and put the IRA unit involved into a tailspin.

The idea behind different tactics was to mystify and disorient the IRA about the origins of intelligence, which was critical to maintaining effective security. Predictably, the IRA sought to exploit every opportunity to identify secret sources of intelligence used against it. It also wanted to know because militant republicanism is a retributive beast. People who crossed it would pay.

In broad terms the significant moments of the military contest from the early 1980s onwards were played out in the southern half of the country in South Region. This was a FRU-free zone where SB managed all well-placed agents and had positioned extra resources. The headline victories against the IRA would happen in border counties in South Region. This is not to diminish SB's effectiveness in containing Belfast or Derry IRA, insurgent brigades that remained active and deadly. Neither is it to ignore SB's ongoing fight against loyalist terrorist organisations, particularly in places ravaged by sectarian tit-for-tat murders. Rather, it is to emphasise how the geography of border counties in South Region favoured the IRA. Hills, forests and endless border crossings with nationalist towns either side, like Dundalk and its on-the-run community, worked against the security forces.

It is therefore unsurprising that in 1982 South Region was the scene of three separate shooting incidents by SB linked to incidents with a cross-border dimension, such as on-the-runs. These resulted in six fatalities and one arrest. Each was a covert operation involving E4 SSU. The outcry from nationalists and the liberal left resulted in four E4 SSU officers put on trial for murder in two separate cases. In acquitting three of them (4 June 1984) in the Craigavon case where three IRA men were killed, Lord Justice Gibson made it clear they were absolutely blameless and commended their courage. In the other trial of the Armagh city incident, Justice McDermott similarly acquitted constable John Robinson (3 April 1984) for the murder of two senior INLA men. INLA leader and on-the-run Dominic 'Mad Dog' McGlinchey was mentioned in the intelligence but missed in the operation. Both judgements, particularly Gibson's, inflamed nationalists.

In the third incident, the 'Hayshed' shooting, a suspected IRA 'volunteer', Michael Tighe was shot dead and IRA man

Martin McCauley arrested. McCauley was convicted for terrorist offences. In 2012 the conviction was overturned due to the prosecution not disclosing in the trial that a listening device was in the hayshed. To disclose such would have informed the IRA about secret methodologies. At the time these were the stuff of science fiction and difficult for terrorists to fathom. Such disclosure would have detracted from their future use.

Eavesdropping, telephone intercepts and listening devices in general were not deployed to an evidential standard. For those monitoring it was intelligence not evidence. The integrity of the product was not guaranteed, as a criminal court requires. They were treated as intelligence-gathering devices and not exhibits. In the same way surveillance operators and well-placed agents did not give evidence in court. If this were the case, there would be no intelligence. And if this type of recording is inadmissible in a criminal court (and many SB detectives were frustrated by this, having listened to IRA men boast about people they murdered), how could it be admissible to prosecute police?

Not all recordings contained intelligence, perhaps 10% to 30%. Most of the time it was background stuff, social chat of no intelligence value. Simply put, SB did not have the people, space or logistical knowhow to keep every recording securely. In any event they were not the property of SB, but MI5. These were products owned by national security. To produce the recording would have set a precedent.

The controversy in the Hayshed case centres on the recording having been destroyed, as this was now deemed material evidence by an investigator (Stalker). The inference from the destruction was that, to hide the fact that there was no need to open fire as both men were trying to surrender. This is a possibility. Yet so is destruction being standard practice in national security interests or the recording corroborated police statements that E4 SSU lawfully opened fire.

McCauley protested his innocence, saying he was out for a stroll and stumbled into a hayshed that just happened to have rifles in it. He knew nothing of them. The court did not believe him.

McCauley is currently on-the-run, convicted in 2004 for terrorist offences by a criminal court in Colombia (training FARC rebels in bomb making). He was caught and convicted along with IRA man James 'Mortar' Monaghan and Sinn Féin's representative in Cuba, Niall Connolly. Known as the 'Colombia 3' they had entered Colombia on false passports and had been in FARC controlled territory for over a month prior to their arrest. McCauley, as with the others, professed his innocence. The court did not believe them. Unable to live in his hometown because the UK has an extradition treaty with Colombia, he lives in the Republic. In the upcoming and long-delayed Hayshed inquest he was entrusted with a copy of the Stalker Report, which has not been made public, under the proviso it was not shared with anyone else.

As a consequence of the trials and three incidents two things happened. First, the deputy chief constable of Greater Manchester Constabulary, John Stalker, was appointed in 1984 to conduct an inquiry into SB practices. This overshadowed the second, the murders of Lord Justice Maurice Gibson (73) and his wife Cecily (67) by a large roadside bomb along the Newry border in 1987. It was the IRA's revenge. Gibson understood the practical and legal dilemma SB faced and ruled accordingly, Stalker did not. Stalker proved a controversial figure. In 1986 he was removed and suspended from duty over allegations of an inappropriate relationship with a leading criminal in Manchester, accusations later unproven. The chief constable of West Yorkshire Colin Sampson replaced him.

Stalker published a book promoting his version of events. He believed he had uncovered sinister practice and was removed from the inquiry on a false charge because of this. Hermon rubbished Stalker's claims, complaining that it was a scandal how Stalker abused his authority by leaking sensitive information to journalists. Stalker's behaviour fell below what Hermon believed constituted a proper police/press relationship. Journalist Peter Taylor supported Stalker's position. And it was Stalker's viewpoint Taylor popularised. Taylor is a superb writer and broadcaster. His coverage of the Troubles led to him being widely regarded as a 'security expert.' What he wrote and said carry great weight, with his words being repeated by other journalists and the media in general. The Stalker/Taylor viewpoint dominated. The press were on Stalker's side.

Stalker was examining SB at a time it was evolving and had recently taken over the lead for the entire security effort. It seems Stalker did not realise this or understand the fullness of the insurgent threat. Most controversy surrounded how SB presented a case in court. The introduction of TCG, E4A and E4 SSU alongside Divisional SB had complicated matters. Previously a single SB detective performed all these functions, knowing the source of the information and therefore what could be disclosed. For instance, the SB detective whom 'Darkie' Hughes spoke at Myrtlefield Park would have sailed through any cross-examination by a defence lawyer probing this area. But E4 SSU officers did not have the same knowledge. They were not as confident. They were unsure what to say. The new process was not as clear as it should have been. 'E' department was in its early days. This was the first time covert operations were really tested in court.

Most significantly, the E4 SSU officers had signed the Officials Secrets Act. But they were now asked questions the answers to which violated this. Not only were they committing a criminal offence under the Official Secrets Act. In their eyes they also faced being put out of 'E' department, having their DV revoked and dismissed from the police. But if they did not answer they would be found guilty of murder. This was the dilemma. They believed the Official Secrets Act took precedence over disclosing sensitive details in court. They knew that their answers would educate the IRA, who desperately wanted to know more.

Their concern about what they might say was that it would put an agent's life at risk, compromise a technical asset or secret technique. Essentially, the evolutionary flaws that increased the risk to agents through police who had not signed the Official Secrets Act, which SB rectified, were now 'de-rectified.' SB's fears were well founded. Almost 50 people were murdered by insurgents for 'collaborating' prior to the court cases in 1984, one every four months. Death because the IRA believed someone 'touted' having heard an E4 SSU officer's testimony was a real danger.

Following the trials and Stalker's inquiry speculation about the true identity of agents was rife in the media and books. Some categorically claim that Eric Dale was an agent in one of the incidents. Dale's family strongly refute this and point out that another person, subsequent to Dale being tortured and executed by insurgents, was also suspected thereby raising doubt of accusing Dale. Another theory publicised was that an agent was involved in one incident and remained in place for at least a year afterwards. Alive to this 'tout hunt' mentality in journalists that played into the hands of the IRA, SB felt compelled to fabricate a cover story for the E4 SSU officers.

To tell the truth on this issue, in SB's assessment, would put someone's life in jeopardy. For the defendants it was a no-win situation. They fabricated their statements. Although the approach dramatically unravelled in court, the judges were sympathetic to the officers' dilemma, having considered the overall context. Almost every commentator, however, interpreted events as covering up a 'shoot-to-kill policy' and 'dirty war' against the IRA. Sinn Féin was elated, raising hopes that it could dispense with SB as they did with previous security initiatives.

So, how valid is the 'shoot-to-kill' claim? An analysis of reactive deployments in the 34-months prior to the three incidents shows that approximately 96% of E4 SSU reactions resulted in arrests. Most involved perpetrators caught in the act of committing a serious terrorist crime. Suspects were routinely apprehended in possession of loaded weapons and/or live explosive devices in a variety of situations. This is the 'red-handed' approach Richards praised. The timing of the intervention secured the physical evidence necessary to prove guilt 'beyond reasonable doubt.' Allowing the crime to develop in this manner increased the sentencing threshold from approximately one to five years to 15-25 years as the offences were much more serious. The Provisionals were being pulverised.

The restraint shown in such scenarios was a point Hermon

highlighted in his 1982 annual report in the police response to disorder during the hunger strikes. A former SB officer with 23 years in E4 SSU typifies former officers' experiences:

> You are relying on people themselves, their own upbringing and respect for life - to do the right thing for people. In all those house entries if you saw someone who was no threat even though they were armed or making a bomb, you didn't shoot. It was only if you believed your life was in danger or that of someone else. I was usually the first in the door; if I had shot everyone I was legally justified in shooting I'd have killed plenty. Personal and family values certainly were important, as were the values of the RUC. You'd be ostracised if you did not comply. You could not be gung-ho. Selection got rid of the cowboys. It was very disciplined. I reckon less than 1% of the unit ever fired a shot in anger.

Selection and training had indoctrinated E4 SSU officers into an arrest-based culture. Arresting perpetrators 'red-handed' was the aim and the norm. This is what an effective criminalisation policy looks like, placing terrorists before the criminal courts and putting them in prison.

Section 3 (1) Criminal Law Act (Northern Ireland) 1967 covered the use of force. This was enshrined in RUC Code Section 34, which contained exhaustive detail about how the courts apply the law, circumstances for using firearms, warning before firing, firing without warning and warning shots when a verbal warning may not be heard. Section 34 was read out in every set of formal orders in E4 briefings. As one former E4 HMSU officer states: "We were not trained to kill and killing someone was the last thing anyone wanted. For a cop it's your worst nightmare." An SAS trooper says of his first encounter with US special forces in Iraq:

> We were at the back of the room in our first briefing. There was a small detachment of us [SAS] but it was mostly Americans [US Special Forces]. Anyway, the guy states the mission was to "kill or capture." We looked at each other thinking he'd got it

mixed up, as you know, anything we ever did in the province the mission was to capture. If you had to kill it was because they'd forced your hand. You know, they'd brought it on themselves. I put my hand up to clarify the mission and he confirmed that it was kill or capture.

The individual circumstances and the actions of terrorist suspects dictated how the SAS responded in Northern Ireland. Former SAS officer Tim Collins confirms this. Shootings were lawful because suspects were shot having posed an immediate threat to life. Aimed shots were designed to stop the threat, not to kill. Once the threat no longer existed the shooting stopped. E4 SSU and the SAS, as with all police and Army, were trained to aim at the upper body. Every other Army and law enforcement agency in the west did the same. This is the largest part of the body that contains most vital organs. Hits in this area usually stop the threat. They also are usually fatal. And as the SAS and E4 SSU trained endlessly on the ranges they were much quicker and more accurate than the rest of the security forces. When it came to a shoot-out the IRA was up against the world's best. These were the 'big boys.' They didn't have their own rules. But to many it appeared they did. This was because they didn't take a step back. There was no hesitancy. If you posed a threat you were in trouble.

In 1990 a small number of E4 were invited across to the US to brief the FBI on counter-terrorism tactics. By chance there was a SWAT competition involving several federal agencies, state police and sheriff's office. The E4 guys were invited to take part in some exercises. One of them explains:

We did rope repelling out of Blackhawk choppers. We'd never done it before so the Americans gave us a crash course. They were brilliant at it. Very slick. We did well but would have needed a lot more training to reach their standard. They then invited us onto the range.

The FBI went first. You'd an MP5 [Heckler and Koch 9mm sub-

machine gun]. It has single shot and fully automatic functions. It was a distance of 25-yards or so. Not far. The targets showed for a brief second then turned. The FBI guy was very good. He hit every target. He got off one shot each time, around a 5-inch grouping in the upper chest. Our guy got two rounds off each time. The grouping was half an inch. For most the second round pinched the hole made by the first. Quick double-taps. They were all in the centre of the chest. The Americans couldn't believe the speed and accuracy. You could see them nudging each other and calling others over to watch.

For us it was nothing extraordinary. It's what we did. You had to be at this level for the people we were up against. Normally it was a lot more dynamic. We'd put in a run before it so your breathing was heavy. And we'd have it as fire and movement, a combat shoot. We'd also have targets pop up that are not a threat. From the obvious one of a woman pushing a pram to a guy wearing a mask and his hands clearly empty. It forced you to actually look over the sights with both eyes at what you are about to engage. Make the right decision in double-quick time. It's a split second thing. Hesitate and you're dead. It's all about making good decisions quickly. Nobody was biting at the bit to pull the trigger. But if it came to it we weren't afraid to.

In Iraq, at least 70% of covert operations ended in insurgents being killed. The same applies to Afghanistan. This is what a 'shoot-to-kill' policy looks like. If there was a 'shoot-to-kill' policy why is Martin McCauley alive? And why was SB so bad at it when it excelled everywhere else? Every policy and guideline, the Whole of Government strategy, training material, personal accounts of former officers, SB's ethos and factual outcomes show that there was no such policy. Claims of a 'shoot-to-kill' policy are utter garbage. What the three incidents all boil down to is the call the officers made at the time. In two criminal trials the Judges declared these lawful.

What then of Stalker's accusations? Addressing these in detail is a 1987 report by Her Majesty's Inspectorate of Constabulary (HMIC). This followed a recommendation by Colin Sampson that HMIC should examine Stalker's recommendations to fully determine their validity. It was an in-depth inspection of SB. The HMI (Her Majesty's Inspector) appointed was former Chief Constable Charles McLachlan, described as someone who "could not tolerate injustice." From McLachlan's examination it appears that Stalker's public criticism was a sanitised version of his report. The HMI invalidates many of Stalker's recommendations and highlights three main areas of concern. First, Stalker's adoption of a theoretical view was questionable:

It is unfortunate that in the harsh reality of policing a community sorely besieged by ruthless political terrorism, Mr Stalker's recommendations may not always be practicable.

HMI described Stalker as having a "rather detached viewpoint" of intelligence. HMI observed that Stalker had treated Northern Ireland as if he was policing Manchester, although Stalker seems oblivious to having done so.

Second, HMI realised that Stalker had raised major concerns about CID's subordinate role to SB. Stalker did not appear to understand why this was. HMI did, listing witness testimony, confessions, supergrasses, surveillance, and sources in identifying that only the last two remained. Both of which were under the purview of SB. McLachlan warned against forcing these also into a situation where they could no longer be used or become limited in worth. He concluded that without them, terrorist organisations would be far stronger.

For someone with Stalker's background, a dominant SB made no sense. He interpreted this as a "force within a force." A catchphrase regularly rolled out thereafter, particularly by critics of SB. HMI feared that Stalker's recommendations posed a significant threat to public safety if implemented. Which is perhaps what Sampson also recognised and why he wanted HMIC involved.

Third and last, HMI was conversant with how secret

intelligence systems presented legal cases. He noted the process was the same as that used in Scotland, describing it as, "the imposition of an artificial evidential commencement in relation to terrorist incidents." HMI endorsed the process, as it protected the source of the intelligence but said that using a "cover story" was wrong, albeit he appreciated the dilemma SB had faced in this regard. HMI noted the 'cover story' aspect was quickly discontinued after the third incident in 1982. HMI was also conscious that quite often the issue of intelligence was raised in open court:

Not necessarily in an effort to obtain an acquittal of the accused but in order to establish whether or not intelligence had been passed. It is not necessary for PIRA to obtain information about the 'identity' of the informant but merely to ascertain whether or not information has been given.

Former SB officers regularly refer to this as a 'fishing expedition' by defence counsel that became the normal legal ploy. This still happens today. In bringing Islamist extremists to court covert operations are made more difficult by the extremist organisations having learned more about covert practices and as a consequence taking evasive measures in future attacks. HMI appreciated that this consideration had to be factored into any proposed use of intelligence involving a covert response, thus reducing the opportunities to initiate a response. HMI also observed that cases were sometimes withdrawn and terrorists escaped prosecution because a source would have been compromised if the case proceeded.

HMI reports that the very presence of SB officers giving evidence in court proceedings was sufficient to trigger an internal security inquiry by the IRA. He recognised that sources, particularly agents, were the intelligence community's most productive asset in countering terrorism and had saved countless lives. HMI, however, was also aware that terrorist organisations went to extraordinary lengths to uncover agents thereby demonstrating the value of such intelligence.

Of the legal aspect, HMI noted that restrictions placed on the RUC for statements of admission during interrogation were greater than in England and Wales. This corroborates the RUC's observation a decade earlier in responding to the Bennett Report (1979). HMI was persuaded that the courts and Northern Ireland's unique legal system afforded less protection for intelligence-led operations than in the rest of the UK. It is a weakness he identifies the IRA and Sinn Féin took full advantage of. HMI viewed this weakness as a high priority problem that Stalker did not deal with.

In the same vein, HMI points out the Scottish legal system allowed for well-placed agents in a much kinder regime for the police. Specific to Home Office 'informer' guidelines (updated in 1977) HMI identified that SB had been badly exposed by Government through national guidelines that were unfit for purpose. Stalker recognised this also but sidestepped it in adopting a generalised idealistic view that had no practical application, according to HMI. McLachlan recommended the Government urgently draft new guidelines for Northern Ireland. He also shows that some other UK forces, like Strathclyde, found them unsuited for organised crime. Regarding the sharing of intelligence HMI was confident that all SB intelligence was shared with CID at senior level:

> On examining a selection of intelligence reports for the month of July 1987, submitted by Uniform CID and Special Branch, it was obvious that the Special Branch contribution was superior as regards general quality, and also provision of information for the CID, about persons responsible for murders and other serious crimes throughout the three regions. These reports are marked "SECRET" and are circulated on a daily basis to the senior officers at Headquarters. As a result all senior management is appraised of current events and intelligence as recommended by the HMI's Report of 1981.

Because Stalker viewed Northern Ireland through a 'normal' policing lens he did not grasp why CID was reliant on SB, the unique systems between the two and why these differed from the rest of the UK. This was unfamiliar territory for the Manchester policeman. He was probably unaware of a succession of reports from Cunningham to Richards and does not come across as appreciating why SB was in the lead or the practical difficulties of the environment. This has led him to draw negative conclusions that the HMIC rated as exposing the public to greater harm if acted on. McLachlan took exception to Stalker using peacetime standards to examine an armed conflict, which he considered "misleading."

Arrests in covert operations were always the aim, but not always possible. Shooting suspected terrorists was the exception. Notwithstanding the woeful communication strategy of the police it was not difficult to establish this. Sadly, few did. Regardless of cheap headlines and sensationalist storylines 'E' department was going nowhere. For the first time there was significant continuity in the security effort. This is what resilience is - withstanding the knocks and keep going forward. One positive from Stalker, the IRA now knew SB had a hard edge and was not afraid to use it.

Local police were better informed about the threat they faced than anyone in a similar position before or since.

Chapter 15
Clever Cops

The Forbes and Fanning Report in 1986, two senior police officers each side of the border, looked at cross-border intelligence co-operation. It shows SB had 640 officers (5% of the force). This is half of what some experts recommend for an intelligence department. Even at its height SB was small. What made it appear bigger was its smart structure and procedures. It punched away above its weight because it was so well connected to the rest of the body. The whole security organisation was hitting the IRA, not just Special Branch. Although punches by SB's executive arm that put the IRA on the canvass got the headlines, it was the constant and unspectacular daily jabs of the uniform frontline that gave it the edge. At the same time the state was making few mistakes. The defensive guard was up. There was no way through for insurgents to land a blow similar to what had floored previous opponents.

Divisional SB supported by the processing element at headquarters harnessed the entire security apparatus by guiding local police and soldiers on suspects, terrorist methodologies and threats. This was critical to pointing the security forces in the right direction in their everyday duties, protecting them and in turn the public. Local police were better informed about the threat they faced than anyone in a similar position before or since. Guidance of this nature accounted for around 85% of all terrorists charged. One retired officer provides an example:

> We had two cars on patrol just outside Dungannon when we got the report of a fatal shooting of a part-timer. The Branch had briefed us months before that the Provos used minor roads. They [SB] also had us briefed on who and what vehicles to look out for. They kept drilling this into us. Because of this we approached from a really weird direction. As a result we flushed the entire gun team out. Four were caught and the weapons recovered. They all got long sentences, including ____, who was the OC of Dungannon.

A part-time member of the security forces was the victim. The gunman was a young upcoming Provo bursting for action. This was his first taste. He worked alongside his victim. Not only was he the shooter, he also provided the target and intelligence on the target. Seen as a model employee, he took time off work that day to meet his ASU. Wearing a mask he returned with a Kalashnikov assault rifle to pump bullets into his defenceless co-worker at close range as another Provo with a Kalashnikov gave cover. And, as one former SB officer says, "He was calm. No panic, no rushing." As a cold-blooded killer he was a natural.

Both police cars were packed with five officers each. This was highly unusual. The drivers had collected a foot patrol of eight due to low cloud cover cancelling their helicopter pick-up. The patrol had been in the 'high country' of Cappagh and Galbally, an insurgent stronghold where police vehicles seldom ventured. But in this instance the risk was manageable, especially as the drivers knew lanes not even on the map. It was not brash but calculated. They drove unmarked police cars. The drivers wore civilian jackets to hide the police uniform. Once they had cleared the station they hung Tyrone GAA paraphernalia on the rear-view mirror. It was a small but important detail, saying to the casual republican onlooker, 'I'm one of you.' Their efforts to blend in were favoured by fine rain and fading light.

The foot patrol had been in the remotest part of the area, keeping out of sight in following the riverbed, hedgerows and avoiding being highlighted on the skyline. In eight hours it did several snap vehicle check points, stopping only a handful of vehicles, none of whom were the usual suspects or their associates. The patrol made its way over fields to the rendezvous point, a quiet road on the periphery of the 'high country.' During pick-up they received the shooting report.

Initial details were sketchy but they reckoned it was the IRA. And they were in IRA country. The killers would be heading their way, looking to get back to any number of safe houses. This was the opposite direction to where the police response should come from - two main police bases in Dungannon. It was the last thing the IRA team would have expected. But there were quite a few country roads to choose from. They took to the less used minor roads and put on the sirens. This was another highly unusual move, as the police normally responded to such incidents without drawing attention to themselves. The risk being, the original attack was to lure police into an ambush.

Less than 10 miles away the sirens spooked the killers. The two cars dropped men off at key spots en route to the scene. The sergeant in charge was extremely competent, an intelligent, unassuming man who led from the front. He was highly respected by his men and senior officers. He gave clear instructions to the control room in Dungannon over the radio about where to send police and army reinforcements. The killers were trapped and quickly caught. It was innovative thinking and actions, and nothing that could be found in policy or guidelines.

Good police work like this by uniform officers meant that forensic evidence was recovered at crime scenes connecting suspects to crimes. No statement from a member of the public was required. The police were self-sufficient. The public had been taken out of the equation. Highly motivated frontline police were quietly breaking the IRA, smaller insurgent networks and loyalist terrorist organisations. On a large scale intelligence was directed in a non-specific way to potential evidence-gathering opportunities. From regular intelligence briefings the professionalism of local police did the rest. Without this SB's executive arm would have been limited. As it was, a strong platform was built, upon which SB's intelligence attack excelled.

Following the 1982 incidents E4 SSU was renamed E4 HMSU (referred to as E4B for administrative purposes). The re-labelling snapped an obvious link with Stalker and also better disguised it being part of SB, a fact mischievously assisted by the HMSU acronym already in use. The existing HMSU was a normal Mobile Support Unit under HQ (uniform) control. There were five. They supplemented DMSUs when needed, such as large public order events, or searches following a terrorist incident. The press and most authors often mistook this HMSU for E4 HMSU. The two, however, are completely different.

The established strength for an E4 HMSU was 21, with a double-sized unit in Belfast and single units in South Region and North Region - 84 operational officers in total. An E4A team was of similar size. There were six E4A teams in total (126 operational officers). Not until 1986 was 'E' department's executive arm complete in all three Regions. E4 personnel were skilled in emergency medical procedures, firearms, driving and map reading. E4A were especially skilled map-readers. On their own and on the move they needed to be accurate about where they and the target were. A wrong grid reference, road name or direction of travel and the target was lost.

E4 HMSU had a force-wide remit for hostage sieges and the close protection of high risk VIPs. If the Prime Minister or member of the Royal family visited Northern Ireland, E4 HMSU provided the close protection and roof-top snipers.

A strict selection and training regime catered for constables, sergeants and inspectors. Ranks above these involved an interview to transfer across. A small number who went through selection attained high rank in SB, which provided a healthy degree of practical covert experience as part of a diverse and broad base of operational knowledge at command level. Despite the arduous entry regime, resulting in a 95% failure rate, the application process was very popular. There was no shortage of people looking to get into 'E' department.

E4A operators were usually unaccompanied in a car, replicating best practice pioneered by the Det. This was called 'one up.' The reasoning was that someone driving alone attracted less attention, particularly true of women of whom each team had at least one. Of one, a former officer recalls:

She was fearless and brilliant. Anytime we needed a risky 'walk-past' she was first to volunteer. The stuff she got away with was amazing. And to be honest, only a female could have pulled it off.

As the IRA hated Special Branch with demonic passion, 'one up' carried great risk. Alternatively E4 HMSU operated in 'crews,' usually three in 'ghost' cars (unmarked, high powered cars not immediately identifiable as police). The boot would be packed with each officer's operational holdall. A 'crew bag' was also in the boot. They had everything to cater for various tactical situations, such as a sledgehammer and stun grenades for a rapid house entry, to the vitals for a long stay, such as sleeping bags, extra clothes, playing cards and PT kit. They were kitted out for most scenarios (day and night), working on the assumption that, when they left base, they might not be back for a time.

A 'job' could take them all over the province for as long as four to five days before being relieved. E4 personnel talked about 'jobs' as opposed to 'ops.' In casual conversation or over an open phone line 'job' carries no connotations of clandestine activity. Food was grabbed wherever possible, usually in a police canteen or fast food restaurant in a pro-police area. Similarly, sleep was grabbed wherever possible, usually in the car and when the target went static for a long period. If held up at a police station, the gym was used one at a time. The police radio and all the kit they had taken off were in grab bags beside them. If called they would be back in the car in one to two minutes and dressed on the hoof. E4's communications were secure and could not be accessed by local police. However, they had local police radios and could communicate with them if needed.

If it looked as if crews would be held up for a time on a proactive job, the crew commander would get TCG to have Divisional SB arrange a bunk room. For the vast majority of time it was a waiting game. Great patience was needed. Most pro-active jobs fizzled out into nothing that involved a reaction, perhaps as much as 75% of them. Sometimes the IRA unit could lose interest, another planned attack could take place, or they considered it too difficult. In such situations, especially those involving munitions, other tactics were used to lessen the risk. For example, recovering the munitions in planned searches by local police or doctoring weapons so they do not work. Some jobs could also drag on for months. Often when they did it was a sign they could also fizzle out. But the situation could change in a heartbeat. It was a rollercoaster of emotions, with far more downs than ups.

When a strike looked probable E4 HMSU had contingencies for every predictable outcome but also knew to expect the unexpected and never assume anything. Thinking and re-thinking contingencies and factoring in time to prepare and plan were constants. Ideally, specialist tactical teams need time to plan and prepare. Agent handlers and TCG were conscious of this. However, from a standing start, E4 HMSU could plan reaction options on the move. From sitting in the house and being called into work on a 'fast ball,' three crews could be on the road within 45 minutes. They would be briefed on the job by TCG as they went towards it and formulate options by the time they got there. Everyone loved the 'fast balls' because they usually resulted in a reaction. And nearly all E4 personnel lived 10 to 15 minutes drive from the Regional HQ. They could be at the outer margins of their region in less than one hour.

There were no women in E4 HMSU. Those who applied could not cope with the physical nature of the assessment and most struggled to attain the necessary competencies with the Smith and Wesson and Heckler and Koch weapons unique to E4. If a surveillance operator was down injured it was E4 HMSU who would physically extract him from the 'kill zone.' Each officer had to be capable of dragging a casualty with one hand, or carrying the casualty over a shoulder, while holding a rifle in the other hand and being able to fire it.

On numerous occasions E4 HMSU were used to stop a gun team or car bomb en-route to target or rapidly enter a house containing armed terrorists. They were routinely placed in perilous positions. SB personnel received 25 gallantry awards from 1977-1987. At least three received a bar to their QGM, which was exceptional. In these and also in awards for leadership and organisational effectiveness (15), SB outstripped (pro-rata) the rest of the force. It is undoubtedly the most decorated area of policing during the Troubles. Former officers, however, regret that too few were recognised, especially at the lower operational ranks in all three specialisms. They claim that what would have attracted an award in the Army or in the rest of the force was treated as routine in SB. Lesser actions against lesser threats in a UK mainland police force attracted gallantry awards.

SB's selection and training regime, learning organisation mentality, along with the intellectual and financial investment ploughed into it by MI5 and British special forces made it the most professional part of the police. This is a crucial point. Petraeus promotes values - organisational and personal – as the most important part of an organisation. He believes that while models, concepts and systems are important; it is all about people. Without the right people everything else is incidental. SB went to extraordinary lengths to ensure it had the right people.

A former SB detective typifies the experiences of most of his colleagues:

Respecting people's rights and as a person yourself you were taught from the background that most of us came from to respect other people's human rights, ... as a police officer ... you were taught to always respect people's human rights, it was there as a natural ingrained order, your supervisory people made sure that you did.

He was clear the main role of the police was to protect life, regardless of race, colour or religion. Several weeks after saying these words in 2010 the Taliban killed him and two young US marines in the same incident. He left behind a wife and young family who deeply miss him. He lived and died by his values. The US nominated him for a Silver Star (exceptionally rare for a non-US citizen) and the British awarded him a posthumous Queen's Gallantry Medal in 2012. His selfless act and that of both marines saved at least 18 lives. A US Blackhawk helicopter bulging with troops was being refuelled, a sitting duck for a Taliban unit armed with heavy weaponry only yards away. It would have been a catastrophic loss of life had he not fired at the Taliban and alerted nearby marines to the attack.

A doctor with extensive experience of treating Northern Ireland police officers for psychological trauma states:

Of all the police I have seen for stress-related conditions from the Troubles Special Branch officers have the highest ethical and moral standards.

E4 HMSU's main function was to QRF surveillance, responding within minutes to a hard compromise (a crowd gathering around a surveillance operator or suspects attacking them) or intercepting the target (such as a car bomb) if directed. The latter entailed two options. First, a 'hard stop.' Ideally, two cars suddenly appear in front of the target car forcing it to stop sharply. Another at the rear, which also suddenly appears, cuts off the escape. It left the suspects in no doubt it was a covert operation. Second, a 'casual stop,' designed to look like normal police. This was for less dangerous situations, such as someone transporting weapons or explosives not for an immediate attack. Examples of both options are listed below. A former E4 HMSU officer states:

We'd been working on this unit for months. At times we thought the strike would go in but there was always a problem with it being too close to the source. Finally everything came together. There was enough distance and steps from the source to make it happen. It was a gun team.

The terrorists were looking a certain type of vehicle to steal from a specific car park. They'd bring it to a location we weren't aware of. So we got the type of vehicle they wanted and set it in the car park. It had state of the art tracking. But oh no, that would be too easy. They didn't take it. They stole another one that didn't match what they originally wanted. At the last minute they'd changed their mind. So E4A had their work cut out. No electronic wizardry just the good old Mark 1 eyeball. The basics.

The guy driving was hyper about being followed. One minute he's sitting at 110mph on a small back road, the next he's doing 20mph on a main road. He doubled back and stopped a few times. But he didn't shake off the team and he led us to the staging area. We had to hold it. This meant an operator being dropped off to get somewhere to watch. It was in a hedgerow overlooking the premises. For us in the car it wasn't so bad, but it was absolutely freezing outside, strong winds, rain and sleet. It was a typical Irish winter. Within minutes he was soaked through. With the wind-chill it was easily minus 10 or 15 [degrees Celsius]. He'd only a light coat, woolly hat and gloves in a small rucksack. The kit we had then wasn't great.

He'd to be treated for hyperthermia by our medics once we got him off the ground. Around two to three hours later the vehicle appeared between two others. It now had a different set of plates. We'd placed two crews on several roads leading away from the premises.

Surveillance gave us a stand-by. Next thing the target vehicle is on one of the roads with a scout car about half a mile in front and a pick-up car the same distance behind. The crews were well hid. We let the front car go past and then jumped on the target vehicle. Which meant the pick-up car would also get away. But missing these two was no issue. Anytime we did manage to stop all three, there was never anything incriminating on the fronting or pick-up drivers. They always walked.

On seeing us the driver slammed on the brakes and hit reverse, only to see the other crew up his arse. By the time he looked back toward us he and his two passengers were staring down two rifle barrels and being shouted at, "Hands in the air, hands in the air, show me your hands, show me your hands." The priority is to see hands. You keep barking these instructions non-stop and pointing the rifle. Subdue them with controlled aggression. We were feet from the windscreen and the two from the other crew were now at the side. It was the perfect 'L' shape. If we did open up we weren't shooting each other. We'd one up the spout [round in the chamber], which was our normal operational load, the safety was off and fingers were on the trigger. It only takes the slightest squeeze and the first bullet's away. The adrenalin is pumping hard, a real rush, but you've got to control it. Don't get carried away by the moment. Let the training kick in. Trust your training.

The front seat passenger had difficulty getting his hands free from a rifle on his lap. He could easily have been shot. The driver's door was locked. So the window went in and the driver dragged out through it. You can't ask him to open it because this would bring his hands down. The other doors were unlocked. They were opened and both suspects dragged out. The rifle on another suspect's lap fell out beside him. It was loaded. Within seconds the three were down flat, faces in the tarmac and grateful to still be alive. Another loaded rifle was on the back seat. Whoever they were going to hit, it wasn't far away.

They were read their rights, replies noted (which were nil) arrested, searched, bagged and cuffed and taken to the Holding Centre for CID to interview. A scene log was started and the scene handed over to local police and CID.

In a casual stop, another former E4 HMSU officers states:

We'd changed our weapons and vehicles, as you had to. You know, wore the Ruger as the sidearm, had Rugger rifles, old Sterling SMGs and the type of radio normal police carried. Our 59s [Smith and Wesson 9mm pistol] and H&Ks [Heckler and Koch MP5 sub-machine guns and Mark 33 rifles] stood out like a sore thumb. We were the only ones who had them. So straight away people knew you were different. We had two armoured land rovers. So there was nothing to give us away.

We'd been working with the Det and they threw up a suspect who had placed a bag in the boot of his car. An operator just thought it looked suspicious. Nothing more than that, we'd no idea what was in the bag. It was a free run and we'd plenty of time to plan. There were no source protection issues. TCG directed us to do a casual stop. We set up a VCP [Vehicle Check Point] on a stretch of road he couldn't turn off. We started to stop vehicles in front of him. For all intents and purposes it looked like local police. An operator was four or five cars behind and we'd crews on side roads. So he was going nowhere.

When he got to Big Jimmy, he handed over his licence. Jimmy was very polite, asked where he was going and started to chat about the car he was driving. Jimmy said he had one similar. So fuel consumption was talked about, how quick it was, cost of insurance and resale value. Big Jimmy cracked a few jokes and the guy nervously laughed. It was all very casual. The guy obviously thought he was on a winner. But this was Big Jimmy. He took the piss out of us the same way. He then went to hand the licence back, but stopped just before it got into the guy's outstretched hand. Then Jimmy says, "Can I get a quick look in the boot please? Sorry for the hassle. Thanks."

The guy opens the boot and there's the bag, a large holdall. Jimmy takes no interest and asks, "Are you pleased with the boot size. Personally, I find it too small. The wife complains about trying to get the pram in. But you know what women are like." You could see the guy is by now a nervous wreck. This has lasted five minutes. But he's still thinking he's got away with it, that this big cop is a half-wit. Then, in between talking about the pram, Jimmy asks, "What's in the bag big lad? Could you open it please?" The guy crumbles. There were several weapons and ammunition in the bag.

The idea behind the casual stop was that the terrorist organisation was fooled into believing they were unlucky, caught by local police at a random checkpoint. As time went on, especially at the court months later, it became clear this was not the case. By that time though, it was too late. The passage of time made it harder for the terrorists to identify the cause, which was particularly beneficial for surveillance.

E4A and the Det simply did not stand out. They were featureless non-descript individuals in featureless non-descript cars. Every sinew of their being was about blending in. They did not need to break cover; E4 HMSU did that for them. This is what E4A, Det and E4 HMSU did.

Because E4 HMSU wore uniform, crews had to balance being close enough to support surveillance operators and far enough away not to be seen. If they were too close they could blow the operation. Too far away they would not get to where they needed to be in time. A TCG operation on proactive intelligence could at any point involve a 'strike' that meant stopping a car bomb/ gun team, or a 'rapid house entry.' It was a dynamic operational environment. Its versatility was the main reason the SAS was not tasked in Belfast from the late 80s onwards. In the words of one former TCG officer:

The troop [SAS] could not match the mobility or range of options offered by the HMSU. They just could not handle the city the same way. The HMSU knew the place inside out.

E4 HMSU was not designed to mimic the UK's elite regiment. Neither did it copy any other police unit. It was unique. The harmony between surveillance and armed response meant that Det operators were less inclined to react themselves thereby softening their old aggressive surveillance habits. Very rarely did E4A or the Det deploy without E4 HMSU back-up. The relationship was based on trust born from knowing each other's capabilities through actual experiences. Regardless of covert control, however, it was the prerogative of surveillance operators and specialist armed response teams (police and military) to respond to unfolding events if they believed life was immediately at risk.

'E' department reaching its heights roughly coincided with 1985's Anglo-Irish Agreement. Although this brought no significant improvement on cross-border security (if anything, security deteriorated) it was important political progress. The Agreement shows that Prime Minister Thatcher, above all else, was a pragmatist. Much to her consternation, however, and also that of Northern Ireland Secretary of State Tom King, the Republic's approach to security remained limp. The Provisionals murdering police and soldiers was not a significant concern for nationalists.

Compensating for nationalist apathy was intelligence-led policing, especially SB's executive arm where covert operations surprised terrorist units. E4 HMSU successes from 1980-98 resulted in approximately: 1,500 arrests, 1,000 weapons and 50 tons of explosives recovered. The arrests were approximately 15% of the annual total. In the same period eight terrorist suspects were shot dead by E4. This means that 99.5% of all suspects in a TCG operation with E4 as the primary responder were arrested. Sixty nine per cent of E4 arrests were against republicans, 30% loyalists and 1% ordinary crime. Republicans were responsible for approximately 60% of all deaths, loyalists 30%, and the IRA committed most terrorist attacks and nearly all against the security forces. When factoring in divisional arrests the split was 60/40 (republican/loyalist). The security effort was disproportionately focused on loyalists.

As designed, the approach kept surveillance teams out of court, important when considering the time and cost to train a surveillance operator against the likelihood of exposing their physical appearance in court proceedings that would have taken them out of a frontline role. It also protected sensitive methodologies, sources of intelligence and maintained the optimum operational capacity of the executive arm. This is not to suggest everything was perfect. A former Head of SB explains why there were problems with the way headquarters was organised:

We had all our best people out on the ground. Our tactics were good, as was our long war of attrition. But by using our best people in the frontline we overlooked the importance of getting good people to do the paperwork at HQ and the Regional HQs. The people we had writing policy and doing the record-keeping bit were not our best people. … Our use of analysis was poor and the officers we picked to head the strategic analysis had no Divisional SB experience but were all E4 people. They did their best but they didn't think like a traditional Branch man and became yet another tactical unit. Our priority was always tactical, dealing with the immediate and short-term, but nobody saw it that way at the time. We had no room to deal with anything else. That's the reality of it.

Although some attacks did happen, SB was preventing 85% of bombs going off in places like London and denying the IRA what they regarded as their ace card in a finale of violence. Central to this was keeping tabs on a duplicitous IRA leadership who, on one hand were talking peace and on the other planning terrorism. Bombs in London where a bargaining ploy designed to intimidate a new British Prime Minister.

IRA 'volunteers' were increasingly witnessing the surprise, restraint and cleverness of their opponent. Against such speed, discipline, accuracy and courage they had no chance, and they knew it. These were regular occurrences. Anything from 20 to 40 seasoned IRA men were freshly put in prison each year by covert operations. They had plenty of time to talk and embellish, as did their fellow inmates on the loyalist wing. Over a decade of accumulative storytelling the SB 'omnipotent' myth spread like a cancer throughout the republican movement.

Having an executive arm this good was a huge confidence boost for the security forces, wider public and government, much in the same way it had the opposite impact on the IRA/Sinn Féin and their active supporters. Such was the progress of SB's executive arm that in the few years before the first ceasefire in 1994 arrests by E4 HMSU almost matched those of the rest of the force. The fact 99.5% of covert operations confronting armed and dangerous terrorists resulted in arrests is remarkable. When adding the SAS it is 96%. Only the SAS had the expertise and firepower to counter the most vicious IRA units. Their E4 HMSU protégé had outgrown them in nearly all aspects. But in a situation liable to involve brute force, the SAS were the world's best. In these instances E4 HMSU supported the SAS.

Whether sitting in a bar in Dundalk, Londonderry, Newry or Belfast, IRA 'volunteers' believed that in 12-months time they would end up behind bars or dead. And it was imprisonment, by far, that was the more likely. Nearly all the prolific killers in cross-border brigades perished at the hands of the SAS. The border was still porous and the Republic still a safe haven. But these IRA units had to come north to murder. When they did Special Branch would know and the SAS would be waiting.

How do you arrest a terrorist pointing a gun at you who doesn't want arrested?

Chapter 16

Deadly Covert Ops

What follows is a chronological list of all covert operations involving E4, the Det and SAS that resulted in one or more fatality from 1974 to 1992. Prior to this the Army, who were in charge of security from 1969 to 1976, struggled to come to terms with what was required in a covert context to tackle the IRA. Innovative IRA tactics had taken the Army and police by surprise and it took time to figure out what an effective covert response entailed. A concept the Army came up with was the Military Reaction Force (MRF).

The MRF was confined to Belfast in a period that endured the most intense levels of violence. One terrorist incident took place every 40 minutes in 1972. It was chaotic and dangerous. The MRF shot dead 10 unarmed civilians in Belfast in 1972 and is not noted for any security success against active terrorists. For those living in republican areas and the IRA it demonstrated the speculative nature of covert operations. The MRF initiative proved counter-productive and was quickly done away with.

Other examples of fatalities in a covert operation at this early stage are SB detective inspector Cecil Patterson (45) and constable

Robert Buckley (30) of the Special Patrol Group murdered by the IRA in Belfast in 1971 and Royal Engineer Edward Stuart (20) described as an undercover soldier murdered by the IRA in Belfast in 1972. At least 13 people were killed between December 1969 when the Troubles started and early 1974 when covert practices through the Det started to take a shape and structure better suited to the environment and threat.

As a SAS soldier says: "How do you arrest a terrorist pointing a gun at you who doesn't want arrested?" In many respects the following list reflects this reality. The list excludes those whom the IRA wrongly perceived as having been engaged in covert operations, such as the murders of sergeant Eric Brown (41) and constable Brian Quinn (23) by the IRA in Rostrevor in 1983 and the particularly brutal IRA murders of corporals Derek Wood and David Howes in Belfast in 1988. Another is SB detective Norman Prue (29) and Army sergeant Robert Maughan (30). They were shot dead by the IRA in Lisnaskea while buying a republican newspaper outside the Catholic Church during Sunday mass. It was a routine the IRA caught onto.

Derry city, 14 April 1974. Det operator **Anthony Pollen (27)** was surrounded by a crowd while taking pictures of a republican march. Derry city IRA shot him dead.

Forkhill, County Armagh, 15 April 1976. One insurgent (South Armagh IRA), **Peter Cleary (25)**, was shot dead by the SAS during a routine arrest operation. Cleary was unarmed. Although not a covert operation it is included because the SAS normally engaged in high-risk covert operations.

Drumuckavall, County Armagh, 16 January 1977. One insurgent (South Armagh IRA), **Seamus Harvey (20),** was shot dead by the SAS during a short gun battle. A shotgun was recovered beside his body.

Silverbridge, County Armagh, 14 May 1977. **Robert Nairac (29)** was a soldier kidnapped, tortured and secretly buried by South Armagh IRA. He is commonly reported as a member of the SAS, and appears to have been conducting 'undercover' work in south Armagh when abducted.

Derry city, 12 December 1977. One insurgent (INLA), **Colm McNutt (18)** was shot dead when, with another assailant, he tried to hi-jack at gunpoint the car a Det operator was driving. McNutt was an INLA leader.

West Belfast, 14 December 1977. Belfast City IRA attacked and shot dead a sole Det operator, **Paul Harman (27)**, stopped in his vehicle at a road junction. His car was set on fire and his firearm taken.

Coalisland, County Tyrone, 26 February 1978. One insurgent, **Paul Duffy (23)** from East Tyrone/Monaghan IRA, was shot dead by the SAS while moving explosives.

Derry city, 10 June 1978. One armed insurgent from Derry city IRA, **Denis Heaney (21)**, was shot dead by the Det while, along with another assailant, trying to hi-jack the car a Det operator was driving. A weapon was recovered at the scene.

North Belfast, 21 June 1978. Three insurgents from Belfast IRA, **Denis Brown (28), Jackie Mailey (31)** and **James Mulvenna (28)** were shot dead by the SAS while attempting to plant incendiary bombs. One innocent Protestant civilian, **William Hanna (27)** was also killed.

Dunloy, 11 July 1978. **John Boyle (16)** was an innocent Catholic civilian shot dead by the SAS while they were watching a weapons hide in which a rifle linked to several murders was recovered. Corporal Alan Bohan and Trooper Ron Temperley were acquitted of murder in a subsequent trial.

Derry city, 11 August 1978. Insurgents from Derry city IRA shot dead Det operator, **Alan Swift (25)**, with automatic rifles. Swift was sitting in a parked car.

Coagh, County Tyrone, 30 September 1978. **James Taylor (23)** was an innocent Protestant civilian shot dead by undercover Army while on a duck shooting expedition.

Derry city, 24 November 1978. One insurgent from Derry city IRA, **Patrick Duffy (50)**, was shot dead by the SAS in an operation that recovered several weapons and bomb making equipment.

North Belfast, 2 May 1980. One SAS soldier, **Herbert Westmacott (28)**, was shot dead with an M60 used by insurgents from Belfast city IRA. The SAS Captain was leading an eight-man team in a reactive operation. The insurgent unit involved surrendered having been boxed in by the SAS. They were arrested and convicted of terrorist offences.

Derry city, 28 May 1981. Two armed insurgents from Derry city IRA, **Charles Maguire (21)** and **George McBrearty (23)**, were shot dead in a short gun battle in attempting to ambush Det personnel. A third assailant was wounded. He was arrested and convicted of terrorist offences, receiving five years imprisonment. Two automatic rifles were recovered at the scene.

Lurgan, County Armagh, 11 November 1982. Three unarmed insurgents from North Armagh IRA, **Sean Burns (21), Eugene Toman (21)** and **Gervaise McKerr (31)**, were shot dead by E4 SSU. At a subsequent trial three E4 SSU officers were acquitted of murder.

Lurgan, County Armagh, 24 November 1982. One suspected insurgent, **Michael Tighe (17)** North Armagh IRA, was shot dead and another Martin McCauley arrested by E4 SSU while in possession of illegal firearms. McCauley was convicted of terrorist offences (the conviction was overturned in 2014). McCauley was also convicted of terrorist offences in Colombia in 2004 where he escaped from custody. He is currently on-the-run.

Armagh City, 12 December 1982. Two unarmed insurgents from the INLA, **Seamus Grew (30)** and **Roderick Carroll (21)**, were shot dead by E4 SSU. Constable John Robinson E4 SSU was acquitted of their murder at a subsequent trial.

Coshquin, County Londonderry, 2 February 1983. An insurgent from INLA, **Neil McMonagle (23)**, was shot dead while confronting a Det operator with another man.

Lurgan, County Armagh, 26 July 1983. **John O'Hare (25)** was shot dead by E4 HMSU following an exchange of gunfire in the armed robbery of a Post Office. O'Hare was not linked to any terrorist organisation. He was armed with a sawn-off shotgun. The inquest jury ruled that it was a lawful killing. His accomplice was jailed for a year having admitted the offence. In 1978 O'Hare was sentenced to eight years for robbery and hi-jacking.

Coalisland, County Tyrone, 4 December 1983. Two armed insurgents from East Tyrone/Monaghan IRA, **Brian Campbell (19)** and **Colm McGirr (22)** were shot dead by the SAS at an arms cache. One insurgent escaped in a getaway car. Bloodstains in the vehicle indicate he was injured.

Dunloy, County Antrim, 21 February 1984. Two armed insurgents from North Antrim IRA, **Henry Hogan (21)** and **Declan Martin (18)**, were shot dead in attempting to ambush a Det observation post. One soldier, **Paul Oram (26)**, was also killed and another seriously injured. Hogan was considered an important activist.

Larne, County Tyrone, 14 April 1984. **Seamus Fitzsimmons (21)** was shot dead by E4 HMSU during an attempted armed robbery. This concerned ordinary crime and not terrorism.

Ardboe, County Tyrone, 13 July 1984. One insurgent from East Tyrone/Monaghan IRA, **William Price (28)**, armed with a handgun was shot dead by the SAS and another two arrested (convicted to nine years each for possession of illegal firearms).

Tamnamore, County Tyrone, 19 October 1984. An innocent Protestant civilian, **Frederick Jackson (43)** was shot dead by the SAS during a gun battle with East Tyrone/Monaghan IRA. Insurgents had been attempting to murder an off-duty UDR soldier. One assailant was subsequently convicted on terrorist offences, receiving a seven-year prison sentence.

Kesh, County Fermanagh, 2 December 1984. One insurgent from East Tyrone/Monaghan IRA, **Tony McBride (27)**, was shot dead by the SAS and another; **Kieran Fleming (25)** drowned evading capture. They were part of a five-man team inserting a 1,000lb landmine. In the ensuing gun battle one soldier, **Alistair Slater (28),** was also killed. Three insurgents escaped across the border. Fleming was an on-the-run living in the ROI having escaped from prison in Northern Ireland. He was convicted of the murder of policewoman Linda Baggley (19).

Derry city, 6 December 1984. Two armed insurgents from Derry city IRA, **William Fleming (19)** and **Daniel Doherty (23)**, were shot dead by the SAS in the process of conducting an attack on an off-duty UDR soldier. William Fleming was the cousin of Kieran Fleming, killed four days earlier.

Strabane, County Tyrone, 23 February 1985. Three insurgents from West Tyrone/Donegal IRA, **Charles Breslin (20), Michael Devine (22)** and **David Devine (16),** were shot dead by the SAS while carrying automatic weapons and in possession of grenades and grenade launchers. Breslin was a senior command figure. Michael and David Devine were brothers.

Rosslea, County Fermanagh, 26 April 1986. One insurgent from

Fermanagh IRA, **Seamus McElwaine (26)**, was shot dead by the SAS while engaged in an operation involving an 800lb landmine. He was the commanding officer of Fermanagh IRA, stood for election for Sinn Féin and was a Monaghan-based on-the-run having escaped from the Maze prison in 1983. Another terrorist was arrested and given a 25 years sentence for possession of explosives and weapons with intent to endanger life.

Loughgall, County Armagh: 8 May 1987. Eight armed insurgents from East Tyrone/Monaghan IRA, **Patrick Kelly (32), Declan Arthurs (21), Seamus Donnelly (19), Michael Gormley (25), Eugene Kelly (25), James Lynagh (32), Gerard O'Callaghan (29)** and **Patrick McKearney (32)**, were shot dead by the SAS at Loughgall while conducting a complex bomb and gun attack on a police station. One innocent Catholic civilian, **Anthony Hughes (36)**, was also killed. The dead included the commanding officer and his deputy, three on-the-runs (McKearney escaped from the Maze prison in 1983) and one former Sinn Féin councillor.

Gibraltar, 6 March 1988. Three insurgents from a specialist IRA GHQ unit, **Mairead Farrell (31), Danny McCann (30)** and **Sean Savage (23)**, were shot dead by the SAS while on a mission in Gibraltar to murder British soldiers with a car bomb. They were unarmed. A substantial car bomb was later recovered near the border in Spain. The European Court of Human Rights found against the UK, judging the deaths violated Article 2 (right to life) of the European Convention of Human Rights. A local Gibraltar inquest found the killings were lawful.

North Belfast, 4 July 1988. One innocent Protestant civilian, **Kenneth Stronge (46)** was killed by the SAS who were reacting to a gun and rocket attack by Belfast IRA on North Queen Street police station.

Drunmakilly, County Tyrone, 30 August 1988. Three armed insurgents from Mid-Tyrone IRA, **Gerard Harte (29), Martin**

Harte (23) and **Brian Mullen (26)**, were shot dead in the process of attempting to murder an off-duty part-time member of the local security forces. Gerard Harte was the commander of Mid-Tyrone IRA. Gerard and Martin Harte were brothers.

North Belfast, 2 September 1989. A member of the UVF, **Brian Robinson (27)**, was shot dead and another wounded by the Det after an incident where a Catholic was murdered. The wounded terrorist received a life sentence for the murder of the Catholic.

North Belfast, 9 November 1989. A member of E4 HMSU, **Ian Johnston (31)** was shot dead by friendly fire during the course of a rapid house entry in which a rifle and ammunition were recovered. The female owner of the house was given a suspended sentence for making her home available to the IRA. A similar charge against a male was dropped.

West Belfast, 13 January 1990. Three members of a crime gang, **Peter Thompson (21)**, **Edward Hale (25)** and **John McNeill (42)**, were shot dead by the Det while engaged in an armed robbery of Sean Graham's bookmakers. Two were wearing balaclavas and carrying imitation firearms, the other was the unarmed getaway driver. Follow-up searches recovered weapons. The verdict of the inquest jury was lawful killing. The jury believed that it was natural for the soldiers to believe the suspects were terrorists and posed a threat.

Kinnego, County Armagh, 18 April 1990. One insurgent from the IPLO, a republican terrorist group, **Martin Corrigan (25)**, was shot dead by the SAS in an armed attack on the home of a part-time police officer.

Loughgall, County Armagh, 9 October 1990. Two insurgents from East Tyrone/Monaghan IRA, **Desmond Grew (37)** and **Martin McCaughey (23)** were shot dead at the advanced preparatory stages of attempting to murder an unknown target. McCaughey was on-the-run and a former Sinn Féin councillor. Grew was linked to IRA murders in Holland. A third terrorist suspect was arrested. A 2012 inquest jury found the killings were lawful.

Strabane, County Tyrone, 12 November 1990. One insurgent from the INLA, **Alexander Patterson (31)**, was shot dead by the SAS during a gun attack on the home of a UDR soldier. Several assailants escaped.

Downpatrick, County Down, 10 April 1991. One insurgent from South Down/Dundalk IRA, **Colum Marks (29)**, was shot dead by E4 while engaged in positioning a mortar along with an accomplice who escaped. The inquest jury found that Marks ignored police warnings to stop (verbal and warning shots) in finding the killing was lawful. Marks was taken to hospital were he died from his wounds. He was the commanding officer of the IRA in Downpatrick. In April 2016 Northern Ireland's Attorney General recommended that the Public Prosecution Service conduct a new inquest.

Coagh, County Tyrone, 3 June 1991. Three insurgents from East Tyrone/Monaghan IRA, **Lawrence McNally (38)**, **Peter Ryan (37)** and **Tony Doris (21)**, were shot dead by the SAS in attempting to murder a part-time member of the security forces. McNally and Ryan were on-the-runs.

Clonoe, County Tyrone, 16 February 1992. Four insurgents from East Tyrone/Monaghan IRA, **Kevin Barry O'Donnell (21)**, **Sean O'Farrell (23)**, **Peter Clancy (19)** and **Daniel Vincent (20)**, were shot dead having attempted to murder police officers in a complex attack against a police station that involved a 12.7 mm heavy machine gun. Three others were arrested and convicted for terrorist offences, and several escaped to the Republic where they were treated for injuries.

West Belfast, 25 November 1992. One unarmed insurgent from

Belfast IRA, **Pearse Jordan (23)**, was shot dead by E4 HMSU having run from a stolen car he was driving. It is claimed forensic traces from his clothing linked him to explosives. A 2014 inquest by a jury failed to reach a verdict on the cause of death. The High Court in Belfast instructed a new inquest (without a jury) should be held. Jordan was the last person shot dead in a covert operation.

From the inception of 'E' department (1976) two incidents involving a reaction to ordinary crime (armed robbery) resulted in an assailant being shot dead in each – John O'Hare in 1983 and Seamus Fitzsimmons in 1984. These are itemised in the chronological list but are not included in the figures we are about to look at, as they are not connected to counter-terrorism. For the same reason the three suspects shot dead at Sean Graham's bookmakers (1990) are also not included.

The list shows a total of 73 deaths in 40 separate covert operations (excluding three ordinary crime) from 1974-1992: 58 insurgents; 6 civilians (4 Protestants, 2 Catholics); 8 security forces and; 1 loyalist terrorist.

Almost all those killed were active terrorists. Even by modern standards the collateral damage was extremely low. The last innocent civilian killed was Anthony Hughes in the Loughgall incident in 1987. While all the civilian deaths are tragic the circumstances regarding John Boyle (16) are particularly heart breaking.

Not outlined in the list, for obvious reasons, former SB detectives who checked it claim that several terrorists killed in separate incidents were agents, without naming them or the incident. They say these agents had not disclosed to their handlers that an attack was to take place.

Of the 58 insurgents killed, 83% were in possession of weapons or explosives. Except for Michael Tighe (a suspected terrorist), all terrorists killed were confirmed as active members of their terrorist organisations. The accuracy of the intelligence was close to perfect. It placed surveillance and specialist armed response teams in the right place at the right time to confront active terrorists who were invariably armed, which is dramatically different to the start of the conflict.

Of note, 88% of all insurgent deaths in covert operations were in border counties. From 1983 onwards eight on-the-runs were killed, whereas there were none previous to this. The numbers show the IRA's dependency on its cross-border offensive. On-the-runs had more experience of terrorism, their average age was 30, in contrast to an insurgent based in Northern Ireland whose average age was 24. The one loyalist terrorist killed was a Protestant. All insurgents killed were Catholics.

An early visible sign that the IRA was losing the intelligence war was in 1986 when the SAS shot dead Seamus McElwaine. This was a year before the Loughgall incident. McElwaine was a Lynagh-type figure. His forte was murdering Protestants who lived in remote border areas. The IRA in Fermanagh never recovered from his loss. McElwaine's death was the first in a series of six incidents from 1986 to 1992 in border counties where the SAS killed 21 of the IRA's top operators. The most spectacular was the Loughgall incident. All were triggered by SB intelligence. They all occurred in South Region. Former SB officers estimate that these terrorists were responsible for at least 650 murders in counties Armagh, Down, Tyrone and Fermanagh, as well as in England and Holland. Cross-border brigades accounted for approximately 73% of insurgent killings from 1979 until the first ceasefire in 1994.

Three separate incidents resulted in murder trials in which two SAS soldiers and four E4 SSU officers where acquitted. No incident in Northern Ireland has been deemed unlawful, although some inquests still remain to be heard. Unhappy with the inquest procedure and police investigation, the families of those killed at Loughgall (supported by liberty-type groups traditionally critical of security) complained to Europe. Strasbourg judged that there were procedural shortcomings under Article 2 (right to life) of the European Convention on Human Rights. The court awarded £10,000 compensation to each family, together with £30,000 group costs. Similar payments have been made under human rights law in some of the other incidents.

Killings in covert operations from 1974 to 1998 amount to 2% of total deaths during the conflict. From 1974 to 1978 the Det pioneered how surveillance could be conducted against an unfamiliar IRA threat. It was a steep and deadly learning curve. Five soldiers operating on their own were murdered testing new operational procedures. The basics early Det operators established revolutionised surveillance. They were added to by the addition of the SAS and specialist police teams in a sophisticated and co-ordinated covert effort that increased in effectiveness as time went on. Another significant landmark was Special Branch taking over the main intelligence-gathering role from the Army when the police regained primacy of security in 1977.

The 40 counter-terrorist incidents catalogued track how the intelligence war against the IRA progressed. A slow and unsure start in the 1970s provided lessons that benefited the covert effort in the early 1980s. Lessons were learned. Mistakes were not repeated. It is important to remember, however, that this is only 4% of all covert operations against terrorists that resulted in an armed response. The outcome 96% of the time was arrest.

February 1992 was the last occasion the SAS was involved in a covert operation resulting in a fatality, which related to four terrorists of East Tyrone/Monaghan IRA just after they attacked Coalisland police station. This stands out when contrasted to the Loughgall incident five years previously. Unlike Loughgall, a village supportive of the police, Coalisland was a town hostile to the police. Within five years of the Loughgall incident East Tyrone/Monaghan brigade had been reduced to conducting attacks within the geographic boundary of its small-support base and even then it failed miserably. By 1992 East Tyrone/Monaghan IRA had been decimated. This released finite covert resources to concentrate on the once invincible South Armagh IRA.

A measure of the inroads SB had made against South Armagh IRA was E4 HMSU arresting one of its leading terrorists, on-the-run Michael 'Mixie' Martin in 1994, and the SAS closely supported by E4 HMSU arresting one of its sniper teams in

1997. Both covert operations took place deep in this republican stronghold. For the IRA's last real bastion of resistance - south Armagh - the writing was on the wall. Had the conflict continued they would have suffered the same end as the other cross-border brigades. And this is significant because south Armagh was the nexus of IRA bomb making. Intelligence advances against it restricted the IRA's capacity to play what they saw as their ace card – bombing London.

As a barometer of the intelligence war the list shows the IRA was on a downward slide a decade prior to their leadership in 1993 asking the British government to help them end the conflict. At their lowest point they sued for peace.

*The police became a sacrificial pawn
of the peace.*

Chapter 17

A Rigged Game

Exhausted militarily, suffering low morale and out of ideas, insurgent leaders asked the British Prime Minister in 1993 for help in ending the IRA's terrorist campaign. The first IRA ceasefire was in 1994 and the formal peace accord in 1998. Loyalist terrorist organisations stopped in response. SB had achieved its objective. It won the intelligence war. By design it was a secret victory. The Whole of Government strategy had worked. The Troubles were over. Saving republican face Sinn Féin loudly and unashamedly declared victory, lauding the IRA as magnanimous and undefeated. Provos were recast as peacemakers. By 2004 the insurgent leadership's secret aim was realised. Sinn Féin was the largest nationalist party and in the power-sharing executive. Half of its elected representatives were convicted terrorists.

The last attempt by the Provos to prevent a pitiful plea to the British was to shake off SB through 'collusion.' 'Shoot-to-kill' tripped off the tongue but was easily refuted. Chicago police shot dead 240 people in four years from 2010 to 2014. Even for the most diehard republican seven terrorists and a terrorist suspect killed by E4 over a 30 year conflict does not speak 'shoot-to-kill.' Sinn Féin propagandists needed something less vulnerable to the facts. 'Collusion' was perfect. True to form, in 1989 Sinn Féin's PR campaign provoked the government into launching an investigation headed by John Stevens, the Chief Constable of Cambridgeshire. This dovetailed with a PR strategy by loyalist terrorist organisations also aimed at tainting SB, mimicking how the IRA, UVF and UDA had secretly collaborated previously to undermine crime squads and the supergrass system.

Unknown to the IRA, loyalist terrorist organisations had few modern weapons and munitions. Loyalists were suffering badly at the hands of SB. After a covert operation in 1988 where E4 HMSU arrested three notorious loyalist terrorists, the judge commended them for having recovered 61 military rifles, 50 grenades and 11,000 rounds of ammunition. The seizure triggered further arrests and convictions. The episode was a severe setback for the murderous ambitions of loyalism's hard men. Prior to Stevens' arrival loyalist terrorist organisations were well contained.

In the eight years before Stevens, one person was murdered for 'informing.' In the same period after this increased to five. Two of the latter victims are credited with the recovery of extensive amounts of weapons and munitions, as well as the arrest and conviction of a significant number of loyalist terrorists. The last loyalist murdered for 'informing' was in 2001, William Stobie, exposed as an agent by Stevens. A new breed of loyalists, like Johnny 'Mad Dog' Adair used Stevens to expose those they suspected of informing. Stevens was the means to get rid of an old guard infiltrated by SB. The Cambridgeshire police officer had played into the hands of loyalism's hard men and impeded SB's capacity to prevent loyalist terrorism, which more than doubled after Stevens.

As with Stalker, Stevens' background was CID and policing in places like Cambridge. Stevens followed Stalker's template, ignoring the threat and assuming consent-based policing exists, where people provide statements to the police and normal investigative practices are always possible.

In the final of three different investigations lasting over a decade, the Stevens team amassed one million pages. Although critical of SB, FRU and MI5 it did not provoke criminal proceedings against intelligence personnel. Instead, a non-legal definition for 'collusion' that ranged from poor record-keeping to conspiring with an agent in murder was constructed. The cynic would say this allowed Stevens to justify a massively expensive and lengthy investigation that produced nothing substantial.

Stevens and his team of England-based CID detectives could not get their heads around SB dominance and the agent concept. They viewed policing the Troubles through the eyes of a British bobby. If it didn't comply with what happened in England it was wrong. A FRU officer interviewed by the Stevens team states, "He [Stevens] was totally clueless about the Troubles. He didn't want to listen." The enormous workload, challenging environment and inadequate resources were ignored. Innovation, initiative, failing to take evidence-gathering opportunities and shortcomings were treated as criminal conspiracies. Stevens was uninterested in why SB dominated and was separate from CID. The McLaughlin (1987) Report is insightful:

Northern Ireland is beset with terrorist strife and political murder can be almost an everyday occurrence. The RUC Special Branch are taken to task because of their not unnatural difficulty in adapting the policing of a ruthless terrorist reality to the pattern allowed by a benevolent conforming society. ... We see much to admire in the RUC Special Branch. Their efforts save many lives. They work under continuous threat of murder. Operational decisions affecting the life and death of terrorists, colleagues, informers and members of the long suffering public have to be made at a moment's notice. All this is done under the threat of critical judgments made with the benefit of hindsight and the application of some 'mainland' policing rules which, in terms of the Ulster reality, seem to have little relevance to that most important basic duty:-a) The protection of life and property; b) The maintenance of order; c)The prevention and detection of crime; and d) The prosecution of offenders against the peace.

The work of the RUC SB applies in relation to all these issues generally, as well as in respect to terrorism. They are a major source of intelligence and guidance to the force in all their duties, as well as being a means of protecting them from terrorist attacks. These efforts at protection also extend to the civil populace in NI, on the mainland and in the Republic of Ireland.

Stevens joined Stalker in not seeing it the way Her Majesty's Inspectorate of Constabulary did, or for that matter, world-class experts and irregular war precepts. The practical foundation on which Stevens based his claims is fundamentally flawed.

The majority of fall-out centres on the murder of Catholic lawyer Patrick Finucane by the UDA in 1989. He was viciously gunned down at his home in front of his wife and young family. Mr Finucane was well known for defending IRA suspects. Under parliamentary privilege Patrick Finucane was named in the House of Commons in a way that highlighted him in sympathy with the IRA. The majority of people reviled his clients and, unfortunately but inevitably, him with them from ignorant quarters. In Ulster's sectarian turmoil the parliamentary statement was damning. Compounding matters, intelligence agencies were aware that Mr Finucane was a potential UDA target. The accusations are, they knowingly stood aside to allow his murder or actively facilitated it and were directed to do so from the top – Prime Minister Thatcher.

The Patrick Finucane murder is 'collusion's' centre of gravity. When one studies 'collusion', however, like republicanism it is riddled with inconsistencies and contradictions. One minute SB officers are master criminals, the next bumbling incompetents, anti-Catholic then anti-Protestant, protecting agents at all costs then sacrificing agents when the cost is too high. If SB could, with extraordinary precision, surprise hyper alert terrorists armed with weapons, a civilian lawyer innocently going about his daily business was child's play. In such a straightforward scenario surveillance and not agents is needed. And if murder was the policy, why did the IRA's permanent leadership survive? They would have been top of the hit list. 'Collusion' is whatever its author wants it to be. But when one knows SB's covert policing tactics as opposed to the myths 'collusion' makes no sense.

Stevens showed the shortcoming of two separate intelligence agencies - FRU and SB. It is a valid point. A review into the murder by Desmond de Silva in 2012 shows confusion between the two worked against protecting Patrick Finucane. It was not ideal, but in an irregular war nothing is. There are no failsafe systems. But the system saved more lives than the alternatives. No conflict since has implemented the type of Threat to Life policy the police is criticised for not having. Much as people like Stevens have tried to impress, the Troubles was not a peacetime context. As with Stalker, Stevens did not provoke a scene change. SB stayed in the hot seat.

None of this is any comfort to the Finucane family. Patrick Finucane was an innocent Catholic callously cut down. Tragically, the preventative option put in place (which regularly worked previously) failed. It was not a case of turning a blind eye, unlawfully conspiring or SB playing God, but an honest failing. If the Finucane family ever get a chance to talk to the SB detectives involved they might realise this. SB were trying to protect Patrick Finucane not kill him.

'Collusion' would be the blame game's centrepiece once peace was agreed. The abstract nature of intelligence is a politically rich target, a way to help prevent republicanism from splitting. Redundant Provos in suits were put to work on a 'collusion' campaign guaranteed to play out favourably in the courts and media. It was war without the killing. 'Collusion' was the post-conflict equivalent of the hunger strikes. It galvanised republicanism, continuing to convince those who took part in and supported the 'armed struggle' that what they did was justified.

Stevens, fortuitously, happened in the transition from conflict to peace. Raising the spectre of a 'dirty war', as Stevens did, was not inconvenient for the British side. Pandering to the

Provos suited, particularly as this was when the British were running down the intelligence effort to give Sinn Féin breathing room. The insurgent leadership persuaded a new Prime Minister that the police and its SB needed disbanded, a longstanding political demand of nationalist leaders. This, effectively, occurred through the Patten Report (1999). The report used Stalker's 'force within a force' line to describe SB, an early indication of things to come. The police became a sacrificial pawn of the peace. It was the other side of the 'peace process' coin that portrayed the Provos as peacemakers.

The RUC being reconstituted as the PSNI in 2001 left many officers feeling betrayed. Critics point out that they received a generous early retirement scheme. SB detectives, however, traditionally worked beyond the 30 year retirement threshold. Retiring early was not financially attractive, particularly for the lower ranks. Most SB officers took it because they were sick of the celebratory manner of Prime Minister Blair, his ministers and spin-doctors with unrepentant insurgent leaders. They no longer felt valued. Sinn Féin portrayed those that remained as the 'dark side,' an impediment to a new beginning in policing. But to secure the peace the policing change was politically pragmatic. There is a perverse irony about prisoners released early and included in the 'peace process' and police retired early and excluded.

What escaped most people's notice, especially unionist leaders, was that republicans and nationalists wanted a new police ombudsman with retrospective legal powers. For a retributive republican movement, replacing the RUC with the PSNI cleared the way for giving the RUC a hammering. Undermining the rule of law did not end with the Belfast Agreement. The republican strategy was about continuity rather than change. A former Deputy Head of SB explains:

You have to hand it to the republican movement; their strategy was far better than ours. Their top thinkers are very bright. Once they realised we had them beaten on the military front they put long-term objectives in place – influencing residents groups, victims groups, human rights groups and whoever they believed would represent their interests. As soon as the shooting ended they dedicated all their efforts to promoting their version of what happened. It is quite brilliant.

Retrospective investigations into the police would be the cornerstone of republican revisionism. Sinn Féin did not need to re-write history - they would get the state to do it for them. Nationalist leaders, local NGOs and others similarly disposed toward the RUC supported Sinn Féin's 'collusion' charter. For them this is what a 'peace process' looks like - SB acted with impunity and must be held to account. There was nothing similar for the IRA (or loyalist terrorists). Equality, enshrined in the Belfast Agreement, did not extend to police. The main statute body progressing 'collusion' is the police ombudsman. Nationalist expectations have not been disappointed. A former Head of SB states:

I spent a full week, 9 to 5, with Ombudsman investigators. They were asking about how SB did this and that and why. Clearly they didn't know how SB operated so I took time to explain it. Everything I did was to help them understand. But when their report came out it was highly critical. Nothing I'd said had been included. They'd dismissed all of it.

Different investigators approached for a subsequent investigation. And I went through the same routine. This time I spent almost two weeks with them. They knew I was annoyed from nothing I'd said having appeared in the other report, which they claimed was wrong. But when this report was published the same thing happened. There was nothing in it from my side. Whilst the investigators placed weight on what I provided the actual Ombudsman discounted it. Believe me, I've tried, but what's the point. It's political.

Another former officer describes the post-conflict arrangement as a "rigged game." Currently, the police ombudsman has lost the confidence of retired police officers. They see it as a politicised body whose investigative integrity has been compromised. The most damning indictment came from a recently retired Head of Crime Operations. ACC Peter Sheridan was the most senior Catholic officer in the PSNI when he retired. A quiet and softly spoken man respected by both communities, he is currently the head of a peace-building charity called Co-operation Ireland. In a televised House of Commons inquiry in 2014 about on-the-runs he calmly expressed bitter disappointment at a police ombudsman report that he considered unfairly misrepresentative of the facts. This rattled the police ombudsman, an office that had never been held to account in this manner. The response was unconvincing. This, retired police officers say, is the problem. The police ombudsman is, essentially, unaccountable.

The description of 'collusion' is so wide ranging as to be meaningless in a criminal justice context. Its main use is political. It has reached the stage where barristers in court argue that, no evidence of 'collusion' is evidence of 'collusion' and historical reports state, not finding evidence of 'collusion' does not discount 'collusion.' Lawyers' arguments are more theatre than fact, and police ombudsman reports more dissertation than investigation. 'Collusion' is a dream for lawyers, journalists and authors of historical reports. 'Collusion' grabs headlines. But on many occassions, what is presented to the public is a failure to understand the limits of intelligence rather than an intelligence failure.

Finding fault is the mindset. A relative of a victim need only believe there was 'collusion' to trigger an investigation. And it seems no-one lodging a 'collusion' complaint to the police ombudsman has been disbelieved. The filter of healthy scepticism normally found in assessing the validity of a criminal complaint is missing. Retired police believe that the ombudsman at the start of an investigation identifies if an agent was connected and then reverse engineers the investigation around the agent's existence to fit conclusions that murders were preventable. If this is the case, evidence is not being followed but an agenda. In an environment where agents were one or two steps removed from a conspiracy to murder, getting links to support such conclusions are easy.

Historical investigations are also contaminated by hindsight bias. A retired police officer published in theories of psychology explains:

Hindsight bias stems from a number of flawed beliefs: 1) The world is more predictable than it really is; 2) We are smarter than others. This comes about because what ever happened was obvious for us to see yet they didn't. Of course we are looking back with knowledge of what did happen and we delude ourselves that they should have seen it because we would have! 3) Others failed to see what was obvious and were negligent in their role.

The impairment is most acute in intelligence. The amount of information available after an event is greater than the amount beforehand. Hindsight is always perfect vision. The 9/11 Commission in the US cautioned members against hindsight bias. There has been no similar awareness or warning in Northern Ireland.

When there is the perception of intelligence having failed, accusations are that you 'should have known.' Only extensive contemporaneous notes can offset this. Failure to keep such makes it more likely the allegation will be made. Insufficient paperwork is an ingredient of 'collusion' and extra bureaucracy a constant recommendation of retrospective reports. This goes against the streamlined bureaucracy needed in counterinsurgency. Officers are needed on the frontline not behind desks. The records recommendations of this kind cause are perhaps 70% of all paperwork in policing today. A peacetime setting can cope but in a conflict this puts life in peril. It slows down the police and prevents them from getting ahead of the threat. Freed from the fear of future litigation, there is an honesty of intent to protecting life in policing a conflict that does not exist in peacetime.

A multi-million pound industry emerged in which law firms, NGOs, academics and a liberal elite have prospered. The state has been thrown into a spin of investigating itself. An historic investigation has more time and resources than the original. It examines police officers with far more rigour than it does the murderers. The British are litigating their way out of the Troubles. As with the Internal Security Solution, most fall-out is local. Republicanism's victim and compensation culture gave it an enormous head start on everyone else.

Few reverberations make it across the Irish Sea, although the arrest of a retired member of the Parachute Regiment in 2015 in connection with a new murder investigation into Bloody Sunday is one of a few exceptions. Only when this happens does anyone on the UK mainland take notice. The British Army is still fighting small wars overseas. Westminster cannot afford to have soldiers they have asked to protect the nation think about being sued afterwards for opening fire in the heat of battle. This is what is happening in Northern Ireland.

Of the liberal elite the track record of Amnesty International is telling. From 1971 to 2013 Amnesty International, a body co-founded by a former IRA chief of staff Seán McBride who later campaigned for people's rights, published 24 reports on Northern Ireland. All, bar one, examine the state and are critical of it. The exception is a report in 1994 when the conflict was effectively over. A small part examines the IRA. Over 43 years Amnesty International devoted almost all its attention on the state. The main protagonist escaped its gaze. Yet the IRA and its political partner controlled republican enclaves. Which, according to the UN, obligated them to comply with the Geneva Conventions, such as the humane treatment of prisoners.

It was hardly a secret that the Provos routinely tortured those it took prisoner and summarily executed almost 100 'collaborators.' Amazingly, or perhaps not, none of this merited a standalone examination by Amnesty International, an organisation committed to highlighting humanitarian abuses. One can see why their approach frustrated Northern Ireland Secretary of State Roy Mason. It was as if the IRA did not exist. Amnesty International where clearly aware of views like Mason's, making their one-sidedness all the more suspicious and disappointing.

Neither did Amnesty International examine the Republic's

role. Yet the border and the Republic's territory were major reasons the insurgency lasted as long as it did, not to mention a morally warped interpretation of terrorism preventing almost every extradition request of a terrorist suspect. In contrast to the paltry amount of weaponry loyalists were left with in the North, the IRA's mountainous arsenal in the South raises uncomfortable questions for Dublin. The Republic showed more appetite to police other borders as part of overseas UN missions than it did its own. This is not to criticise police, soldiers and prison officers in the Republic, some of whom the IRA also murdered, but successive governments in Dublin.

In conflicts since WW2 the Geneva Conventions have been widely ignored, mostly through the arbitrary execution of prisoners or aerial bombings causing civilian casualties. Northern Ireland's police did not execute prisoners. Neither did the Army bombard on-the-runs in the Republic. The difficulty with the Geneva Conventions is that they were written for conventional battlefields and armies, not an unconventional war like the Troubles and organisations like the IRA.

Modern battlefields are shopping centres, tube stations, music concerts and remembrance services. The parties to whom the Conventions apply, like the IRA and its political partner Sinn Féin, are uninterested in complying with humanitarian rules. But this is what set the police and Army above them. They accepted the rules, played by them, engaged with the system and put in remedies when they fell short. The IRA and Sinn Féin did not. Regardless of systematically and deliberately violating humanitarian laws the IRA desperately wanted to be seen as an army, hence the contradictory and hypocritical language of republicanism. One sentence is about respecting human rights the next condones murdering a prisoner.

The men who directed the executions of 'collaborators' also concocted 'collusion.' The idea is to drag the police down to the IRA level, to show that the police were just as bad as the Provos – 'one is as bad as the other' moralising. Taint SB and you taint the RUC and entire security effort. For republicans, success is not the families of innocent Catholics or IRA men complaining about 'collusion' but the families of police, soldiers and innocent Protestant civilians. Increasing the 'collusion' victim pool increases the legitimacy of the IRA.

All of this was to accommodate the IRA and Sinn Féin with a way out. But it was bigger. Nationalists also needed a way out. Consequently, the only side that had something to give in the peace deal was the majority of the population that wholeheartedly supported the rule of law and opposed the insurgency. The British government represented their interests. The IRA was in demand mode. It needed its prisoners out of jail and secret promises not to pursue on-the-runs. All the Provos had to do was be the same as everyone else in a civilised democracy – abide by the principles of non-violence and consent. They had to stop murdering. And the leaders of the Catholic community had to fully support the rule of law.

The sense of national pride in the police and security forces in general is something the 'peace process' has sought to destroy, to instil shame on having supported the rule of law. NGOs like Amnesty International follow suit. Local academics write papers that compare the Troubles to brutal dictatorships in South America and Africa. One of the lesser inquiries into a single victim cost roughly the same as that spent on 19,000 victims of apartheid in South Africa. Legal aid payments in Northern Ireland are the highest in the world. The scope, length, financial cost and extent of inquiry are unprecedented and wildly disproportionate when considering the police were responsible for 1% of all killings, all of them deemed lawful.

Republicanism means never having to say sorry. Sinn Féin blames an evil Special Branch that directed agents in loyalist terrorist groups to slaughter innocent Catholics. To fight this, IRA terrorism was justified. To have been in the IRA or supported it and withholding support for the police were not bad things. 'Collusion' soothes the conscience of people holding this view and exploits the emotional distress of those who do not but are desperate for answers about a lost loved one.

'Collusion' sees loyalist terrorists as idiots incapable of murder without the intelligence agencies putting a gun in their hand and telling them who to shoot. Republicanism is conditioning wider society into retrospectively accepting that the handling of agents was 'collusion.' Instead, in reality, it was a lawful undertaking with the least hard-line terrorists in a bid to stop their more violent colleagues. Agents saved many lives and sometimes their crimes were tolerated. SB had its failings. These, however, must be considered against the intent to protect life and an effective track record in this regard.

The active support of republicans and passive support of nationalists for the IRA and the IRA's reliance on the Republic as a safe haven were security drawbacks SB overcame. Systems and procedures were devised that tiptoed around nationalist sensitivities. Policing was compensating for Irish nationalism's failings and the immaturity of all political parties in Northern Ireland. In a peace agreement dependent on placating republicans and nationalists it was not in any political parties' interests to embarrass either on this count. Which is why historical investigations get away with framing a fictional context.

Knowing how SB operated, the character of the people, selection and training, ethos, mission and actual outcomes, means that on so many levels 'collusion' is nonsense. This is not what SB was or did. It is deeply insulting to officers and their families. 'Collusion' is an illusion, a dictionary definition popularised at the expense of the truth. Perception has become reality. For a second generation of Troubles journalists 'collusion' is a fact. But facts do not leave room for possibilities.

In various subtle ways the 'peace process' has tainted policing and dehumanised SB officers. They are treated like war criminals. Their remit was to defeat the Provos and loyalist terrorist groups, not to counter a propaganda strategy to tarnish policing once the conflict ended. That was the British government's job. The difficulty was that SB came with an expiry date – Good Friday 1998. There was no political capital to be made by dying in the ditch to protect SB's reputation. Politically, the prudent path was to let republicans have their way.

In 2012 British Prime Minister David Cameron apologised for the state failing to protect Patrick Finucane. He also apologised for Bloody Sunday. Both were the right things to do. Why then, do Sinn Féin not apologise for IRA terrorism or the SDLP for not supporting the police? Do unionists get off for discriminating against Catholics for 50 years and creating the conditions that made a conflict likely? Who holds Amnesty International to account for ignoring the main human rights abuser? What about the authors of misleading reports and sensationalist journalism? Should the Republic of Ireland be investigated for its security failings? How many lives could have been saved if courts in the Republic extradited terrorists? Should the proprietors of Irish-American bars in Boston and New York be prosecuted for financing terrorism? How liable is Libya? And what about all those who withheld information about terrorist crimes from the police?

Political parties, politicians and others loudly claim credit for the peace but are deafeningly quiet about accepting responsibility for the conflict. There is no collective responsibility, political or otherwise. That said, one should never ever lose sight of the fact, which 'collusion' is designed to do, that a small, unpopular insurgent network started and sustained the Troubles. It created chaos. Instilling fear and spreading confusion were its tools. The Provos and their political partner have got away with, literally, murder.

Those who made it difficult for the police now judge the police. It is Orwellian. Looking for a culprit inside Northern Ireland suits Northern Ireland. But the culprit chosen has no bearing on reality. The thin blue line that held the country together when politics failed is a soft target. The people who least deserve criticism have been criticised the most. Perplexed by this a former Head of E4 states:

There is an effective perpetuation of the political agenda to attack and demonise the RUC and particularly SB with current politically motivated selective historical inquiries. These claim to put events in the context of the conflict at that time.

However, they invariably do not. The RUC is judged against current standards in a perfect world, on a presumption that they had full knowledge of what was happening and with unlimited resources

Historical inquiries have created the impression that a conflict can be casualty-free, an insurgency wished away and there are no bad people except for police.

Compensation claims, judicial reviews, inquests and inquiries benefit from being linked to 'collusion.' It raises the profile of a case or report, accesses legal aid and increases media coverage. Running alongside this republicans represent that the IRA was unfairly criminalised. A 'volunteer' killed or injured by his own bomb in committing or attempting to commit mass murder is a victim. They want the state to provide a pension for them. Groups that follow the republican line agree.

The Belfast Agreement needed a scapegoat. Security fitted the bill. 'Collusion' is the Provisionals projecting what they would have done had they been the state. Republican propagandists simply had to sow the seed. As the 'Great Communicator' US President Ronald Reagan said, "When you're explaining, you're losing." 'Collusion' forces an explanation.

'Collusion' is a key part of a 'peace process' criticised for its underhandedness. Secret side deals with the IRA have brought it into disrepute. Of this a senior figure of the Thatcher government (Lord Tebbit) states:

In my view the combined security forces had done a very good job in Northern Ireland and the IRA was all but totally defeated. The organisation had been penetrated by the security forces up to and including the Army Council itself. Senior IRA members had been induced (one way or another) to become informers on their colleagues. The net was also closing on one of the most senior figures in the IRA. Indeed, I understand that a file had been sent to the office of the prosecutor linking him to eight separate murders, but it had attached to it a note to say

that in reaching his decision the prosecutor might wish to take
into account that the individual concerned was expected to be
a delegate at the (then) projected talks on a cease fire. Those
talks eventually led to the so-called Good Friday Agreement. And
it led to the On The Run letters and I believe other unpublished
guarantees given by Mr Blair.

Lord Tebbit reminds us that the IRA was forced to negotiate and how far the Prime Minister went to secure peace. 'Collusion' distracts from this, IRA brutality and a duplicitous long war strategy. The difficulty, especially for people like Norman Tebbit who has had to care for his wife Margaret, permanently paralysed by the Provos' Brighton bomb, is that the IRA was not compelled to say sorry. How do you forgive someone who does not want forgiven? Someone who insists murder is right? If there is no repentance there is no reconciliation.

The 'armed struggle' was evil, immoral, sectarian, unlawful, unethical and wrong. But do not say this out loud. It annoys republicans, and you do not want to do that. Ultimately, the 'peace process' boils down to placating Provos. It is not a peace process but an appeasement process. The main benefactor by far has been the republican movement. But there has been no reciprocity. Not until republicans deal with their demons can a genuine peace process begin and inverted commas removed from the term.

In the Belfast Agreement republicans took advantage of a Prime Minister impatient to have the hand of history on his shoulder. Tony Blair and his team ignored SB assessments that the insurgent leadership was taking them for the proverbial ride. Republicans could bend further than the Prime Minister was prepared to go and there was no danger of a split, about which Prime Minister Blair was anxious, as was US President Bill Clinton. The iron grip the IRA leadership had over the republican movement made a significant split in republicanism a non-starter.

The British had superb leverage with the prisoner and on-the-run issues. What was needed was a dignified apology by the republican movement and admission that what they did was wrong.

249

This would have brought closure and reconciliation. Contesting who was right or wrong, which 'collusion' personifies, would have been avoided. And it would have sent a clear signal to others that the 'armed struggle' is not worth copying.

To make the 'peace process' work a morality bypass was needed. Disbelief also had to be suspended. In a world where insurgency is increasingly popular, applauding and rewarding extremists who used an ideology to legitimise murder would have wider consequences. It is a dangerously confused message. The 'peace process' fascinated fundamentalists like al-Qaeda's leader. As one intelligence war ended others began. Iraq would have its Troubles. So, how did this work out for a British government still back-slapping from bringing peace to Northern Ireland? Why is Northern Ireland still blighted by a rebranded IRA? And how did any of this influence al-Qaeda's attacks on 9/11?

*Insurgents do not abandon their terrorist
campaign out of goodness.*

Chapter 18

Al-Qaeda and the IRA

Al-Qaeda and the IRA are cut from the same cloth. In 1992, after the IRA shattered London's calm by devastating the Baltic Exchange, it issued this statement:

Because it is a prime target symbolic of the Thatcher years. Let's face it, if someone was to bring down the Twin Towers of the World Trade Centre in Manhattan it would be a severe blow to American prestige.

The audacious attack was Sinn Féin strengthening its political strategy and spelling out how great the IRA is to supporters in Irish-America. In case any remote observer missed the message of striking at the heart of the evil empire, similar 'spectaculars' occurred in Bishopsgate (1993), Canary Wharf (1996) and Manchester (1996). The explosions killed six civilians, including schoolgirl Danielle Carter (15), injured around 500, a large number seriously, and cost the taxpayer at least £2 billion. Responsible for all of them was the last properly functioning IRA brigade - South Armagh. It was the desperate and depraved throes of a dying insurgency.

Bombing England for many Irish republicans and planes flying into buildings in America for many Sunni Muslims was giving the oppressor a rightful taste of their own medicine. 9/11 marked the start of al-Qaeda's Global Insurgency against the US and the west. Besides the awful carnage of that day, America was awakened to the frustrating reality that insurgency forces people to choose sides, and it is not always clear what side people are really on.

Hot on the heels of the intelligence war against the IRA was the Global War on Terror and conflicts in Afghanistan and Iraq. On television screens al-Qaeda's mesmerising attacks in New York surpassed IRA attacks in London, and bombs in Baghdad's dusty roads replaced bombs in Belfast's kerbed streets. Terrorism had moved on in sensational style. Al-Qaeda was the IRA on speed. Insurgency, a term new to most, was on everyone's lips. Few, however, understood it.

Adding to the not knowing was the shenanigans of the Belfast Agreement, which was the IRA's political exit a benevolent Whole of Government strategy facilitated. Feeling no obligation to return the generosity, Sinn Féin heralded the Provos as 'peacemakers'. This set the post-conflict tone. The 'peace process' was not about recovering counterinsurgency lessons. A security-free Northern Ireland model emerged to explain to the world how peace was achieved. Although a partial picture it was the rising tide that lifted all political boats. In a conflict it is an account that should come with a health warning – NOT FOR USE IN AN EMERGENCY.

All the Agreement's accolades were for politicians and terrorists. Without question the third party brokerage of US Senator George Mitchell, contribution of insurgent leaders, Irish Taoiseach and local political parties must not be devalued. But winning the intelligence war is what made peace possible. An irregular war cannot be ended without an effective security response. Ask governments in Baghdad and Kabul.

From a militant's perspective the Northern Ireland model says terrorism works. Today's peace-breakers are tomorrow's peacemakers. They see it reaffirming their belief that the west is politically weak (afraid of getting bogged down in an unpopular and lengthy war) and morally bankrupt (will change the definition of right and wrong when politically expedient to do so). Given that al-Qaeda's leader had an addiction to the BBC news and interest in the NI 'peace process,' did he envisage himself being feted at the White House and Downing Street like Sinn Féin's President? Gerry Adams promoted the 'armed struggle' as successful and justified. 'We beat the Brits' language of the Belfast republican was music to the ears of the warlord. Did the jihadist see the odd 'spectacular' in London and regular terrorism in Northern Ireland a combination worth copying?

Did the IRA inspire 9/11? Have Provos shaped al-Qaeda's near enemy/far enemy long war? The prophetic 'twin towers' analogy in 1992 makes it difficult to discount. You cannot propagate the airwaves with 30 years of hate-filled bile and continue to justify murder and think it has no adverse impact in places you have never been and on people you have never met.

Wars in Afghanistan and Iraq painfully laid bare the novelty of the UK's new thinking. Attempts to build police capacity in southern Iraq were based largely on British bobby style policing. It was an unmitigated disaster. Colonel Tim Collins believes that Prime Minister Blair's Cabinet got "carried away" by the euphoria of the 'peace process.' He states:

> *British Army officers were dismayed that Government were much too insistent in pursuing a deal with Shia militants in Basra and paid less attention to security, much to the alarm of the Americans.*

The British approach in southern Iraq against a determined Shia insurgency funded and equipped by Tehran was a short-term fix that skipped security in going straight to talks with terrorists. There was no long-term strategy or any credible attempt to build up local forces to a point that a rule of law approach could take over. The main lessons from the Troubles had been ignored or dismissed. For many, it was a case of, no sooner were the British in

Iraq than they wanted to leave.

As one US officer states, "The Brits withdrew into their bases. They paid the Mahdi army more not to attack them than the Iranians did for attacking them." British policy in Iraq focused on the political end-game of an irregular war and not the long, hard security slog that precedes it. In 2003, the British got as far talking to Shia militants as they did in Northern Ireland with the IRA in the early 1970s. This is what the start of an irregular war looks like, insurgents are bullish and convinced they will win, which was the case in Iraq. It is inexcusable the British did not know this. Political bribes extorted by terrorists at the end of a conflict in Northern Ireland had given way to financial bribes extorted by terrorists at the start of a conflict in Iraq.

The British approach was out of sync with that under direct US leadership. General Petraeus prioritised security as the means of progressing politics, economics and good governance. How the US confronted the Mahdi army at Najaf (2004) forced its leader (Muqtada al-Sadr) to adopt a passive approach. The prospect of obvious defeat pushed Muqtada down a political path that was not his preferred intention. General Petraeus mirrored Prime Minister Thatcher's approach and not that of Prime Minister Blair. There was, however, one important difference; Prime Minister Thatcher used a robust police model that built upon military successes, eventually took over from the military and was something the military could support.

In Iraq, the British failed to establish a permanent police presence as the means of denying territory to insurgents, something they had excelled at up to then. The same people who brokered the Belfast Agreement presided over strategies in Iraq and Afghanistan. Having gained power in 1997, when the Troubles were effectively over, they had limited experience of conflict. The Northern Ireland model encapsulates their thinking. Set aside was how the British traditionally did 'boots on the ground.' This was not about big numbers but a small military force building a police organisation to support. With a downsized Army one would have expected this to be an ideal tool to develop in a world where governments are loath to put their troops in harms way.

The UK uniquely had the most recent version of a rule of law approach at its fingertips, a sustainable solution that had just defeated the type of threat now faced afresh. But the British did not use or promote it. Political intoxication with a 'peace process' that marketed Prime Minister Blair's global profile (and others like his main advisor Jonathan Powell) is one reason. Such a police force in Iraq or Afghanistan would have angered republicans they had bent over backwards to please. Thinking the RUC model redundant, unworthy or preferring the British bobby style of policing are other reasons. Whatever the reason, it is a damning omission of the government and in keeping with it having sent troops to Iraq with inferior equipment and limited resources. It was a government characterised by spin, not substance.

The findings of the Iraq Inquiry in 2016 heavily criticised Prime Minister Blair and his government, particularly their failure to learn the security lessons of the Troubles. Another reason is the Army had shrunk and had to do more with less. Although the advent of HUMINT satisfied an intelligence gathering capability, it went against the longstanding principle that local police are better at this than foreign soldiers. The Army had neither the same need nor means to construct an SB and RUC-type force.

A lack of information is also a reason. Security experts like Brigadier Kitson were content to write about Malaya and Kenya but not the Troubles. They understood the fullness of the IRA/Sinn Féin threat, especially the link with respectable third parties. Anything written would be forensically examined. Words would be misrepresented, selectively quoted or taken out of context in order to criticise the writing and the writer. Litigation in a generous legal aid system is also a real risk.

Even without writing about the Troubles, Kitson had a lawsuit lodged against him in 2015 due, it seems, to his books on other conflicts. Northern Ireland is the world's claim capital. It is no surprise the Army could not wait to leave and did not formally document its experiences. Only when it had time to draw breath following a withdrawal from Iraq and drawdown in Afghanistan, has there been a realisation that the lessons from the Troubles are missing. The Army Counterinsurgency field manual (2009) sees this as a "stark omission."

Northern Ireland remains plagued by violence, albeit nowhere near as bad as it was. Given the hatred of SB by republican and loyalist terrorists, and the way SB has been kept in the public eye by critical historical reports, few detectives have written books. Their home is Northern Ireland. Many are still terrorist targets. Accustomed to not being in the limelight they prefer to keep it that way. There are authorised histories of MI5, MI6 and books explaining the National Intelligence Model but nothing similar about SB. At least with soldiers, what happened in one conflict can be handed down informally by word of mouth in another. But cops as a rule do not deploy to a different war zone to police it. What they know invariably stays where they served. And police forces do not publish irregular war manuals.

In modern conflicts commanders need to defeat an insurgency and at the same time build local forces. The ultimate aim is a rule of law approach. This is what General David Petraeus had to do. A gifted leader, the desired end-state was never realised. This took almost 30 years in Northern Ireland. He was given five. There was simply no time to build a police force that could cope with the threat, a task made more impossible by using inadequate police models. Imagine a British government elected in 1970 on a manifesto of pulling troops out of Northern Ireland by 1980 and publicly setting this deadline to achieve success. This was General Petraeus' dilemma. Insurgents simply outwait their enemy.

In both Iraq and Afghanistan the US was the main force and led the overall effort. The US is unbeatable in a conventional war but it was the unconventional it faced. An IRA-type campaign by Sunni insurgent networks in Iraq derailed any notion of quick victory. The vast majority of US deaths were caused by IRA tactics that Sunni insurgents copied, like roadside bombs. Insurgents started at the top of their learning curve. Counterinsurgents started at the bottom. Even if the US had been prepared, which it was not, it had no time to close the gap.

Those confronted with an insurgency's harsh reality soon understood that conventional police models from the west were unsuited. As a US marine explains: "If we policed this place like it was Boston, there wouldn't be too many cops left." The place in question was Haditha, Iraq. Sadly it had been policed like Boston and there were not many cops left. Iraqi police were murdered with ridiculous ease. Policing was virtually extinct. General Petraeus had military counterinsurgency field manuals but no 'rule of law' handbook and the phone from the UK was silent. Despite this the SB concept made it into the US system. If the British had no interest the US did.

In Iraq, US marines were in the worst of the fight in Anbar province on the Syrian frontier. Syria was a safe haven for Sunni insurgents. Amid Anbar's chaos a bright marine major with an insatiable work appetite and several tours under his belt studied the Troubles. When others slept he read. In 2006 he came across the RUC SB and knew his marines needed it. This, he passionately believed, would save lives. Coincidentally the Irregular Warfare Support (IWS) in Washington DC at the same time was also in research mode and came to the same conclusion. What both unearthed is what most of the world did not know. The IRA lost an intelligence war against their old foe, Special Branch, and had been steadily decimated in the process.

Although bombs in England were the final convulsions of a failed insurgency, it was a political masterstroke by its leaders. The IRA did atrocities. Sinn Féin did apologies. A permanent leadership of super-terrorists controlled both, switching between each depending on the audience they sought to influence. They authorised the attacks then denied this. The British believed them. The deceit allowed these men to distance themselves from the IRA threat and use the lie of a fully functioning IRA as a bluff. This gave them equity in the negotiations they did not merit. Lord Tebbit touches on why so much confusion exists of how the Provos were brought to heel:

As you will know it was the intention of Margaret Thatcher to make Airey Neave her Secretary of State for Northern Ireland, but he was murdered by INLA on the eve of the 1979 Election. I knew him well and knew that he intended to achieve the total and complete military defeat of the IRA before moving on to talks about a political settlement. Sadly Major and Blair fell for the IRA's "cease fire" gambit to save the skins of their leaders.

Total and complete military success was not the annihilation of the IRA but winning the intelligence war plus forcing the IRA to say sorry and what they did was wrong. Afterwards peace talks would begin. Special Branch delivered the intelligence win. The British government, however, did not live up to the ending envisaged by Neave, an expectation shared by most police. And the talks allowed IRA leaders to avoid a tightening security net likely to result in their prosecution.

The way the secret victory was followed up politically meant the republican movement did not taste the bitterness of defeat from which it could have exorcised its demons for the benefit of republicanism and wider society. How IRA men no longer under the Sinn Féin whip have done this is to individually admit the 'armed struggle' was futile and a needless waste of life.

For practitioners like the major who know the horrors of insurgency first-hand, they see the secret victory. Insurgents do not abandon their terrorist campaign out of goodness. They need pushed. And there are few better at pushing than the US Marine Corps. They can be your best friend or worst enemy.

In 2007 the US Marine Corps tested the SB concept in Anbar. The Armed Services Committee (2010) in Washington DC assessed it:

The committee applauds the Irregular Warfare Support (IWS) program achievements supporting both unconventional and irregular approaches to warfare. The committee is especially interested in the "Attack the Network" approach used in the Republic of Iraq and the Islamic Republic of Afghanistan... The doctrinal program was based on a previously successful

European model [RUCSB] and began as a research and development pilot project. Proven to be immediately effective in disrupting terrorist network activities, saving lives.

Similar plaudits are expressed in official reviews and inspections of SB during the Troubles and in secret IRA communiqués. At the point of need and judged at the time, practitioners revere it and opponents respect it.

As historical inquiries criticised SB operational practices the same practices were being used in conflicts and praised. In an irregular war, as a matter of necessity, the threat determines the response. Unlike those in charge of historical inquiries, soldiers and police cannot ignore the presence of al-Qaeda or the Taliban or they are dead. Civilians under insurgent control run the same risk. This is what the major was dealing with. No-one saw anything when marines were gunned down in busy neighbourhoods, when teenagers were abducted from school and beheaded for talking to soldiers and when cops were murdered at Friday prayers. This is the reality. This is irregular war.

Almost all the tactical options historical inquiries have presented as a replacement to those that were used increase the risk to life. It shows how intellectually vacant the post-conflict era is in terms of what works in an irregular war. To compile all the options historical inquiries commend is to glimpse the conventional policing mindset and see that it is a mismatch for an unconventional setting. At every level peacetime policing is different from policing an irregular war.

All of this is alien and somewhat intimidating to police who have only worked peacetime streets. In America and Europe terrorist attacks are infrequent. Few police officers experience one. In a conflict cops confuse and forget terrorist incidents because they have known so many. The risk appetite in a conflict is also greater, with many tactical responses deemed proportionate regarded as disproportionate in a peaceful environment. Iraq's insurgency broadly followed the IRA template. The rule of law was the main target. Local police were murdered on a massive scale. General Petraeus drafted a strategy almost identical to that in Northern Ireland, without knowing this. As often happens, too many police departments were set up and few shared information. Too many intelligence agencies slow down the intelligence attack. Fragmentation of this type is unhelpful anywhere, let alone in tribal societies like Iraq where patronage and corruption are part of the culture.

The creation of different departments created false geographic boundaries, playing into the hands of terrorists. A senior Iraqi Intelligence Officer states: "al-Qaeda in Iraq know Iraqi police boundaries. They know and exploit our boundaries." Insurgents murdered his father and brother, both in the security forces. Another, who had escaped three murder bids by insurgents and lost his wife and young son in one, notes that insurgents "have no borders. He swims between police boundaries." The approach inhibited operational effectiveness, not that Iraqis knew any better. They had just emerged from decades of dictatorship. They assumed what they were told was right. Their advisors were mostly from police backgrounds in places like Kent and California. In the kingdom of the blind the one-eyed man is king.

On the political front the US established an old Stormont. A Shia dominated government in Baghdad discriminated against a Sunni minority in a way that made 1960s unionism look charitable. What resulted was eminently foreseeable.

Examining the Troubles in an international context helps to show why small residual insurgent networks like the Real IRA and Continuity IRA have replaced the Provos. For them the Provos failed. But if the Provos could not beat the 'Brits' these smaller groups certainly cannot. The difficulty is that, Sinn Féin condemns dissident republican terrorism today but justifies Provo terrorism yesterday. There is no clear moral blue water between the current brand of IRA and the former. The confused message and danger it creates is most obvious when contrasted to the ideology of extreme Islamists.

As long as Sinn Féin continues to justify IRA murders militants will be encouraged. But for Sinn Féin to admit killings were a needless waste of life is to admit they were unlawful and agree with what the IRA despised most – the rule of law. There is no prospect of this happening as long as republicans see votes in blaming the 'Brits' and an old guard hangs onto power. Only when a new generation of Sinn Féin leaders take charge is some form of IRA apology likely, after which meaningful reconciliation can begin. It is much easier to say sorry for something someone else did.

Looking at other conflicts shows the effectiveness of an intelligence-led approach in Northern Ireland, further exposing the republican myth of brutally repressive security. As can be seen with the refugee crisis today across Europe, people flee harsh regimes in large numbers. A country's population can decrease by as much as 50%. A Catholic population that increased by almost 10% during the Troubles does not imply British repression and brutality.

The Internal Security Solution is a success story. Beyond reasonable doubt was the legal benchmark. Eighty-five per cent of terrorist attacks were prevented, in the process of which three times as many security forces were killed as insurgents. It is the world's most human rights compliant counterinsurgency. But for a politically correct leftist lobby this is not enough. Political correctness neutralises the UK's capacity to help places like Iraq by over-indulging on human rights. Human rights are crucial, but brief guidelines in simple language relevant to the correct context.

Overseas police missions are more concerned about protecting themselves against litigation than the end-user protecting life. Mountains of doctrine are given over in a 'we've told them so' mentality. Building a police force becomes a directionless numbers game and tick box exercise. In Iraq, hundreds were packed into large tented classrooms, subjected to hours of torturous powerpoint and passed 'good to go.' In so many ways quantity is prioritised over quality.

Iraq's many police departments were paper tigers blown down by the first insurgent breeze. This is a main reason why the west failed in Iraq, is destined to fail in Afghanistan and will continue to fail if there is no change. Iraqis and Afghans are honourable and clever people. They deserved better. So did brave American and British armed service personnel and those of other coalition nations.

Today, places like Helmand where much British and American blood was spilt in hard fighting against the Taliban have been cheaply handed back to the Taliban. There was no policing approach coming in behind the military to consolidate hard-won gains. What is the point of taking ground if you do not hold it? When you do not the insurgency spreads. Very soon it is at the place you have retreated into. People think of that place being Baghdad or Kabul but it is also New York, Paris or Brussels. Insurgent threats need to be treated at source. This is where the main effort needs to be.

It is a worthy thing for any nation to aspire to a British bobby police model. But is this realistic in one prone to conflict? This is not to suggest the RUC police model and its SB is the fabled silver bullet. Yet no policing effort in recent irregular wars has been as effective, which is what has proved so illusive. In Northern Ireland a proven police intelligence model was made extraordinary by some of the world's finest police chiefs, intelligence experts and special forces. This is a good start point for future interventions, something for smart people to revise and repair.

General Petraeus says that terrorist incidents in Iraq peaked at "220 per day," six times greater than the Troubles peak of 36. Conflicts are more violent and policing solutions harder to find. Effective counterinsurgency is about keeping your mistakes to a minimum, getting the big questions right, and there is none bigger than selecting the right police model. In the Troubles, the police held society together when politics was not functioning. People can put up with bad politics as long as there are tangible benefits in security and stability.

In Iraq and Afghanistan, the US introduced a formatted version of SB. To date SB has not been road tested in full 'E' department mode or as part of a single police force. It has not got out of first gear. The RUC model remains current. Investing in this is a worthy endeavour but unlikely in a post-conflict arrangement where the protectors are persecuted and the aggressors applauded. It's the republican way. Historical inquiries will soon match IRA bombs in London in cost to the taxpayer. Northern Ireland is trapped by its past, often incapable of helping itself never mind anyone else. Perhaps a future British government wearisome of the spoilt 'peace process' child and mindful of the need to tackle threats like Islamic State might reclaim and update it. Probably, however, it will be the US who continue to lead.

The EU has also proved incapable of getting it right, their agencies preferring police with no experience of insurgency to 'teach' people like the Afghans. This in itself is not a deal-breaker because these are usually high calibre people. But when you combine it with an unsuited police model and policing practices, it is a fatal mix. Brussels' red tape and factionalism holds little hope that this will change. The same applies to the UN. This is not to undermine the good name of the EU or UN but to highlight that international missions of this kind are limited in what they can achieve. They are symbolic rather than practical.

Another aspect is the private sector. Iraq was the first contractors' war. Many firms made enormous profits. Snake oil salesmen mis-sold policing solutions to officials where doing something was more important than doing the right thing. Resources were recklessly thrown at a problem that was not understood.

Casualties in Iraq and Afghanistan have resulted from professional ignorance, commercial opportunism and political arrogance. That such bankrupt policies and practices were allowed to proceed does little to promote the benefits of western world intervention in armed conflict.

Even today, there is not an agreed legal framework flexible and comprehensive enough in which properly trained military and police can effectively deliver the rule of law in the aftermath of a military campaign. This is because people with no experience of policing a conflict dominate the debate. As a result, human rights have come to shape the discussion and dictate the response.

While there is universal agreement that intelligence is central to defeating terrorism, and that the best intelligence is from people within terrorist organisations, bodies like the EU and UN (as with most others) duck the big question – drafting an adequate law for intelligence-led policing in a conflict. If the RUC did not accept guidelines designed for ordinary crime, how could Iraqis or Afghans? For this is what human rights mean in a conflict, complying to rules that have no bearing on reality and being criticised for non-compliance. This is why Iraqis and Afghans have been given the full human rights treatment.

Policing in a normally functioning democracy can cope with human rights that have swung too far towards criminal offenders, but a society suffering under an insurgency cannot. All of this is to the detriment of international humanitarian law, which for decades has served us so well in armed conflict.

Throughout the world the British are known for fair play, tolerance and decency. These are values important to uphold in a conflict, but not to the lofty extent Europe demands. In WW2, the British were first to Europe's rescue. Commonwealth nations and the US followed. After WW2 the European Convention on Human Rights was drafted to prevent regimes like those of Hitler and Mussolini re-emerging. The convention was part of the post-war fix. Germany and Italy, and those in bed with them needed new rules. The British did not. What they had worked well. In an irregular war these old values codified in law need to move in parallel with policing at a pace that can overtake the threat. Europe's approach prevents this by interpreting human rights in a system where terrorists are treated as victims. For many UK voters in 2016, this was one factor that did little to persuade them to stay in the EU.

Outside of Northern Ireland, SB has protected life, whereas the IRA has much foreign blood on its hands. Besides influencing al-Qaeda and insurgents in Iraq, IRA relationships with terrorist groups in Spain (ETA) and Colombia (FARC) saw spikes in terrorism in these nations. Hezbollah and the PLO are other alliances. Terrorism has a tiresome constancy and predictability.

Little is new. Scale and settings change but the basics stay the same. The IRA is only a step behind the Islamic State.

A covert operation by the SAS supported by E4 HMSU deep in bandit country was the decisive action that ended the IRA's border campaign. This netted the arrests of four active terrorists and provided vital information on personalities, hide-outs and methodologies. It was a crushing blow for South Armagh IRA. Overwhelmed by the evidence against them, the defendants pleaded guilty on the first day of the trial. Such was the excellence of covert operations. Convicted for multiple murders they received sentences that should have kept them in prison for 25 years. They were released under the Belfast Agreement having served no more than two.

In 1994, an RAF helicopter crashed in the Mull of Kintyre. It was the RAF's biggest peacetime disaster, 29 perished. The passengers were the UK's top security experts, a mix of MI5, SB and military. Ten were police, including the Head of SB, Brian Fitzsimmons. Had the Chinook crash been a decade earlier it would have been an enormous boost for the IRA and a huge setback for security. As it was, by 1994 the IRA was in no position to carry on, due in no small way to these men. Like so many of their colleagues they did not see the RUC awarded the George Cross in 1999 for sustained bravery. They had the world's most difficult policing jobs.

In the RUC memorial garden in Belfast is part of the 'Man in the Arena' speech by US President Theodore Roosevelt. It reads:

It is not the critic who counts; not the man who points out where the strongman stumbles, or where the doer of good deeds could have done better. The credit belongs to the man in the arena, whose face is marred by dust and sweat and blood; who strives valiantly; who errs, and comes short again and again, because there is no effort without error and shortcoming; but who does actually strive to do the deeds; who knows the great enthusiasm, the great devotions; who spends himself in a worthy cause; who at the best knows in the end the triumph of high achievement, and who at the worst, if he fails, at least fails while daring greatly, so that his place shall never be with those cold and timid souls who know neither victory nor defeat.

Blessed are the peacemakers.

Acknowledgements

The arguments and analysis in this book are based on the generous input from people in my personal and professional life. I am indebted to them. Writing about intelligence during the Troubles is tricky. On four occasions I took the liberty of merging several factual accounts into one: the 'hard stop'; 'soft stop' by Big Jimmy (not his real name); doctoring a gun; and an agent driving a car bomb. This was to protect the sources and/or agents involved. Along the same lines, I did not ask about the origins of intelligence and nothing was volunteered.

I am grateful to professors Henry Patterson and Arthur Aughey, General David Petraeus, Colonel Tim Collins, former ACCs Raymond White and Peter Sheridan, Lord Tebbit, Billy Brown, Terry Walkingshaw, Paul Hillis, Rogelio Alonso, Marco, Zu, Toddy, Oscar 1, LW, Ernie Waterworth, Richard McKimm, Niall Crozier, Cindy Barrilleaux and my literary guru Austin Hunter. I am also grateful to the University of Ulster, Police Libraries in Belfast and Bramshill, Police museum in Belfast, Northern Ireland Retired Police Officers Association and PSNI (C3, Crime Operations).

This book is broadly based (with significant updates and additions) on PhD research I did at the University of Ulster titled, RUC Special Branch: How Effective was it at defeating an insurgency? The PhD will interest those looking for book references and academic articles. On this, it would be remiss of me not to point out that nearly all the deaths listed are from *Lost Lives* by David McKittrick et al and *Constabulary Heroes* by Sam Trotter. Where there are differences in accounts, I sided with Trotter. A lot of the RIC section is from *Police Casualties in Ireland 1919-1922* by Richard Abbott and David Galula's classic *Counterinsurgency Warfare* underpins much of the irregular war aspect.

In 2006 I met some inspirational people in Irregular Warfare Support (IWS) and the US Marine Corps. Drew Lomax of IWS (now called CTTSO - Combating Terrorism Technical Support Office) and Greg Tyson (US Marine Colonel) are two of them. DC is another. In searching for ways to counter insurgencies in Iraq and Afghanistan they complained that there was no book on the Troubles from a practitioner's perspective. There was nothing to help them. A bit late, but here it is.

Lastly: to my wife and family. You made this possible. I love all of you very much.

INDEX